A Concise Companion to
Contemporary British Fiction

Edited by James F. English

KU-208-806

Blackwell
Publishing

© 2006 by Blackwell Publishing Ltd
except for editorial material and organization © 2006 by James F. English

BLACKWELL PUBLISHING
350 Main Street, Malden, MA 02148-5020, USA
9600 Garsington Road, Oxford OX4 2DQ, UK
550 Swanston Street, Carlton, Victoria 3053, Australia

The right of James F. English to be identified as the Author of the Editorial Material in
this Work has been asserted in accordance with the UK Copyright, Designs, and Patents
Act 1988.

All rights reserved. No part of this publication may be reproduced, stored in a retrieval
system, or transmitted, in any form or by any means, electronic, mechanical,
photocopying, recording or otherwise, except as permitted by the UK Copyright, Designs,
and Patents Act 1988, without the prior permission of the publisher.

First published 2006 by Blackwell Publishing Ltd

1 2006

Library of Congress Cataloging-in-Publication Data

A concise companion to contemporary British fiction / edited by James F. English.
    p. cm.—(Blackwell concise companions to literature and culture)
  Includes bibliographical references and index.
  ISBN-13: 978-1-4051-2000-5 (hardcover : alk. paper)
  ISBN-10: 1-4051-2000-2 (hardcover : alk. paper)
  ISBN-13: 978-1-4051-2001-2 (pbk. : alk. paper)
  ISBN-10: 1-4051-2001-0 (pbk. : alk. paper) 1. English fiction—20th century—History
and criticism. 2. English fiction—21st century—History and criticism. I. English, James F.,
1958– II. Series.
PR881.C658 2006
823'.91409—dc22

                                                                2005012329

A catalogue record for this title is available from the British Library.

Set in 10/12pt Meridien
by Graphicraft Limited, Hong Kong

For further information on
Blackwell Publishing, visit our website:
www.blackwellpublishing.com

SWANSEA LIBRARY UNIVERSITY

Contents

Contents

Notes on Contributors

John Brannigan is senior lecturer in the School of English in University College Dublin. His most recent books are *Orwell to the Present: Literature in England, 1945–2000* (2003) and *Literature, Culture and Society in Postwar Britain, 1945–1965* (2002). He has recently completed a book on the novelist Pat Barker, to be published in 2005.

Robert L. Caserio, author of *The Novel in England, 1900–1950* (1999), is most recently a contributor to the new *Cambridge History of Twentieth Century English Literature* (2004). He heads the English department at Penn State University.

Cairns Craig is Professor of Scottish and Modern Literature at the University of Edinburgh and Director of the Centre for the History of Ideas in Scotland. He writes on Scottish literature and culture, on critical theory and the history of criticism, and on Irish and American modernist literature. His books include *Yeats, Eliot, Pound and the Politics of Poetry: Richest to the Richest* (1982), *Out of History: Narrative Paradigms in Scottish and English Culture* (1996), *The Modern Scottish Novel: Narrative and the National Imagination* (1999), and *Iain Banks's Complicity* (2002).

James F. English is Professor and Chair of the English Department at the University of Pennsylvania. He is the author of *Comic Transactions: Literature, Humor, and the Politics of Community in Twentieth-Century Britain* (1994) and *The Economy of Prestige: Prizes, Awards, and the Circulation of*

Cultural Value (2005). From 1999 to 2004, he was editor of *Postmodern Culture*. He is currently working on a study of race, class, and the problem of translation in UK–US cultural trade.

John Frow is Professor of English at the University of Melbourne. He is the author of *Marxism and Literary History* (1986), *Cultural Studies and Cultural Value* (1995), *Time and Commodity Culture* (1997), *Accounting for Tastes: Australian Everyday Cultures* (with Tony Bennett and Michael Emmison, 1999), and *Genre* (forthcoming 2005).

Dominic Head is Professor of Modern English Literature at the University of Nottingham. He is the author of *The Modernist Short Story* (1992), *Nadine Gordimer* (1994), *J. M. Coetzee* (1997) and *The Cambridge Introduction to Modern British Fiction, 1950–2000* (2002).

Andrew Higson is Professor of Film Studies at the University of East Anglia in the UK. He has written and/or edited several books on British cinema, the most recent being *English Heritage, English Cinema: Costume Drama Since 1980* (2003), and, as editor, *Young and Innocent? The Cinema in Britain, 1896–1930* (2002). He has also published numerous essays, including work on the concept of national cinema.

Nico Israel is Associate Professor of English at Hunter College, City University of New York. He is the author of a book, *Outlandish: Writing between Exile and Diaspora* (2000), and of essays on such figures as Conrad, Adorno, Rushdie, and Stevens. He is also a frequent contributor to *Artforum International* magazine and has published more than 50 catalogue essays, previews, and reviews for contemporary art exhibitions. His next book project, tentatively titled *Globalization and Trauma*, will explore intersections among literature, contemporary art, and critical theory in the post-1945 period.

Suzanne Keen is Professor of English at Washington and Lee University. She is the author of *Narrative Form* (2003), *Romances of the Archive in Contemporary British Fiction* (2001), and *Victorian Renovations of the Novel* (1998). Her most recent book, *Empathy and the Novel*, is due to be published in 2006.

James Procter is lecturer in English Studies at the University of Stirling. He is the author of *Writing Black Britain, 1948–1998* (2000), *Dwelling Places: Postwar Black British Writing* (2003), and *Stuart Hall* (2004).

Bruce Robbins is Professor of English and Comparative Literature at Columbia University. He is the author of *Feeling Global: Internationalism in Distress* (1999), *The Servant's Hand: English Fiction from Below* (1986), *Secular Vocations: Intellectuals, Professionalism, Culture* (1993), and is co-author of volume 5 (nineteenth century) of the new *Longman Anthology of World Literature* (2003). He has edited *Intellectuals: Aesthetics, Politics, Academics* (1990) and *The Phantom Public Sphere* (1993) and co-edited *Cosmopolitics: Thinking and Feeling beyond the Nation* (Minnesota, 1998).

Richard Todd is Professor of British literature after 1500 at the University of Leiden, The Netherlands. He is the author of *Consuming Fictions: The Booker Prize and Fiction in Britain Today* (1996), and a short monograph, *A. S. Byatt* (1997) in the British Council's "Writers and their Work" series. He has published widely on a range of aspects of non-dramatic British literature in the early modern period, and on contemporary "Booker-eligible" fiction.

Patricia Waugh is Professor of English Literature at the University of Durham. Her publications include *Metafiction: The Theory and Practice of Self-Conscious Fiction* (1984), *Feminine Fictions: Revisiting the Postmodern* (1989), *Practising Postmodernism/Reading Modernism* (1992), *Harvest of the Sixties: English Literature and its Backgrounds, 1960–1990* (1995), *Revolutions of the Word: Contexts for the Study of Modern Literature* (1997), (with David Fuller) *The Arts and Sciences of Criticism* (1999), and most recently *The Oxford Guide to the Theory and Practice of Literary Criticism* (ed., 2005). She is currently completing a book entitled *Literature, Science, and the Good Society*.

Introduction: British Fiction in a Global Frame

James F. English

Until quite recently, it was common practice to treat "contemporary" British fiction as synonymous with fiction of the entire postwar period. In their historical sequences of British literature classes, English departments would usually assign just a single course number to British novels of the later twentieth century: there were the various courses on modernism and modernists, and then there was one final course treating the aftermath or postscript – British fiction since the death of Woolf (and of modern experimentalism), since the emergence of the welfare state, since the collapse of the empire. This scheme seemed serviceable enough, given that one could always rearrange the precise contents of the contemporary/postwar bookshelf (removing John Braine or Ivy Compton-Burnett, adding Salman Rushdie or Jeanette Winterson). But it also came to seem increasingly at odds with ways of defining and addressing the contemporary that were becoming dominant in other fields, including fields with which English itself was ever more closely intertwined.

Starting in the mid-1980s, such influential writers as the historian Eric Hobsbawm, the geographer David Harvey, the economist Giovanni Arrighi, the sociologist Anthony Giddens, and the literary critic Fredric Jameson published major works that pointed to the 1970s as the fulcrum point of a decisive historical shift, affecting the spheres of economics (with the re-agglomeration of wealth, the rise of speculative finance, the global spread of neoliberalism, and the resultant collapse of welfare provisions); ideology (with the fading of all the great emancipatory narratives handed down from the Enlightenment, the rise of multiculturalisms, relativisms, anti-foundationalisms); society (with the rapid proliferation of new identities, new ethnicities, new demands for social recognition, both below and above the level of the nation-state); and culture (with the emergence of global telecommunications networks and a host of new technologies and media and entertainment genres, coupled with rapid transnational conglomeration of the culture industries) – to touch on just a few points of this now familiar narrative of the emergence of a postmodern, postindustrial, postcolonial, and postnational era. The very fact that, by the early 1990s, these kinds of books – Giddens's *Consequences of Modernity* (1990) or Harvey's *The Condition of Postmodernity* (1989) – were sometimes included on the syllabi of advanced English courses signaled concomitant shifts that had been occurring since the 1970s in the discipline itself: toward "theory," toward history, toward politics, toward cultural study in general, or at least toward some notion of greater interdisciplinarity.

As this way of periodizing "the long twentieth century" gained general acceptance, it opened a new vantage on the "contemporary" within literary study. With respect to British fiction, a rough division imposed itself on the curriculum, with "postwar" now tending to mean the Movement, the Angry Young Men, the first generation of feminist novels, and the period of great acclaim for such individual authors as Graham Greene, Anthony Burgess, William Golding, and Iris Murdoch (all perennial contenders for the Nobel Prize through the 1970s). "Contemporary" seemed to refer to a quite distinct literary scene: the immigrant and postcolonial writers (already beginning to be taught in a parallel or shadow curriculum, whose relation to "contemporary British fiction" was left awkwardly undefined), the Scottish and Welsh New Waves, the brash new celebrity authors who won Booker prizes and appeared in *Granta* magazine's "Best of the Young British Novelists" (in 1983 and 1993). Dividing the two moments was a kind of sea change in the very terms of cultural value and cultural temporality, such that contemporary British fiction could be embraced as the scene of something radically new and decisively more important and vigorous than what had come before. It was as though the fiction of postwar Britain had never actually *been* contemporary until now; it had finally, in the 1980s, managed to assert its contemporaneity, which seemed also to mean its worldliness, its recognition of and within a global literary geography.

Granta had helped to promote this sense of a more than merely generational upheaval and transformation, announcing in its inaugural issue of 1979 that we were witnessing nothing less than "the end of the English novel [and] the beginning of British fiction." This was certainly a bit of sloganeering, cultural hype of the sort that would itself come to be strongly associated with the new stage of literary history it purported to describe. But the slogan was effective because there was in fact a perceptible waning of English dominance within the canon of contemporary British fiction (and even, in a different way, within the apparatus of canon-making), and because this re-arrangement involved, in turn, an altered place for British fiction on the wider field of literature in English – or, as it was coming to be called – the literature of "global English." It involved, that is to say, a remapping of the whole "world literary space" (Casanova 2005: 72), the entire transnational scene and system in which British fiction was now being produced and received.

The present volume is an attempt to provide a concise overview of this new situation of British fiction as it has taken shape since the 1970s, and especially since 1978–9, when the election of the Thatcher government effected a sudden and intense acceleration in the pace of change, aligning Great Britain with the fast track of free-market glob-alism and thereby forcing a massive rearrangement of the cultural sector. Our emphasis in this volume, therefore, is less on any particular canon of contemporary authors or works than on the social, political, economic, and ideological determinants of canonicity itself: on the changing shape of the literary field, the new positions of privilege or marginality that have opened on that field, and the new practices or styles of play that literary people – not only authors, but critics, pub-lishers, and so forth – have developed in response. We have tried to avoid exaggerating the extent and uniformity of the transformations that have occurred since the late 1970s. Literary fields are always subject to inertia – committed to reproducing certain forms, certain habits of writing and reading, certain relationships of power and value – even as they adjust actively to altered circumstances. While rapid and dramatic post-1970s transformation is indeed evident in a number of the chapters that follow, such as Richard Todd's on the new arrangements in publishing and bookselling or Cairns Craig's on the "devolution" of Scottish fiction, there are other chapters, such as Patricia Waugh's on the situation of the woman writer or Bruce Robbins's on the academic novel, in which continuities are emphas-ized as much as change. Taken as a whole, however, this Companion argues for an important historical break in British fiction roughly coincident with the "Thatcher revolution" and tied to changes not just within the UK but in the relationship of the UK to the world.

Something of these changes is evident in the very problem of nomenclature. As the *Granta* slogan suggests, the worrying of differences between English literature and British literature, between British literature and Commonwealth literature, between Commonwealth literature and postcolonial literature, came during the early Thatcher years to seem increasingly urgent. The term "Black British" emerged originally for reasons of political strategy, to unite various minority constituencies into a "counter-hegemonic bloc" (to use the language of those years), but it was taken up in literary and other cultural spheres partly for reasons of commercial and curricular convenience, as a rough and ready way of situating a diverse and as yet uncataloged array of writers, artists, and works. A third- or fourth-generation Londoner of African descent; an Irish-identified native of Belfast whose father had emigrated from Pakistan; a recent illegal immigrant from Jamaica doing casual labor in Glasgow; or the daughter of a wealthy Parsi businessman, educated in Mumbai and Geneva but now a resident of Holland Park – subjects as differently positioned as these could, if they entered the literary field, be shelved and taught together under the sign of "Black British" writing. Of course, as James Procter details in his chapter here, this was an unsustainably reductive formulation. But in straining to assert, across many and various lines of difference, a kind of sameness in difference itself, the idea of Black British literature succeeded in highlighting the relative homogeneity and insularity of Englishness proper, and thereby in recasting the English novel, in the contemporary context, as something small, local, and perhaps dwindling into inconsequence. Having long enjoyed its position as the dominant term lurking within "British" literature, English was suddenly subjected to an unwonted and diminishing scrutiny.

This was compounded by the strong emergence in the 1980s and 1990s of Scottish, Welsh, and Northern Irish fiction, which not only succeeded in gaining broader readerships but also in more sharply differentiating themselves, formally and linguistically as well as thematically, from the accepted norms of the English novel. Within the space of just a decade or two, British fiction had divided and proliferated into a whole range of commercially and symbolically important subcategories – "white" as well as "black" – among which the English novel could not even be firmly maintained as the primary or central one. Furthermore, while British fiction was undergoing this process of productive destabilization and fragmentation, other anglophone literatures outside the UK (though all of them of course rooted partly in the long history of British imperialism) were staking ever larger claims on the attention of Britain's readers, critics, and literary institutions.

Prizes and awards, themselves a constitutive element of the contemporary literary scene, provide a useful gauge of these changes. When William Golding won the Nobel Prize in 1983 (to rather muted applause among British literati, whose attention had already shifted away from the mid-century novelists of ideas), he was the seventeenth English-language author to receive the prize. Seven of these were British (as was Elias Canetti, who wrote in German). Since then, English-language authors have received the honor even more frequently than before (7 times in 22 years), but only one of them has been British – and that one, V. S. Naipaul, is a Trinidadian émigré whose eagerness to be identified with Great Britain, and indeed with England, made his selection by the Swedish Academy deeply controversial. Of course it is no secret that the Nobel Prize has sought, since the 1970s, to broaden the cultural and geographic scope of its legitimating power; we would expect to find African American, South African, Nigerian, Caribbean, and other anglophone authors traditionally disadvantaged by their position in the "world literary space," increasingly represented among the Nobel laureates. More striking is how closely Britain's domestic fiction prizes have followed this same pattern of increasing recognition for non-English and even non-British authors. From its founding in 1969 up until 1980, fully two thirds of the winners of the Booker Prize were native English, while in the 24 years since then, not even one third have been. The only two-time winners of the UK's most coveted novel-of-the-year prize are the South African J. M. Coetzee (who now lives in Australia) and the Australian Peter Carey (who now lives in New York City) – unless we count the Indian-born Salman Rushdie (also now living in New York City), who won the 25th-anniversary "Booker of Bookers" in addition to his 1981 prize for *Midnight's Children*. Even this degree of globalization has been seen as insufficient by the Booker's current sponsor, the Man Group, which has launched a new "international" Booker prize for which US novelists as well as foreign-language novelists in English translation are eligible. Several of the so-called Baby Bookers, prizes that sprang up during the 1980s and 1990s, have assumed this more global orientation from the start. The Orange Prize for Women, for example, has been open to US and Canadian authors since its founding in 1996, and like the Booker has been won by non-British novelists

5

two times out of every three. But the shift is evident, as well, in Britain's oldest and most staidly traditional prizes: the James Tait Black fiction prize, which dates back to 1920, was for example awarded for the first time in 2003 to an American author (Jonathan Franzen for *The Corrections*). What these winners' lists clearly indicate is that British fiction exists today in a dynamic relation with an increasingly global field of fiction in English. While this relation has arguably disadvantaged the English novel as such – the strictly "domestic" novel – it has made possible new articulations and productive antagonisms between Britain's literary culture and the wider world. Far from withdrawing into resentful isolation, Britain's institutions of literary study and consecration, as well as its fiction writers themselves, have entered into active forms of engagement with this more extensive field of anglophone literary production.

The more global situation of British literature registers to varying degrees in the chapters that follow; it is not in every case a major or even an explicit point of emphasis. But as a way of briefly sketching the contents of the volume while also contributing one further line of inquiry, I will indicate some of the ways that the three main parts and the twelve individual chapters may be seen, even as they map the contours of the British fiction scene in all its national particularity, to suggest a global framework within which those contours have assumed their contemporary shape.

Institutions of Commerce

Every chapter of this volume attends to the *institutional* dimensions of British fiction – to the administered system of cultural, educational, political, legal, and commercial institutions whose fundamental role in the production of literature is too often overlooked or repressed by critics. But the three chapters that make up Part I, "Institutions of Commerce," offer the most detailed treatment of these institutional aspects in regard to the business side of fiction. Because they focus on the economics of the fiction industry, their relevance to broader narratives about the globalization of culture and media is readily apparent. Richard Todd's chapter on "Literary fiction and the book trade" traces the rise of booksellers, over the last quarter century, to a position of unprecedented dominance in the system of literary production. What he describes in terms of a "concentration of power around the retail axis," with a concomitant eclipse of the power of authors, editors, and publishers, not only applies to other national markets but would never have occurred in the UK if the domestic bookselling environment had remained as insular as it was up until the 1970s. It was precisely because of the globalization of retailing generally and of book retailers like Borders and Amazon in particular, and the concomitant global imposition of neoliberal ("free market") economic policies, that such longstanding domestic barriers or protections as resale price maintenance were gradually weakened and then undone in the mid-1990s. For all their concreteness and particularity in the national context, the trends Todd describes, with their far-reaching impacts on the kinds of fiction that can succeed and achieve recognition in contemporary Britain, fit squarely into the broader narratives of post-1970s globalization.

This is not quite the same as saying that such trends support the narratives of *Americanization*. One of the recurring features of contemporary British literary journalism is the denunciation of any major alteration or abridgement of traditional literary practices as an effect of Americanization. But, as John Frow and I argue in connection with the rise of literary celebrity culture in Chapter 2, Britain must be seen as a formidable agent of change in its own right, and not simply as a passive absorber of American (or for that matter, European) influences. Particularly in the realms of high-literary promotion and publicity, London has been in many ways a more vigorous incubator of innovation than New York or Los Angeles. American literary people, from magazine publishers to bookstore managers to prize administrators, have since the early 1980s often looked to London as the site of new and strikingly successful commercial deployments of authorship, of high-literary branding, of cross-media synergy, and of journalistic scandal. The Booker Prize, with its many pages of pre- and post-announcement newspaper coverage, its national television audience, its capacity to link book culture with the bookmaking culture of Ladbrokes and William Hill, not to mention its sheer impact on book sales, is the envy of literary society in North America and throughout the English-speaking world.

Britain's cultural apparatus has also been singularly successful, as Andrew Higson describes in his chapter on fiction and the film industry, in leveraging literary success in London into cinematic acclaim in Los Angeles or Cannes as well as into global box-office receipts. Those Booker Prize winning novels have, with disconcerting regularity, ended up as Academy Award winning films: notably *Schindler's Ark, The*

Remains of the Day, and *The English Patient*. And, as Higson points out, even the novels that have been adapted into art-house or cult films (such as Irvine Welsh's *Trainspotting*) have thereby gained recognition from a much larger and more international audience than they had originally. Higson accepts neither the perennial criticism of Britain's film industry – that it is too dominated by literary form and literary sensibility – nor the more recent claim that Britain's traditional literary values are being eroded by Hollywoodization and cinema obsession. What he describes is a more complex interleaving of the two cultural forms, which has enabled British fiction to achieve much broader global recognition without surrendering its relative autonomy at the local level.

Elaborations of Empire

As is evident in the chapters of Part II, however, the global success of Britain's local literary institutions – the enduring and indeed augmented power of London's prizes, journals, publishers, and publicists – must be weighed in the context of empire and its politically fraught aftermath. There is nothing politically innocent about London's leading position on the field of world literature, nor about the tendency of its literary institutions to rely on partnerships with or sponsorship from transnational corporations. The consecration, under such corporate auspices as Booker plc and the Man Group, of a particular canon of postcolonial fiction (Salman Rushdie, Ben Okri, Keri Hulme, Arhundati Roy, et al.) has been explicitly critiqued as a form of neo-imperialism. Through London's literary institutions, the difficult and continuing struggles around the world against colonial burdens and impoverishments are translated into a readily global-marketable form of "exotic" airport literature for cosmopolitan readers – a new way, in effect, for metropolitan business interests to impose their imperial control on, and extract their imperial profit from, the periphery (Huggan 2001).

But, as Nico Israel argues in the chapter that heads this part, the transnational dimensions of postcolonial fiction in Britain are more complex than such critiques suggest. The very emergence of the postcolonial novel as a recognized category in literary London required the prior emergence of postcolonial theory: a truly international phenomenon, involving the assimilation and redeployment of continental (especially French) philosophical critiques, by intellectuals of colonial origin, mostly educated in the literature departments of British and

North American universities. Israel stresses, as well, the uneasy but critical convergence and overlapping of postcolonial theory with the Black British political movement, itself driven in large part by the pronounced demographic changes to London from the late 1970s onwards. The increasingly heterogeneous complexion of the city, he notes, can be readily seen in the contrast between "the television images of London's citizenry during the 1982 wedding of Prince Charles and Lady Diana, and then, 15 years later, of the mourners for Diana Spencer after her death; during that time London had become, even in its celebration of royal rule, a strikingly more 'multicultural' city." It is not just the tendency toward greater transnational corporate involvement in canon-formation, but also these tendencies toward greater intellectual and demographic heterogeneity that have been reshaping the institutional framework of British literature.

James Procter's chapter deals at length with this proliferation of differences in the domestic population, showing how the "new ethnicities" that began to be discerned in Britain in the 1980s have both made their mark on the British literary scene and, in the course of doing so, struggled to assert their particularity within an international commercial and symbolic marketplace where ethnicity as such, ethnicity in general, functions as a kind of commodity. "As difference gets incorporated, reworked, and pieced out according to the logic of late global capitalism," Procter remarks, "it is worth asking whether (ethnic) difference is still capable of making a difference."

Where Israel and Procter focus primarily on literary deployments of difference with respect to Britain's growing immigrant populations, Cairns Craig and John Brannigan focus on the repressed system of differences that had always underwritten the "United" Kingdom. Craig traces the rise of cultural and specifically literary nationalism in Scotland, attending to the important parallels between the recognition accorded to Scottish novelists within contemporary British literature and the devolution of political authority to Scotland within the UK system of governance. The effect of Scottish fiction writers' strong (if also complexly ambivalent) assertion of cultural and linguistic difference, Craig observes, was not merely to challenge the traditional literary history of British fiction, in which Scottish novelists are treated as "regional versions of the development of the English novel"; it was also "to make the more menacing claim that Scotland had not, through the years of Union, been successfully integrated into a unified British culture, and to project, therefore, its continuing potential for separate development." Which is to say that Scottish writers began, in the

1980s and 1990s, to situate themselves in something like a postcolonial relationship to British literature, joining Scottish literature with the other "new" literatures in English that had been likewise gaining symbolic legitimacy and commercial viability.

In Northern Ireland, as discussed by Brannigan, this process of simultaneous literary and political self-assertion from the margins has had to reckon not only with the longstanding (colonial) disparity between the cultural capital of Belfast and that of London, but also with a transnational mediascape of more recent vintage that has succeeded in fixing Belfast within "a global iconography of terrorism and atavistic, tribal war." Yet Brannigan sees the current peace process, initiated in 1993, as clearing a new literary space within this global mediascape, a space "continually haunted" by the region's collective narratives of "loss, trauma, and elegiac desire," yet nonetheless "open to imaginative transformation." Brannigan's larger argument here is not just that the new political situation which affords Northern Ireland greater autonomy of governance has made possible the emergence of a new, post-Troubles literary generation. Like Craig, he insists also on the capacity of this new literary situation to provoke, in its turn, the emergence of a still more promising political environment, one in which the Northern Irish imaginary is no longer locked in the agon of empire. We see the beginnings of this emergence, perhaps, in the increasingly common representation of Belfast not in terms of a provincial relationship to London but as one of the up-and-coming cities of unified Europe.

Mutations of Form

Part III of this volume considers the ways that categories of author and relations of genre have shifted over the last three decades. The chapters in this part continue to examine the institutional and commercial dimensions of contemporary fiction which are the primary focus in Part I; genre categories are, after all, produced and sustained by academics and booksellers, and the hierarchies that determine their relations to one another (above all, their recognition or non-recognition as "serious," "literary" fiction) are likewise adjudicated in the universities and the marketplace. This final cluster of chapters continues, as well, to explore the questions of identity, representation, and political power that provide the main focus of Part II; categories such as "queer fiction" or "women's fiction" are obviously no less entangled with such matters than are "Black British" or "postcolonial." Distinct categories of fiction, or of authorship, invariably correspond to, and assist in constituting, distinct social groups.

But this is only to indicate the coherence of the volume as a whole, which maintains certain core emphases (institutionality, canonicity, the struggle over literary value among differentially positioned classes or groups) even while varying the points of most direct concern. In the case of Suzanne Keen's chapter, the concern is with the putative renaissance and refashioning of historical fiction in Britain since the 1970s, and with the actual range of discrete types of novel and classes of reader that the generic term "historical fiction" misleadingly claims to unite. With respect to the globalization hypothesis, Keen documents convincingly the orientation of the more "serious" or philosophical strain of historical fiction – the so-called "New Historical" fiction of the 1980s – toward a canon of world literature (in particular, Latin American magic realism) rather than toward a strictly domestic literary scene. But the alternative, lower-status strain of historical fiction – women's historical romance – is equally a "world" genre, among the most readily transportable across national borders, as its prominence in the airport bookstalls attests. This more conventional and popular form of historical fiction, Keen argues convincingly, is scarcely vestigial or in danger of being eclipsed by its more celebrated counterparts on the "literary" side of the aisle. Despite their neglect in most accounts of the contemporary historical novel, women's historical romances are thriving right alongside the New Historical fiction, and are continuing to shape the ideas of the past – including a durable nostalgia for Britain's colonial past – that are in turn shaping the politics of the present.

Patricia Waugh's chapter takes up the question of how the figure of the "woman writer" and the quasi-generic category of "women's fiction" have shifted since the first wave of the modern women's movement back in the 1960s. Here once again we can readily see the global dimensions of the changes she describes. Both feminism as a political movement and the woman writer as a politically charged literary figure had been established internationally by the late 1960s, but with relatively little awareness of the problems entailed in positing unity or solidarity across lines of national, cultural, and ethnic difference. By the early 1980s these problems had risen to the surface and become acute for feminist writers of fiction and nonfiction alike. The difficulty lay in the need to reckon with the differing cultural, economic, and political circumstances of women in the different

11

localities of feminist writing and activism, while also maintaining the viability of the "woman writer" as a world literary figure; both the politics of contemporary feminism and the mandates of contemporary literary commerce involve a certain investment in this universalism. As Waugh discusses, the recent and massive success of chick lit on the world women's fiction market – spearheaded by the Bridget Jones franchise, and capturing not just a popular market but many readers of "serious literary fiction," as well – has suggested to some observers that the postcolonial-inflected feminisms of the 1980s have failed, and it is the postfeminism of the young, white professional class in Britain and North America which has managed to universalize its values. Ultimately, Waugh rejects this version of literary history, seeing chick lit as something of a sideshow and arguing that feminist writing has in fact arrived at a moment of productive synthesis, "working over the expressive realist thesis of the early years and the antithetical deconstructions of the 1980s and early 1990s, to return to a reconsideration of experience, rights, and subjectivities, in the context of a new era of globalization and multiculturalism."

Like chick lit, which has its antecedents in the whole history of the novel of manners since Austen yet has nonetheless managed to seem new, "queer fiction," the subject of Robert Caserio's chapter, only "emerged as an identifiable and important literary category in Britain in the 1970s and 1980s," despite a long history of homosexual authors writing on the theme of homosexuality. What was new in the emergence of "queer fiction," at least initially, was less a mode of writing than a mode of reception, a new social and commercial framework for the recognition of gay and lesbian writing. The key condition of possibility for such recognition, Caserio argues, was "a concerted movement toward full-scale public acceptance of homosexuality." But the great irony of his account is that "at the very moment of this gay and lesbian bid for a public world," i.e., the mid- to late-1970s, "the public world itself began to disappear." And he attributes that reversal, which has indelibly marked queer fiction for the last two decades, to the arrival in Britain of the global neoliberal agenda of privatization: "The advent of Thatcherism in 1979 signaled an end of collective-minded progressive values that might have offered homosexual men and women full standing as citizens. Privatization – of everything from state industry to personal 'choice' of sexual orientation – became the order of the day." Nor has a decade of New Labour governance done much to reopen the public sphere to gay literature and culture, especially given the Blair government's determined "alliance with a presidency that has renewed public aggression against American gays and lesbians." A genre that emerged internationally, "with American inspiration," is still struggling to find its place on an international field that began almost immediately its deep tilt toward privatization and conservative religious values.

If the contemporary moment in British fiction has been marked by the emergence of such literary categories as queer fiction, New Historical fiction, Black British fiction, and postcolonial fiction, it has also seen the eclipse of what had been, in the early postwar decades, one of Britain's most distinctive and critically esteemed genres – namely, working-class fiction. In addressing the reasons for the genre's rapid decline and virtual disappearance, Dominic Head stresses once again the Thatcherite religion of privatization, efficiency, and individual enterprise. The neoliberal economics imposed, as it were, through Thatcher's government by global capital, meant in practice the dismantling of trade unions, the abrogation of the welfare-state social contract, and the collapse of traditional working-class communities. Since the 1980s, the British labor force has been characterized by an expanded middle-class salariat oriented toward feverish consumption; a new "servant class" of menial service workers, employed on a "casual" basis to cater to this more prosperous bourgeoisie; and a so-called "underclass" of "truly disenfranchised" individuals lacking all prospects of work. Yet Head is careful not to offer too reductive an account of the relation between political and literary histories. He points out, on the one hand, that the working-class novels of the 1950s and 1960s were already far more ambivalent in their representations of class identity and unity than is usually acknowledged, and, on the other hand, that the dominance of contemporary fiction by "middle-class" writers is neither a new circumstance nor, in itself, a lamentable one, given the increasing diversity of ethnicity, regional or national background, religion, political outlook, and so forth that is today enshrouded by that category. According to Head, the real story with respect to fictional representations of class in Britain, whether we are looking at the old working-class realism or the new novels of underclass experience or the enduring strain of bourgeois social concern, is that of "deep contradictions" in the very notion of class identity.

In the volume's final chapter, Bruce Robbins makes a somewhat related argument with respect to the academic novel. Though campus satire has shifted markedly in both emphasis and tone since the Thatcher government initiated its radical corporate-style reform of the higher educational sector in the mid-1980s, the genre has continued to be structured by an essentially town/gown opposition that expresses a more long-term legitimation crisis of the academy in general and English departments in particular. The root concerns of the academic novel have undergone more of an intensification in the contemporary period than a true revision. But there has also been a kind of extensi-fication, or broadening of geographic scope, with respect to both the production of campus novels and their thematics. Robbins points out that the Thatcherite "rationalization" of the universities "was of course part of the larger international movement that has come to be called 'globalization,' [and] its symptoms are thus to be found on the same global scale." He points to recent academic fiction from South Africa and Canada in which the Literature department is faced with familiar Thatcher-era demands to improve its efficiency and utility.

Robbins also notes, however, the impact of another important aspect of globalization in regard to the academy. Higher education has, since the 1970s, become vastly more international in terms of the actual populations of students and faculty, with British universities in particular succeeding in attracting ever larger contingents of tuition-paying foreign students while also finding employment abroad for the redundant products of their doctoral degree programs. The academic novel has, by way of response to this new circumstance, tended to present the British academy through the eyes of a foreign visitor or observer. Yet, rather than establishing a greater satiric distance from the professoriate, these novels have almost revived the pastoral form of campus fiction that characterized the first half of the twentieth century. Comments Robbins, "It is as if British higher education, un-dervalued by its own government, had turned to that hopefully more complimentary reflection of its value to be found elsewhere in the world, where demand for its wisdom and credentials continues to run strong."

It is appropriate that this volume should end with a consideration of the complex and increasingly transnational relationships between British fiction and the academy. Robbins's essay, and I hope the volume as whole, gives us the opportunity to reflect, as we should, on our own institutional homes and their role in determining the values that obtain on the field of contemporary literature. Literature is not after all a discrete object, out there, which we readers and critics contem-plate and interpret; it is a space of ongoing symbolic combat in which what is at stake is less the outcome (the canon) than the very terms or rules of the game. "Contemporary," "British," and even "fiction" are all in this sense fighting words; and we scholars, wherever we may be situated, are active participants in the struggle to determine their meanings.

References

Arrighi, Giovanni (1994). *The Long Twentieth Century*. London: Verso.

Casanova, Pascale (2005). Literature as a world. *New Left Review*, 31, January/February, 71–90.

Giddens, Anthony (1990). *The Consequences of Modernity*. Cambridge: Cambridge University Press.

Harvey, David (1989). *The Condition of Postmodernity: An enquiry into the origins of cultural change*. Oxford: Blackwell.

Hobsbawm, Eric (1994). *The Age of Extremes: A history of the world, 1914–1991*. New York: Vintage.

Huggan, Graham (2001). *The Postcolonial Exotic: Marketing the margins*. New York: Routledge.

Jameson, Fredric (1991). *Postmodernism: Or the cultural logic of late capitalism*. London: Verso.

Part I

Institutions of Commerce

Chapter 1

Literary Fiction and the Book Trade

Richard Todd

Most scholarship on British fiction focuses on the form and content and social meanings of literary works rather than on the business of their acquisition, publication, marketing, and sales. Literary-critical methods have undergone considerable innovation since the discipline of English studies emerged in its modern form after World War I (Hawkes 1986: 51–72, 120–6), but even with the rise in recent decades of a new range of critical theories and methods, the discipline has never afforded much space to the nuts and bolts of literary commerce. The one great exception to this disciplinary rule has been the work of John Sutherland who, since the publication of his *Fiction and the Fiction Industry* in 1978, has virtually made the subject his own, producing a very substantial body of books, articles, and occasional pieces devoted to the British book trade in its commercial aspects. What follows is thus heavily indebted to Sutherland's pioneering work, even as it sharply deviates from the main pathways along which the discipline of English has developed.

Those more standard disciplinary pathways have, with respect to contemporary fiction, been oriented toward politics. Critics have recognized that recent decades have seen a boom in the fiction market, with a host of important new authors, modes, and schools of fiction writing. But they have assumed that this rise in the market for, and in the level of excitement surrounding, contemporary British fiction can be largely explained by the kind of political tensions that literary criticism uncovers and elaborates with respect to individual works:

tensions attendant on the rise of identity politics, for example, or on the emergence of postcolonialism more generally. There is some justice in this view, since much of the boom has derived from what we now think of as the "empire writing back," together with the various reactions against that development. Certainly, the corporate media have stressed this aspect of the contemporary literary scene as much as literary critics have. Still, as I shall argue, the politics of fiction cannot tell us the whole story of what has been happening in Britain's literary culture over the last quarter century. There is much we can learn by examining in detail the commercial forces that underlie the writing, publication, and retailing of fiction today.

I propose to examine these forces in the framework of a triangle, of which one point is formed by the author and agent working together, another by the publisher, and another by the retail industry. I shall begin with the assertion that in today's climate it is the retail industry that has the upper hand, and shall go on to discuss the consequences of this concentration of power around the retail axis.

In fact it may be asserted from the outset that literary fiction today, like all fiction, is more retail-driven than ever before. From the commercial point of view, the biggest change in the book trade since the end of World War II was the abolition of resale price maintenance (RPM) upon the expiration of the Net Book Agreement (NBA) on 17 September 1995. In March 1997 the NBA was formally abolished as a "restrictive practice" under the terms of the law, and its application is now illegal (Dearnley & Feather 2002: 16–17, who find no reason to argue that what they term the "abrogation" of the NBA has damaged the book trade in any way). It is true that before 1995, it was standard practice for retailers, with publishers' permission, to offer remaindered or damaged stock, specified contractually, at discount. It is also true that in the years immediately prior to 1996 various bookstores, notoriously Dillons, had been daringly offering sporadic discounts on the retail price of books (Todd 1996: 95–6) – and of course the terms of book club memberships allowed circumvention of the existing legislation. But, despite the exploitation of these and other legal loopholes, perhaps stimulated by the aftershock of the aggressive business behavior that had become the norm in Britain in the 1980s – the Thatcher decade – there was no "free market" in the American sense. That is to say, the retailer had no formal freedom to price new fiction from the date of publication or pre-publication itself. Such a free market was surely a theoretical terminus of Thatcherite thinking, and the space for it might not have been created had British politics taken a different direction in 1979.

With the abolition of RPM everything changed, and the retailer was quick to make use of the now legal possibility of lowering the recommended retail price (RRP) as much as was commensurate with sound commercial sense. (As we shall see, even that criterion has undergone a remarkable degree of flexible interpretation.) Moreover, books in Britain, unlike those in much of the rest of the EU, are not subject to value-added tax, which is usually around 6% but in certain countries can exceed 20%.

Figures culled from a variety of sources – and it must be admitted that, though best guesses, these can only be estimates – suggest that a hardback literary fiction title retailing at 10/6 (53 pence) in 1955 amounted to 10% of an average weekly wage of £5. To gain an idea of how purchasing power has altered, one need only consult the data on inflation, which show how historically exceptional were the inflation figures of the second half of the 1970s (Twigger 1999: 12–15). The reason was a combination of a rapidly falling pound and a major oil crisis during 1973–4. Against an index of 100 for 1974, 1955 comes in at 40.9, and 1998 at 592.3. Extrapolating forward to 2005 at around 3% or 4% inflation per annum would give us a figure near 700: in other words, retail prices in general have risen sevenfold in Britain in the past 30 years since the oil crisis, and seventeenfold since the mid-1950s. In the 20 years before the oil crisis, retail prices only rose by a factor of two-and-a-half. This latter period includes the 1956 Suez crisis, but at that time, although there was petrol rationing in Britain, the pound was at a fixed rate to the dollar ($2.80). It would remain so until being devalued to $2.40 in 1967, although in retrospect it can be seen to have been persistently and increasingly overvalued against the dollar and the stronger European currencies even after the 1967 devaluation.

Today's RRP for a similar hardback title to an imaginary 1955 one might be around £17, whereas the weekly wage (which varies far more greatly than it did in 1955) is now on average around £500 (nearer £650 in London): these figures (which are rather higher than for the US) are based on official ones for 2001 (www.usd.edu/business/globalu/countries/uk), with considerable fluctuations either way. Today's hardback literary fiction title, sold at its RRP, therefore represents about 3% of the average weekly income. But of course this is not customarily the case. In today's world an RRP of £17 may well in practice mean a price nearer to £15 (a 12% discount) or even £12 (a 30% discount). In these cases the proportion of average weekly income drops to 2.5% and 2%, respectively.

None of this, of course, is to mention the explosion of the paperback phenomenon of the past two decades. Paperbacks have been available for 70 years, since the founding of Penguin by Sir Allen Lane (1902–70) and the launching of the first 10 titles in 1935, each costing the same as a packet of cigarettes. The phenomenon gradually, and then increasingly rapidly, took off, and spawned many other paperback imprints along the way, most of them emerging in the past 10 to 15 years, a few vanishing into oblivion. It is worth noting that the price difference between a hardback and a paperback version of the same title has actually fallen considerably during the past 50 to 70 years. The following points may help to explain why.

Literary fiction usually appears in the so-called "B format" (198 × 126 cm) and often in a pricier matt-lamination finish. The "C format" is less precisely defined in the book trade but "is most often used to describe a paperback edition published simultaneously with, and in the same format as, the hardback original" (Publishers Association 2005). The time difference between first appearance in hardback and subsequent paperbacking has fallen, typically, from about two years in the 1970s to a matter of months, weeks, or even – as we can see (by definition) in the case of the "C format" – simultaneity today. Increasingly, Penguin is concentrating on other of its strengths, and giving up the rights to contemporary literary fiction titles to imprints such as Vintage: this change is having significant copyright implications.

Necessitated by the literary fiction publisher are therefore careful calculations of numbers of hardback stock and aggressive marketing of lead hardback titles. Fewer loss-leaders are to be found (Gill, personal communication, April 29, 2004). Above all, however, it is paperbacks that the death of the NBA has affected. Indeed, the purchasing power comparisons in hardback fiction given above are seen to be flawed when we consider the proportion of the retail industry paperbacks take up today compared to 50 years ago.

Improvements in technology, particular the development of IT, and a general increase in wealth among those sections of the British public who consider themselves as book buyers and book readers have clearly played their part. Postwar austerity in general (food rationing was not abolished in Britain until 1954, by which point her ravaged European neighbors were already enjoying the benefits of the Marshall Plan), and the paper shortage in particular, are outside the living memories of more than half the British population. But all the same, the fact that a hardback title in 2004 is probably five times cheaper in real terms than it was half a century ago is a remarkable statistic. Note that this is before the 10%, 20%, or 30% paperback discounts now to be met with are factored in, let alone the "3 for 2" actions that characterize the retail of paperbacks at the present time. If 50 years ago a new fiction title in hardback amounted to 10% of the average weekly wage (no new *literary* titles appeared in paperback in Britain, although genre-fiction titles did) a new "3 for 2" title in paperback amounts to less than 0.01% of the average weekly wage today. In the summer of 2004 Amazon.co.uk was offering up to 55% off the RRP of a large selection of recent or even new, that is, non-remaindered, books. Who will pick up the tab? Or rather, how will the book trade economy remain viable in the sense of maintaining a dynamic balance between its various components? One of the purposes of this essay is to look more closely at this dynamic and consider some possible answers.

The large discounts and "3 for 2" actions have their effect, of course, on authors' royalties. (What follows goes only for home sales, not the export market, where the royalty situation is more complex and book prices vary from country to country.) One might at first be tempted to think that the author is the beneficiary of the huge sales that actions such as "3 for 2" must be witness to. But it is the publisher who funds the discounts, and they affect the author's pocket implacably. Let us take any imaginary reputable literary fiction publisher. (For the sake of convenience, it is to be assumed that London is the locus for Britain's publishing world as far as literary fiction is concerned.) Under normal circumstances, a royalty of 10% might be paid over the first 2,500 to 3,000 copies sold; this would rise (according to the so-called "royalty escalator" built into a standard contract) to 12% over the next 2,500 to 3,000 copies sold, and it will peak at 15% thereafter. (A royalty of 20% is not unknown but extremely exceptional – although royalties on English-language literary fiction in translation can be as high as 50%. The extra cost of translation – although most translators are notoriously badly paid – must be factored in here.) Paperback (including trade paperback) royalties might typically be 7% over the first 25,000 copies and 8% thereafter (Todd 1996: 18n; Franklin, personal communication, April 30, 2004). Let us suppose a high-selling hardback title with an RRP of £17 is discounted at 30%. At £17, the royalty due per copy reaches the 15% level (that is, over 5,000 to 6,000 copies have been sold and the royalty escalator topped out), so that per copy the author might expect to earn £2.55.

Instead, the title now retails at just short of £12; on a 15% royalty the author nets just under £1.80, a loss of 75p per title and a decrease of 4.4% on the RRP. Assuming the author has been paid a substantial advance and the advance has been earned out, it is easy to see that, where a 30% discount is in effect, the royalty payable on each additional 10,000 sales will no longer be £2,500 but only about £18,000.

Moreover, if a discount has been available on stock, or a proportion of it, *already* covered by the advance, that advance will clearly not go as far as it would have done without the discount. In the example given in the previous paragraph, the author pockets *at most* less than a third of what might have been expected once the advance has been earned out – or, to put it another way, the advance simply has to stretch further. In an analogous "3 for 2" action, a trade paperback with an RRP of £8 is now going to retail at £5.33. Assuming the escalator has been reached, the royalty of 8.5% would gross the author 68p per copy at RRP, and 45p on a "3 for 2" basis, a loss to the author of 23p, or 30% per copy. It is not inconceivable that 100,000 or more copies might be shifted in a "3 for 2" action, in which case the publisher and ultimately the author would stand to lose £23,000. This may seem hard to believe, but it is no exaggeration to suggest that a very high-selling paperback title such as Monica Ali's *Brick Lane* (2003) or a longer-selling title such as Louis de Bernières' *Captain Corelli's Mandolin* (1994) – of which one million copies were sold in the home market in the first five years after publication (Gill, personal communication, April 29, 2004) – may have discovered its advance eaten into, and its subsequent generated income through royalties dramatically lessened, by amounts such as these figures suggest. In Ali's case, however, one is obliged to admit that she was benefited by her looks, and will have done very well in terms of subsidiary rights that emphasize the author's physical, mediagenic appearance. When we get to the kind of lasting achievement of de Bernières, translation rights will have gained substantial extra income, and in this particular case, film rights as well. By 2001 *Captain Corelli's Mandolin* was available in 11 languages, and de Bernières is reputed to have earned enough from just this one title never to have to work again. Fifty years ago, with truly notable exceptions such as William Golding's *Lord of the Flies* (1954), or George Orwell's *Nineteen Eighty-Four* (1949), this would have been almost unheard of – they are truly notable exceptions because they occupy a permanent place on a perpetual international high-school and university syllabus. While the success of de Bernières is still unusual in the world of literary fiction, these days it is by no means unique.

In the present climate, publishers are all the more alive to cost-cutting possibilities: while the NBA was still in force it was not uncommon to see upmarket trade paperbacks, in B or C format, with a flap that extended inside both front and back covers, allowing room for biodata and blurb, in much the way a hardcover jacket still does. Today, such flaps add 35% to the cost of the cover and, furthermore, slow down production by 10 days (Franklin, personal communication, April 30, 2004). Publishers, in other words, are being forced increasingly onto the back foot.

They have means of fighting back, as may already have become clear above. One survival strategy has been conglomeration. Thus a number of independent publishing houses have now been taken up by a conglomerate such as the Random House group, so that the actual number of independent literary fiction publishers housed in different premises, usually in the Bloomsbury area of London, has halved in the past 10 years. The narrowing of this element of the book trade corresponds to the rapid opening of retail outlets (Gill, personal communication, April 29, 2004), a point to which we will return. The design of a book's jacket can make a difference in sales of several hundred percent (Franklin, personal communication, April 30, 2004), and indeed the retailer can influence the publisher on book jacket design. An established literary publisher can make use of a "totemic" author as a strong marketing asset. It will be no surprise to learn that publishers aggressively promote "lead" authors and titles at the expense of those lower down a given seasonal list, and that they make no secret of this practice: indeed it has been suggested that chain stores may not even stock the lower five on a list of ten (these would, of course, be available through Amazon or other online retail outlets). Publishers can afford to price down lead titles but at the same time they find themselves increasingly under pressure to reinvent the backlist (Franklin, personal communication, April 30, 2004).

By now it will be evident that most people in whatever sector of the book trade are agreed that it is useful to see its shifting dynamics in terms of a triangle involving authors, publishers, and retailers. This whole triangle, it must be stressed at the outset, involves to a very large extent what happens to a fiction title before it is even seen by the consumer. At the top of the imaginary triangle, then, is where a given fiction title originates, with the author – who, today, almost invariably works in cooperation with an agent. ("Slush-pile" titles

– unagented and unsolicited manuscripts circulating around several publishing houses, often simultaneously – have always been with us and will not be treated further here. It is estimated that these number about 800 at any one time (Gill, personal communication, April 29, 2004)). From the agent the manuscript goes along one line of the triangle to the publisher. If it is a title that the agent feels needs to be competed over, there will be an auction. This rarely occurs with a debut title, however (Franklin 2002: 276). If there are likely to be rival bids, a title is submitted, usually by an agent, to a number of selected publishers in order to secure the best offer or highest price. The process is vividly and excitingly described in a recent essay by Dan Franklin, the publishing director of Jonathan Cape (2002: 273ff).

All this may sound straightforward, but the relationship between the best agents and the most successful publishers depends on an indefinable attribute that resists more precise description than to say that the partnership "clicks." The good agent has, and continues to learn to acquire, a nose for what a particular publishing house's "line" is, what is "right for our list" (Franklin 2002: 276). This, of course, applies particularly to debuts and second novels.

Because it is not easy to find in print – outside the established journals of the book trade, such as *The Bookseller* – a first-hand account directed at the laity from what Franklin refers to as "the 'sharp end' of the literary business" (Franklin 2002: 270), his essay is all the more welcome in making clear to a lay readership that the higher the financial stakes (and we are still of course talking about literary fiction: Jonathan Cape has one of the strongest literary fiction lists in Britain), the more dynamic *and reciprocal* the axis between author/agent and publisher is. Put simply, in an extreme potential bestseller case (much more risky for a literary fiction publisher than for a genre fiction publisher) the publisher has to gamble with the company's money, offering an advance (possibly, indeed these days increasingly probably, involving a two- or three-book contract) that may run into hundreds of thousands of pounds. The £500,000 threshold was notoriously set by Martin Amis for *The Information* and what became *Heavy Water* in 1994. Seven-figure two- or three-book title advances for literary fiction are now not unknown.

The publisher has to be so sure the title is worth it that the gamble will pay off in terms of royalties, serialization and other kinds of rights, and the Holy Grail of transformation into the visual media: TV or – better still – film. As we will see, the faster this gambling process at the sharp end becomes, the more difficulties are simultaneously being placed in the way of such a publisher, since in the present retail-driven climate, the retailer (whether online or on the high street) prices ever more competitively. Indeed, the discounts and special offers now available are, quite simply, unprecedented. Let us not forget that retail outlets now include bookstores at airports, where top-selling fiction titles may be stacked in a dumpbin containing as many as 50 to 100 copies, or in supermarket chains, notably Tesco. These are locations that precisely encourage impulse buying at point of sale, particularly if the book or books in question are part of a "3 for 2" action, and even more so given that the public exposed to these outlets will be more likely to have been affected by the "word of mouth" factor, of which more in due course, than is the more "conventional" purchaser of literary fiction (Gill, personal communication, April 29, 2004). All this aggressive retailing in turn gives the high-stakes literary publisher the feeling that she or he is constantly walking on a treadmill, and that an end to this aspect of a dynamic process is far from sight.

It can, of course, all go unaccountably and horribly wrong, as for example with *Bear Me Safely Over* by Sheri Joseph and *Well* by Matthew McIntosh in 2003, titles of which few readers are likely to have heard. Both examples, hyped in the book trade world but commercial failures when it came to sales, meant big losses for their publishers. They are cited in Kate Figes' regular *Bookseller* feature, which now appears at the end of each year in the *Guardian*: the reasons given for the flop are never the same in each case, and all rest on unpredictable factors (Figes 2003).

To return to the less sharp end, and the more usual kind of situation: let us assume that the agent and publisher have reached agreement on a first title (this may involve some rewriting, or other editorial changes). Let us assume further that that agreement has found expression in terms of commercial success (which of course is a widely varied concept). It follows that a partnership between author and publisher will likely be built up. In this way the agent can be seen as having helped consolidate what may, in 10 to 15 years' time, be a strong backlist, an increasingly desirable commodity. At debut stage, however, the agent can play an important role in physically introducing author to potential publisher if, for example, the agent has set up an auction involving three or four publishers, but as already made clear, this kind of situation is the exception rather than the rule for a first novel (Franklin 2002: 274ff, personal communication, April 30, 2004).

Here, to consolidate the picture, I will abstract some information I am grateful to have obtained from correspondence with publicity expert Gail Lynch while researching my 1996 study *Consuming Fictions*. Little of this information has changed in broad terms in the intervening decade. It relies on the inescapable fact that part of the publishers' gamble is deliberately to select, without compromise, a handful of titles each season that will be promoted as leads. Only lead titles are seriously promoted in the sense of being allocated a substantial marketing and publicity budget. The criteria for being considered as a lead author vary. If a debutant, the writer must be "promotable" – in other words, good-looking and preferably telegenic: this will certainly affect the sales conference. If she or he is an experienced writer, the author must be a well-known personality and/or have a strong track record. This seems unfair, and most people would agree that it is: but it is an inevitable consequence not just of the death of the NBA (Anonymous 2004) but of living in a culture so strongly determined, indeed determined as never before, by the power of the visual image.

It is vital that promotion of a lead title be seen to be going on inside the publishing house as well as outside. Mobilization of the publisher's sales force is essential to ensure loyalty within the house. About nine months prior to publication a promotional portfolio will be assembled. Its nature depends on that of the book. According to Lynch (cited in Todd 1996: 98), the main aspect of the portfolio is what is known as a "presenter," a color brochure usually four to twelve pages in length. This is all part of what is known in the book trade as a "blad." The "presenter" will feature a photograph and biographical details of the author, as well as other material relevant to the title being promoted. A notable item is what is known as "packshot." This is a color photograph that shows the book, the poster, and other related items. Increasingly this is now being presented direct to retail outlets, as it can be put together on a webpage. Formerly it would require the intervention of sales representatives at sales conferences, although the latter do of course still take place.

Among expenses not spared in promoting lead titles is the circulation of bound proofs. In most cases this will be between 100 and 200, but the number can exceed this. The astonishing figure of 1,000 bound proofs of Salman Rushdie's *The Moor's Last Sigh*, each individually numbered and signed, was reached in 1995, when it seemed that Rushdie might establish a precedent and win the Booker Prize (now the Man Booker Prize) twice. On that occasion he did not, nor has he done since, but the feat has subsequently been achieved, by J. M. Coetzee in 1999 and by Peter Carey in 2001. About five months before publication these bound proofs are sent to what are known as "long lead" magazines (middlebrow glossies, literary journals) and their reviewers, freelance journalists, and TV and radio contacts. Again, as we shall see, an increasingly important factor in this, as in so many aspects of the book trade, is "word of mouth" (Todd 1996: 99, citing Lynch).

Several weeks before publication, the promotional campaign hits the media, in the form of leading full-length or mixed-item TV arts programs, as well, increasingly, as radio outlets. The general view is that these, more than published reviews, are likely to enhance the word-of-mouth factor. In various ways these specific media outlets contribute, too, to the reader's sense of being increasingly, as the twentieth century has ended and the twenty-first begun, part of a "meet the author" culture. Book signings and readings in bookstores have gradually become major features during the past 10 to 15 years. It may seem odd, when one considers the immense amount of time and preparation that goes into promoting a lead title, that the object of the exercise, having got massive amounts of stock into the store, is to get it out again as quickly as possible. At the moment of publication everything hangs on what Kate Figes (1995) has termed "those crucial six weeks," for if vast amounts of stock have not been shifted within that period, a great deal of time and money have been wasted. Accounts from the first half of the 1980s show how the Booker Prize emerged as an especially powerful lever in this process, capable of increasing sales quickly and dramatically. In 1983 and 1984 a Booker win meant sales within six to eight weeks of between 10,000 and 40,000 in paperback for Salman Rushdie's *Midnight's Children* and Thomas Keneally's *Schindler's Ark* (later to be released as, and filmed by Steven Spielberg as, *Schindler's List* – and becoming, eventually, the most successful Booker winner ever in terms of subsidiary rights). This "Booker effect" has become even more powerful over time. By the 1990s, Roddy Doyle's *Paddy Clarke Ha Ha Ha* must have shifted eight to ten times as much stock as the Rushdie or Keneally novels in the same eight-week period. Within a year of winning the Booker, it had sold over 330,000 copies in hardback and an even higher number in paperback.

Nowadays this sort of rapid turnaround (promotion into the bookstore, retail out of it) is more diffuse, and reminds us that for the purposes of the present argument the literary fiction title is a commodity. It is a luxury (even now), like a CD or a DVD, and not a necessity, like food, and we shall see towards the end of this essay how the triangular relationship between author/agent, publisher, and retailer impacts on the client towards whom the commodity is directed. In an age where the increasingly conglomerate nature of the retail trade had or has still led some to fear that the small independent will die out altogether, it is worth pausing over the success formula of one small independent. The London Review Bookshop is tucked away in a side street, Bury Place, off the imposing front of the British Museum. It is not the sort of store one would accidentally walk past, which it would be if it were situated on Great Russell Street itself. It was launched in May 2003 in the face of an expectant press: if anything could staunch the threatened hemorrhaging of small independents, this was it. And so it has proved, with the store surviving into its third year intact and in a state of promise. The big chain bookstores – Waterstone's, Blackwell's, Borders, W. H. Smith, and even Ottakar's (targeted as it is away from the urban centers at the smaller market towns) – might expect to stock over 50,000 titles, and in the case of the biggest Waterstone's in Piccadilly, well over 100,000. The London Review Bookshop carries around 20,000 titles, usually in one or two copies, allowing it maximum scope for face out (rather than spine out) display, so that one can browse much more comfortably than in a rival chain store (Heawood 2003; Stilwell, personal communication, May 13, 2004). When I spoke to him, its director Andrew Stilwell emphasized the importance of the bookstore's customer base. Active subscriptions are between 40,000 and 45,000 – and lapsed ones (and thus the means to reach at least some of their owners) are over 100,000. Prior to the opening of the store, the LRB's publisher Nicholas Spice calculated that it would require only 4,000 of these motivated subscribers, purchasing seven books a year, to allow the store to stay in profit (Heawood 2003).

Given the central, if reclusive, setting of the London Review Bookshop in Bloomsbury, part of its policy has been to arrange more events than any of its rivals among the chain stores. It is estimated that sixty to eighty such events are held annually, with the summer being the quietest period. They reflect what is covered in, and of importance to, the LRB, where they are advertised, and thus cater directly to the LRB's readership. "A glass or two of wine" is offered – not a unique gesture but still something of a risk in a bookstore with such variegated stock displayed face out. Some events will be publishers' launches, others debates or "conversations." There are concessions for LRB subscribers. These events have turned out to be the one item that defines the London Review Bookshop above all other such stores. They tap strongly into the "meet the author" culture, and are often more confrontational, less genteel, in style than their chain-store counterparts, precisely because the store's staff can be pretty certain what kind of reading public they are going to host. Andrew Stilwell suggested to me that to get an idea of what the store might be like without events, one could do worse than think of the old-style independent, unconglomerated Blackwell's in Oxford's Broad Street in (say) the 1970s (Stilwell, personal communication, May 13, 2004). Since only one or two copies of a given book are stocked by the London Review Bookshop, the rapid ordering of stock is paramount. Clearly it would not be feasible to order via Amazon: the cost of delivery would drive the store out of business – and as it is, the London Review Bookshop has only very lightly and discreetly started discounting its stock.

Stepping back from the retail arm of the author/agent–publisher–retailer triangle for a moment, we must be aware that not to be selected as a lead does not of course mean that the author–publisher relationship cannot continue on affable terms. Indeed, given that the majority of publishers' titles are not going to be promoted as leads and that this is a matter of general knowledge, maintaining good relationships between author (and agent) and publisher is seen by both parties as a matter of great importance, since it may develop into a career-long cooperation. Such cooperation is, of course, not new: consider William Golding's association with Charles Monteith at Faber (even during Golding's unproductive 1970s), or Iris Murdoch's with Norah Smallwood (and later, somewhat less harmoniously, with Carmen Callil) at Chatto & Windus – or even Muriel Spark's less orthodox introduction to Macmillan: her first novel *The Comforters* (1957) was actually commissioned on the basis of her reputation as a poet and short-story writer (something that would be most unlikely to happen today) after an intervention from Graham Greene, and its success consolidated by a favorable response from Evelyn Waugh. But if the first two examples particularly, like others from the 1950s, seem familiar, the familiarity is deceptive. Although one can look at today's backlists of Jonathan Cape, or Bloomsbury, or Chatto & Windus, or Faber & Faber, and find loyal and doubtless contented writers of a younger generation, such as Ian McEwan, Caryl Phillips, Alan Hollinghurst, and Kazuo Ishiguro, respectively, to name four almost at random, striking differences may be discerned.

What has changed? Today all the last four examples will have been agented and carefully copy-edited (Murdoch's refusal to be edited is now legendary), and perhaps most significant, two of the three houses mentioned (Cape and Chatto) have been subsumed into the Random House group for reasons mentioned above, principally survival. Survival includes not just commercial survival: it means ever more insisting (Franklin, personal communication, April 30, 2004) on one's distinctive "look" or "feel." When I spoke to Dan Franklin about this point, he was adamant that I should not use the word that all too temptingly comes to mind – what is distinctive about his own house, Jonathan Cape, is most emphatically *not* a sense of "brand." No publisher of serious literary fiction would disagree with him – although what retail industry pressures may cause in the future cannot be forecast, and here is another example of where the "triangle" is constantly in dynamic motion.

If the publisher is not a brand, that cannot be said of the author. In Franklin's office was the entire Martin Amis backlist, newly repackaged with a very distinctive look. It does seem as though "branding" individual authors is not only *not* "a bad thing" (consider the instance of Iain Banks and Iain M. Banks), but actually essential if a backlist as well as the newest title is to continue to make its way as being recognizably by the same author. Again, this sort of thing is not new, but the importance of keeping the backlist in the public eye is a measure of the strength of the retail industry. The case of Amis is unusual in many ways. Apart from the controversial advance on *The Information* (1995) and the ensuing debate, often unpleasant in nature, most in the book trade would consider the paperback design of that novel to have been a disastrous commercial miscalculation. It seems to have been based on a failure to realize how small (if incredibly enthusiastic) Amis's readership base really is (in Britain it is mostly male, for one thing). Consisting of a large lower-case black "i" on a bright blue background, the paperbacked *Information* omitted to give any information about the title on the jacket.

Of the four literary fiction publishing houses mentioned above, only two, Bloomsbury and Faber & Faber, are still fully independent. One could easily find reasons why they have continued to buck the trend and survive as independents. Faber benefits from a lengthy and distinguished list of authors, many from overseas, and some remarkably litigious literary estates, including those of T. S. Eliot and James Joyce. The difficulty of securing permissions from these estates has been a nightmare for many scholars but a positive boon for the publisher. Bloomsbury's gamble with British author J. K. Rowling and the Harry Potter books tells its own story. Just to give an idea: something in the order of 1.78 million copies of *Harry Potter and the Order of the Phoenix* were sold at its launch alone, that is on one day in June 2003 (www.booktrade.info/index.php?category=news&feed=All&newsitem=4201). In addition Bloomsbury has published and continues to publish writers from North America who have proved remarkably successful in Britain and indeed the Anglophile EU, such as Margaret Atwood, Donna Tartt, and Jeffrey Eugenides.

Returning from the two least powerful axes of the triangle referred to above, the author/agent and the publisher, we are now better positioned to see how they are axes whose fortunes depend on the third. For both would agree with the third, the retailer, that in today's book trade it is indeed the retailer who has the whip-hand. Online retailing took off in Britain in the late 1990s, with the establishment of a British website, Amazon.co.uk, a subsidiary of the American Amazon.com. There is also a German Amazon site used by many mainland Europeans. Today many publishers have set up their own websites (which include retailing opportunities), as have major bookstores, which thus remain on the high street as well as existing in cyberspace. Since the Amazon.co.uk website is probably best known to readers of this essay, the discussion must now focus on it, along with the changes in customer behavior that can be discerned over the past decade or so. To gain a better understanding of how Amazon has positioned itself, however, some knowledge of the history of the battle for the high-street customer during the early 1990s is appropriate. In many ways it is part of a general corporate phenomenon that has characterized the last quarter century (Monbiot 2000).

For most of the twentieth century the most famous retail outlet for books in Britain was Foyles in Charing Cross Road, traditionally one of London's centers for bookstores of all sorts, including specialist stores such as Zwemmers and a host of second-hand bookstores. There were far more small independents than there are today. Today, London's most successful are probably the oldest, the original Hatchard's (founded in Piccadilly in 1797 by John Hatchard), and the London Review Bookshop discussed above in the context of strategies of survival that independent bookstores need to develop and rely on today. During the past decade there has been much jockeying for position among the bigger conglomerates: perhaps the most celebrated titanic struggle was Waterstone's takeover of Dillons, as a result of which there are now approximately 200 branches of Waterstone's in Britain (including the north of Ireland). Ottakar's is approaching the three-figure mark, but has (to date) no online service and – as mentioned above – has sought its niche market in Britain's market towns. Borders and Blackwell's are somewhere in between, and although there are probably more outlets of W. H. Smith, this firm cannot be thought of as "only" a bookstore.

This essay has attempted to survey literary fiction in Britain today in terms of a triangular conception of the book trade. A book originates with an author and her or his agent; from there it moves on to the publisher who purchases it; from there the publisher attempts to get a return on his or her investment in that purchase by working with (in every sense) the retail arm of the book trade. As we have seen, at this moment in the first decade of the twenty-first century, it is the retailer who is calling the shots, and we have given as the main reason for this state of affairs the abolition of RPM. This, however, so baldly stated, belies the extent to which as early as the 1980s and 1990s something of a renaissance in the retail trade could already be detected: it may be traced to the 1980 Booker Prize "two-horse race" between William Golding (who won) and Anthony Burgess (the first time there began to be talk of "favorites"), and Salman Rushdie's defining win with *Midnight's Children* in 1981.

However, as already indicated, this dynamic triangle could not exist without the consumer or client, the purchaser of the commodity that all three points of the triangle have worked together to produce. Once the product is in the bookstore, or online on your Amazon webpage, you can choose to purchase it or click on it or not. But how does the customer who likes to be considered a book buyer and book reader find out what's in and what's out? Contrary to popular belief, reviews appear to make little difference. What does make all the difference, as already suggested, is that evasive quality, whose workings few would claim to understand, "word of mouth."

Ten to fifteen years ago a fad sprang up, seemingly out of nowhere, and spread across much of Britain. The "reading club" or "reading group" was a typically middle-class and typically feminine phenomenon. A group of young to middle-aged to elderly women would take turns to host an evening, perhaps once a month, at which a previously agreed-upon title would be discussed, informally, unpretentiously, unacademically, and non-competitively. In this manner, acquaintances being what they are, a chosen book, if deemed a success by the group (the criteria are inscrutable), would spread by word of mouth. People might then see others reading it on public transport (it is amazing, given the conditions in which they are doing so, how many London tube travelers can be observed reading while on their journey). The extent to which this alternative reading group "canon" was itself recognized by the retail trade is an interesting case of an insoluble "cause and effect" paradigm.

At about the same time that this *Gestalt* shift was taking place, a shift that was really a form of democratization – the fiction title, usually "literary," was coming out of the academy and into the household – could be observed in the direction of mediatization. The first, or at least most celebrated, TV discussion of a book (not necessarily a contemporary or even a fiction title) that was not part of a highbrow arts program was sponsored by Oprah Winfrey. If her agenda was to get middle America to pay attention to African American fiction, it worked. Of course, only a small number of Oprah books was written by African American authors, and Toni Morrison was probably her hardest sell. Oprah's mission, she said, was "to get America reading again."

In Britain, Oprah – whose book club has subsequently undergone various changes – has been eclipsed by Richard and Judy's Book Club. Amanda Ross, who runs Cactus TV, came up with what might have seemed a risky proposal at the time but has turned out to be a brainwave. She decided that there was a niche slot for the husband-and-wife team Richard Madeley and Judy Finnigan, former daytime talk show hosts for Channel 4, to host a popular book show at 5 p.m., "tea-time" viewing not considered propitious for any kind of serious TV (Thorpe & Asthana 2004). The show first went on the air in 2002. As Oliver Bennett put it in the *Independent*:

> What is their magic ingredient? For it seems that *R&J* mobilises the rump of British readers. Sure, the Booker, Whitbread and Orange awards shift [their] product, but if a *Publishing News* survey is to be believed, an astonishing 1.8 million people have picked up books as a result of *R&J* exposure. "In terms of immediate impact on sales, nothing tops *R&J*," says Scott Pack, chief buyer at Waterstone's. "It's wonderful for the industry," adds Joel Rickett of *The Bookseller*." (Bennet 2004)

It must be pointed out that not all Richard and Judy recommendations are novels. The interesting feature of their lists is the relatively high proportion that would be considered literary novels – admittedly not at the Lawrence Norfolk end of that spectrum. Journalists may have condescendingly referred to Richard and Judy as "the saucy, perma-tanned First Couple of sofa television" (Bennett 2004). But from quarters where snobbery might have been expected, it was not forthcoming: thus the *TLS*'s David Horspool described the couple's first 10-week book club list as "not particularly lowbrow" and the *LRB*'s Thomas Jones felt it represented "the quality end of easy reading" (Bennett 2004). There will never be agreement about manner, but Richard and Judy were felt to be neither condescending nor superficial. Adverse publicity, in fact, seems to have come from those who believed that the formula chosen by Amanda Ross could not succeed. Books that have already "made it" tend not to do particularly well after Richard and Judy exposure whereas unknown titles often do.

In effect, the Richard and Judy Book Club is turning out to be the suburban reading club writ large. If Vanessa Thorpe and Anushka Asthana are to believed, "Essex is the book club capital of Britain," and:

> Book clubs . . . demand to be taken seriously as a social phenomenon as much as a commercial phenomenon because they are increasingly functioning as an equivalent to a Rotary or Masonry for women. They are effectively Old Girls' networks, where important deals are done and job opportunities are discussed. They also provide support for women who might otherwise be isolated. (Thorpe & Asthana 2004)

An anecdote stemming from the reception of the Richard and Judy Book Club concerns a man who, on his own admission, had not opened a book for 40 years, dipped into a title on their list, and decided he would spend the rest of his life reading much more. This may be an exaggeration, but there can be no doubt that if authors, agents, and publishers feel pushed into a corner by the retail industry at this particular historical moment, they should take consolation from what today's events suggest. Literary fiction, if this analysis of its presence in the book trade is correct, and despite the fears of those at the sharp end of the book trade, is opening, democratizing, and in general extending the customer's imaginative and societal franchise. Word of mouth, in however odd and unexpected a manifestation, has come of age.

Acknowledgments

In this essay I have also tacitly drawn on earlier conversations with the following, most of which took place while I was researching *Consuming Fictions*: Jonathan Burnham, Liz Calder, David Godwin, and Peter Straus.

References and Further Reading

NONFICTION

Anonymous (2004). Editorial leader. Narrowing the range. *The Bookseller*, 5 January.

Bennett, Oliver (2004). Never judge a book by its clubbers. *The Independent*, 28 June.

Dearnley, James & Feather, John (2002). The UK bookselling trade without resale price maintenance: an overview of change 1995–2001. *Publishing Research Quarterly*, 17(4), 16–31.

Figes, Kate (1995). Those crucial six weeks. The Sunday Review. *The Independent on Sunday*, 12 November, 32–3.

Figes, Kate (2003). The ones that got away. *The Guardian: Books Review*, 20 December.

Franklin, Dan (2002). Commissioning and editing modern fiction. In Zachary Leader (ed.), *On Modern British Fiction* (pp. 270–83). Oxford: Oxford University Press.

Hawkes, Terence (1986). *That Shakespeherian Rag: Essays on a critical process*. London: Methuen.

Heawood, Jonathan (2003). Small, but perfectly formed. *The Observer*, 27 April.

Leader, Zachary, ed. (2002). *On Modern British Fiction*. Oxford: Oxford University Press.

Monbiot, George (2000). *Captive State: The corporate takeover of Britain*. London: Macmillan.

Publishers Association (2005). Glossary of book trade terminology. Available at: http://www.publishers.org.uk/paweb/paweb.nsf/pubframe!Open.

Sutherland, John A. (1978). *Fiction and the Fiction Industry*. London: Athlone Press.

Thorpe, Vanessa & Asthana, Anushka (2004). If you want a best seller, read her lips. *The Observer*, 2 May.

Todd, Richard (1996). *Consuming Fictions: The Booker Prize and fiction in Britain today*. London: Bloomsbury.

Twigger, Robert (1999). Inflation: the value of the pound 1750–1998. House of Commons Research Paper 99/20, 23 February 1999. Available at: www.parliament.uk/commons/lib/research/rp99/rp99-020.pdf.

FICTION

Ali, Monica (2003). *Brick Lane*. London: Doubleday.

Amis, Martin (1995). *The Information*. New York: Harmony.

de Bernières, Louis (1994). *Captain Corelli's Mandolin*. London: Secker & Warburg.

Doyle, Roddy (1993). *Paddy Clarke Ha Ha Ha*. London: Secker & Warburg.
Joseph, Sheri (2003). *Bear Me Safely Over*. London: Virago.
Keneally, Thomas (1982). *Schindler's Ark*. London: Hodder.
McIntosh, Matthew (2003). *Well*. New York: Grove.
Rowling, J. K. (2003). *Harry Potter and the Order of the Phoenix*. London: Bloomsbury.
Rushdie, Salman (1981). *Midnight's Children*. London: Jonathan Cape.
Rushdie, Salman (1995). *The Moor's Last Sigh*. London: Jonathan Cape.

Chapter 2

Literary Authorship and Celebrity Culture

James F. English and John Frow

Salman Rushdie dramatically emerges from two years in hiding to join Bono and U2 onstage at a sold-out Wembley stadium concert; the band later records a song based on Rushdie lyrics and sharing a title with a Rushdie novel (that novel in turn featuring a rock band partly based on U2). Martin Amis receives a generous advance for a satirical novel about the contemporary London literary scene, spending a portion of it on high-end dental surgery in New York; both his income and his dentistry are given weeks of coverage in the British newspapers and on book-chat TV, with people reputed to be models for the characters in his novel making public statements regarding his ethics and his finances. Zadie Smith, whose autograph becomes valuable after the smash success of her first novel, writes a second novel about a man who collects and trades autographs of the famous; a friend of hers, on whom this character is partly modeled and to whom the novel is dedicated, attends her book launch, where he finds his own autograph in demand among Smith's autograph-hunting fans.

Writers like these – and one could add Helen Fielding, Nick Hornby, J. K. Rowling, Arundhati Roy, Will Self, Jeanette Winterson, and a handful of others – are not simply successful or acclaimed novelists; they are *celebrity novelists*, novelists whose public personae, whose "personalities," whose "real-life" stories have become objects of special fascination and intense scrutiny, effectively dominating the reception of their work. And their celebrity, predicated as it is on images and narratives in the media, has increasingly become an object of fervent media attention in its own right, serving as a major nodal point for discussion and debate about the condition of British literature. Is the celebrity of these authors commensurate with their literary achievements? Has their celebrity corroded their talent, ruined them as writers – and perhaps ruined us as readers, as well, focusing our collective attention too much on the lives of the literati and too little on literature itself? Has British fiction as a whole been degraded by the culture of celebrity in which it now appears to be so thoroughly embedded?

Over the past quarter century, such questions have become staples of literary journalism and, allowing for somewhat different framings and emphases, of academic study, as well. Such attention is not unwarranted – literary celebrity is indeed an important phenomenon, closely linked to a whole range of changes that have been taking place in contemporary British society. But we should not allow all the attention that has lately been directed toward this topic to persuade us that the phenomenon as such is something strikingly new. Literary celebrity has a long history, and one that is thoroughly, if problematically, intertwined with the construction of the British literary canon, shaping the careers of Johnson, Sterne, and Burney in the eighteenth century, of Byron, Dickens, and Wilde in the nineteenth, and of Wells, Waugh, and even Joyce (who was twice featured on the cover of *Time* magazine) in the first half of the twentieth – to name just an obvious few. The very possibility of a modern (post-patronage) literary field has depended less on the production of a new kind of literature than on the production of a new apparatus of authorship capable of focusing popular excitement and fascination on certain figures, certain constructed personalities. And the fact that there has been both overlap and striking divergence between this set of celebrity figures on the one hand and the authors who over time command greatest esteem among other writers and critics on the other has meant that fame of this sort, though apparently unavoidable, has always presented itself as something of a "problem" for literary study. What has occurred since the 1970s is that this problem has come to seem more acute and more urgent, and to occupy a more central place in the discourse on literary value. As Leo Braudy observes in the afterward to his capacious study *The Frenzy of Renown*, while "fame has been the subject of much writing and visual art for centuries, . . . the peculiarly widespread preoccupation with its shapes and distortions is our own. We didn't invent fame, but we have become almost swallowed up by its insistent presence and by its paraphernalia" (Braudy 1997: 599).

Celebrity and the Economics of Culture

How do we account for this greatly intensified focus on the form and figure of the celebrity in cultural life generally, and in the British literary world specifically? In its broadest contours, this transformation of the cultural sphere must be understood as a matter of economics. But the economics of culture is too often reduced to cultural economism – both by mainstream arts and business journalists and by academic culture critics. To take one example from the former group, the editors of *Forbes* magazine are quick to declare that "money is still the most important metric of celebrity." A business magazine known for its lists of the world's largest companies and wealthiest individuals, *Forbes* has lately taken to publishing an annual index of the world's top celebrities, mostly "cultural" figures of one sort or another – and it is notable that for the past two years the highest-ranked author on that list, the sixth highest person overall, and the third-highest in the frequency with which she is referenced on television, has been the British novelist J. K. Rowling, whom *Forbes* has also recently, and not coincidentally, welcomed to the "Billionaire's Club" (a distinction which neither the Queen nor even Stephen King has yet attained). Much of the burgeoning academic scholarship on literary celebrity would essentially endorse the *Forbes* metric in regarding celebrity as a euphemized or thinly disguised form of money: it is the *personality form* of money, which appears on the fields of cultural activity wherever artists have come to be dominated by commerce. The seeming ubiquity of the phenomenon is thus read as a symptom of the ubiquity of the commodity form itself: with the increasing commodification of fields such as music, video, film, literature, sport, dance, radio, television, theater, gaming, and the internet – their unification in a vast global "entertainment" market – has come ever more powerfully elaborated and synergistic devices of publicity and promotion. The phenomenon of the literary celebrity, as the example of Rowling would seem to make clear (given that Harry Potter is fast closing in on Star Wars as the dominant art/entertainment "franchise" of the last quarter century), has more to do with intensified media conglomeration, increasingly sophisticated and conscious brand management, expanding intellectual property rights, and, at bottom, the massification of capital, than it does with literary practices (reading, writing, criticism) or literary value "as such." "Celebrity," Loren Glass has argued, "makes authorship a corporate affair" (Glass 2001: 672).

In the British context, this narrative of the commodification of literature and the concomitant elaboration of a corporate-managed literary star system can be readily mapped onto resonant nationalist narratives of declining British self-determination in the face of rising American economic and cultural hegemony. The "blockbuster" paradigm that first emerged in American-based publishing houses during the 1970s, and the corresponding emphasis both on short-term profits and on a thoroughly rationalized business plan even for what we think of as high-cultural production, are seen as propelling a global shift in literary life toward the kind of polarized, winner-take-all economy that characterizes American society in general. An ostensibly traditional British system in which many productive and talented novelists were provided with a modest living on the basis of the cultural or aesthetic value of their work was thus (according to this view) supplanted by an American-style system, in which a tiny handful of authors become figures of great wealth, renown, and visibility. Having in effect won the jackpot of this new system, these lucky few become not just "household names" but owners of widely leveraged and highly lucrative "brand names." Apart from signing multi-book contracts and film-rights deals (which may go so far as to specify certain narrative features thought to be constitutive of the brand), these authors might appear in major films as "themselves," or endorse a particular malt whiskey in magazine ads, or tour with a rock band to promote some philanthropic cause, or authorize a board game based on the characters from their fiction: all of these extensions of the brand carefully managed, to avoid "dilution," by a "superstar" agent – most likely, an American agent. Their literary peers, meanwhile, however indistinguishable or even superior in terms of perceived artistic merit, struggle ever harder simply to get their works into print.

This way of understanding and critiquing the rise of literary celebrity culture in Britain is not altogether invalid. The increasingly rationalized and sophisticated business of celebrity-construction has been carefully detailed by Look (1999), Rein, Kotler, and Stoller (1987), and others. But jeremiads against commodification, whether or not they specify America (or "American-style" capitalism: as though capitalism as such had some other, more benign trajectory) as the immediate source of the problem, tend to go wrong in several ways. To begin with, in emphasizing the link between literary celebrity and Americanization, they overlook the fact that literary celebrity culture has long been more intense and frantic in Britain than in the States. *Harper's New Monthly Magazine* warned in 1860 of the British penchant for "talking about the private history of public men – prying into their bathing tubs and counting the moles upon their necks . . . peeping at keyholes and listening at cracks," and called for Americans to resist this decadent tendency "for the honor of the guild, for the fair name of literature" (Avery & Maunder 2001: 1). In recent decades, it has been Britain that has produced most of the innovations in such institutions of literature as prizes, festivals, book-chat radio and TV programs, and so forth. The US has been playing catchup since at least the early 1980s, when the director of the American Book Awards journeyed to London to try to learn from Martyn Goff, chief administrator of the Booker Prize, how to generate some excitement and publicity over a literary award (a goal that appears still to be out of reach for the American prizes).

More significantly, insofar as they call for a reversal or rejection of corrosively anti-literary trends, these attacks on the brand-naming and celebritizing of British literature depend on an aesthetic ideology in which the ideal, the goal, and oftentimes the golden age of the past is defined in terms of a "pure" artistic value uncontaminated by commerce or hype. The root interdependence of aesthetics and economics within what Barbara Herrnstein Smith has famously called the "double discourse of value" – an interdependence most thoroughly mapped and theorized in the work of Pierre Bourdieu – is thus conveniently removed from view (Smith 1988: 30–5; Bourdieu 1996). Moreover, in their characterization of the current arrangements of literary production, these narratives of cultural commodification tend to overstate the congruence or perfect alignment of what remain distinct (though, as always, interdependent) economies of fame, money, literary reputation, and so forth. The blockbuster authors, after all, are neither the most famous personalities nor the most highly esteemed writers among other authors and critics. As the example of Rowling indicates, extraordinary commercial success can sometimes lead to widespread interest in the figure of the author herself, just as this kind of popular attention to the person can be leveraged into commercial success for the work (hence the proliferation in recent decades of novels by politicians, movie stars, and other celebrities drawn from beyond the literary field; Madonna has recently joined Rowling in the ranks of children's authors). But most of the world's best-selling authors (Nora Roberts, John Grisham, Robert Ludlum) are merely names: powerful brand names, to be sure, but lacking the aura of "personality," possessing no resonance as public media figures, and hence not functioning as celebrities at all. And, by the same token, many of the most visible, media-attracting writer–personalities, from Martin Amis to Will Self, enjoy no more than middling book sales – at least by the standards of the blockbuster. Furthermore, neither of these registers – celebrity or commerce – aligns perfectly with that of recognition, or prestige among those (the appropriately credentialed literary experts) who are empowered to confer artistic legitimacy (Lang & Lang 1998). By the time of her death in 2000, Penelope Fitzgerald was being praised by well-positioned critics in the pages of influential literary journals like *TLS*, *LRB*, and the *New York Times Book Review* as Britain's greatest living writer, and her work was being taught by scholars on both sides of the Atlantic. Yet she remained decidedly invisible to an instrument such as the *Forbes Celebrity Index* in terms of both media profile and income.

It should be added, as well, that the commonplace and generally alarmist narratives of cultural commodification tend to conceive of literary celebrity as something wholly generated by the machinery of commerce and put to work in such a way as always to advance the interests of corporate profit – an error which Richard Dyer, in his pathbreaking 1979 study of cinematic celebrity, *Stars*, had already identified as the chief weakness of such classic texts as Daniel Boorstin's *The Image* (1961). Over-emphasis on "the machinery of [stars'] production" (Dyer 1979: 13) means a neglect of other kinds of interests that come into play as, for example, when writers themselves strive, not only through media appearances but in their very practice as writers, to manipulate the form and function of celebrity and to short-circuit some of its usual effects (Margolis 1995; Moran 2000; Pattanaik 1998); or when particular constellations of fans emerge, imposing their own interpretations of the celebrity image as a way of promoting their own social and psychic agendas (Ferris 2001; Fiske 1989); or when the semiotics of a given text break loose from both authorial intention and corporate handling, inducing profound social and political effects (Wicke 1998). Just as scholars of Hollywood's star system have had to recognize that movie stars are produced not simply by the industry's commercial machinery but also by actors' performative strategies, audiences' acts of consumption, and the sheer power of the cinematic image (Gledhill 1991; McDonald 1998), literary scholars need to be wary of overly narrow theories of cultural production.

If in what follows, therefore, we attempt to sketch out an economics of literary celebrity in contemporary Britain, it is with the understanding that the economics here is rather more complex than the usual clamor over literature's new "star system" suggests. We want to be clear that British fiction is, like any field or subfield of cultural activity, not simply the site of a grand struggle between art and money but a complex system in which different kinds of agents or players (from writers and critics and journalists, to prize administrators and sponsors and judges, to librarians, teachers, and school administrators, to booksellers, book-club organizers, radio producers, and TV programmers, to various kinds of purchasers, borrowers, and readers) conduct transactions involving distinct forms of capital (economic, symbolic, journalistic, educational, political, social), all of which are partially but none of which is perfectly fungible with the others (Bourdieu 1986). These cultural agents do not all have the same goals; certainly not every transaction aims at maximizing money profit. When we consider the rise of literary celebrity against the backdrop of changes that have taken place in this whole system over the last few decades, it is not very illuminating to say that literature has become "more commercial" or to conceive the situation in terms of an ideally free or autonomous literary space increasingly "penetrated" by the logic of commerce. It is necessary, rather, to accept from the start a more multidimensional model of the literary field, and to propose that both the individual and the institutional agents involved in literary production (which means the production not just of books, but of the regimes of literary value) have come to act more strategically, and the kinds of transaction and exchange that transpire among them are becoming more sophisticated – more "advanced," perhaps, in terms of the historical logic of cultural value. The intense celebrity culture of contemporary British literature, in short, is a symptom not of homogenization and simplification ("it's all about money now"), but rather of increasing complexity in the way that literary value is produced and circulated. Even if that complexity may be resolved into a net gain for commercial interests over the past few decades, we need to take into account the openings and opportunities that celebrity authors might represent for other sorts of interests to advance themselves.

We can take the measure of this process of complexification by comparing the growth of the fiction industry in Britain to the growth of what we might term the literary-value industry, that is, the whole set of individuals and groups and institutions involved not in producing contemporary fiction as such but in producing the reputations and status positions of contemporary works and authors, situating them on various scales of worth. The past 30 years have witnessed substantial growth in both areas, but the latter has greatly outpaced the former. In the 1970s, the British publishing industry had yet to recover fully from its decimation during World War II and from subsequent prolonged paper shortages; only in the early 1980s did the industry begin to publish significantly more new fiction titles each year (about 3,500) than it had done in the mid- to late-1930s (Todd 1996). Since that time, there has been a gradual expansion (to about 7,000 new titles per year), and total sales of fiction books have likewise increased, by about 50 percent in real terms.

While these numbers represent a relatively robust period in the history of British fiction publishing, they pale in comparison with the growth and diversification of the literary-value industry. The universities, to begin with, had yet in the 1970s to produce any substantial critical literature on postwar fiction or even to extend the literary curriculum beyond 1939. Academic journals and literary magazines specializing in contemporary literature were few and obscure, and the mainstream book reviews for the most part served a conservative function, presenting more obstacles than opportunities to emergent strains of fiction. There were only a handful of literary prizes and awards, none of them at all well known or capable of exercising a significant effect on the literary field – with the single exception of the Booker Prize, which had been founded in 1969 precisely to fill this perceived vacuum, and which was just beginning, in the early to mid-1970s, to make a sizable impact (English 2004).

By the start of the new century the situation was radically changed. Before she was elected Prime Minister in 1979, Margaret Thatcher had been minister of education in the shadow government, and the impact of her government on the higher educational sector was, and continues to be, profound. For reasons too complex to discuss here, the literary wing of the professoriate has become both more contemporary in its scholarly emphases and more productive of scholarly writing. Most universities now offer a whole range of courses in contemporary fiction; doctoral programs produce more new specialists in this than in any other literary field; critical studies of contemporary fiction, particularly in its relationship to theories of empire and postcolonialism, have proliferated many times more rapidly than works of fiction themselves – as have new scholarly journals devoted primarily to contemporary writing. Outside the university, the literary magazines, which had been struggling through cuts in Arts Council funding and had just witnessed the collapse of Ian Hamilton's *New Review* (1974–8), made a stunning comeback with the 1979 launch of *Granta*, a glossy book-sized quarterly that in its first year heralded "the end of the

English novel [and] the beginning of British fiction." The founding of the *London Review of Books* that same year represented a similar renaissance in mainstream cultural criticism. Most tellingly, literary awards, led by the example of the Booker Prize (which was first televised on BBC in 1976), have become so ubiquitous since the late 1970s that jokes about there being more prizes than authors are now a cliché of literary journalism.

One should place particular stress on the explosive growth of book awards because they go to the heart of the new institutional arrangement. It is not just the relative expansion of existing institutions that has been transformative of the British fiction scene, but the new strategies at work within and between these institutions, and their increased willingness and capacity to articulate their agendas with one another. Always concerned with the evaluation of literature, the institutional apparatus has became increasingly embedded in what Todd characterizes as a "general atmosphere of canon formation" dating from the early 1980s (Todd 1996: 9). Rather than simply surveying, reviewing, recommending, and critiquing new fiction, these institutions have devoted themselves increasingly to the production of competitive forums, ranked lists, best-of selections, and other quite overt forms of win/lose distinction which either reinforce or counterpose one another. Early in its existence, *Granta* collaborated with the Book Marketing Council to devote an issue to what it called the "Best of the Young British Novelists" (1983). The issue attracted so much attention, to the magazine as well as to the authors selected, that the device was repeated in 1993 and again in 2003; today, BYBN is perhaps what *Granta* is best known for. The first BYBN list managed to anticipate the future winners of, and thus to join forces with, the Booker Prize in the very period of that prize's cultural ascension, while its second iteration reinforced the perception of a male bias in these kinds of consecration and thereby contributed to the founding, two years later, of the Orange Prize for Fiction by Women. Other overlapping and interrelated devices of this sort include the Waterstone's Book-of-the-Month promotions (launched in 1990 and expanded to include a Book-of-the-Century selection in 1995, then reborn as a monthly book-club promotion tied to the Orange Prize); the increasingly ubiquitous top-10 and top-100 best-novel lists; the discernible shift in book-chat radio toward "Book of the Month" (Radio 3), "Book Choice" (Radio 4), or "Big Read" listeners' poll (BBC) formats; and the dramatic expansion of the literary festival circuit (which has made increasing use of tie-ins both with radio polls and with prize shortlists;

organizers of the London festival have gone so far as to include a "Lit Idol" contest modeled on the TV program *Pop Idol*).

All these devices are notable for their capacity to link canonicity with seriality, and thus to assure that, at regular intervals, today's "best" will be displaced by a new winner. Indeed, their mutual co-operation typically takes the form of conscious synchronization; they assure the effectivity of each other's schedules and the rationality of the "literary calendar" as a whole. The pace at which determinations of literary value are made is thus sped up to match the what's-hot/what's-not logic of the fashion system that governs consumption of everything from clothing to nightclubs to automobiles, and whose expansion into new social arenas has been called a determining characteristic of postmodern society (Harvey 1990).

But while this vastly expanded (and still expanding) array of symbolic instruments and institutions can be seen to operate as a fashion system or an "industry" of literary value production, it is far from monolithic in form and function. What this system does is not to create consensus but rather to produce points of contact and contradiction between different scales or registers of value. Joe Moran has argued that celebrity authors are typically figures who "straddle the divide" between literary coterie and mass readership (what Bourdieu (1993) calls the "restricted" and "general" fields of production), and whose "ambiguous" or "crossover" position thus captures "tensions involved in the production of literary celebrity between the legitimacy of culture and the . . . sanction of the marketplace" (Moran 2000: 6–7). Such tensions frequently erupt in the form of what Janice Radway (1990) and Joan Shelley Rubin (1992) have called "scandals of the middlebrow," scandals revolving around charges of inauthenticity, impurity, or selling-out on the part of an author whose too complete or comfortable popularity is thought incommensurate with true literary genius.

From the Signature to the Brand Name

The necessity for contemporary celebrity authors to embody a kind of (scandalous) cultural impurity, to be always located at the intersection of competing regimes of value, may be understood in terms of a broader historical shift over the last century from a model of authorship dominated by the signature to one dominated by the brand name. The major historical reference point for this shift is the Hollywood star system, and particularly that moment after World War II when stars began to take commercial control of their on- and off-screen personas. In her analysis of Hollywood contracts in this period, Jane Gaines found an increasing specification of the actors' rights to market their image, taking over sources of revenue such as merchandising tie-ups and product endorsements which had previously been the prerogative of the studios. At the same time a range of new legal mechanisms, particularly the US right of publicity, which allows public figures to control the exploitation of their image, consolidates a set of property rights in the representation of commercially valuable personal identities. This shift, she argues, is something like a move from a regime of copyright to a regime of trademark, in the sense that "while copyright law still upholds some remnant of the older cultural valuation of individual enterprise and creativity, the trademark unapologetically stands for market expansion and control" (Gaines 1991: 211).

Yet a similar shift had been evident well before this moment, although less systematically, in the world of writing. Glass documents Mark Twain's attempts to register his name and signature as a trademark, as well as the incorporation in 1908 of his legal person (the Mark Twain pen-name) in the Mark Twain Company. This move, as Moran notes, was designed to protect the value not just of his books but of a range of subsidiary products with which his name was associated, including "postcards, cigars, tobacco, whisky, a patented self-pasting scrapbook and a board game, 'Mark Twain's memory builder'" (Moran 2000: 23). His "inspiration that his name could be considered a trademark or brand name," Glass writes,

> reveals his acute understanding of how this emergent legal discourse corresponded to changes in the cultural meaning of authorship. Whereas copyright is based in a legal relation of property between the author and the text, the authorial name or signature as a metaphorical form of trade mark explicitly acknowledges a cultural relation of recognition between the public and the text. (Glass 2001: 689)

Twain's action thus responds to the role played by his immense popularity in the constitution of his texts, and more broadly to his "peculiar location, late in life, between a restricted field of cultural production that mandates a posthumous reputation and a general field of cultural production that mandates contemporaneous mass cultural celebrity" (Glass 2001: 672).

It is this "peculiar location" that defines the place and the scandal of celebrity in the domains of "high" culture in contemporary Britain. For the domains of "popular" culture these tensions do not exist in the same way, and celebrity has been deployed ever more extensively as an uncomplicated way of selling product. The major impetus perhaps came with the concerted advertising campaigns for Swinging Britain in the 1960s, with the Beatles and a host of lesser figures at their center. The culture of celebrity now pervades the tabloid press, where gossip about figures known only by their first names has largely displaced traditional news, and it drives much of television, dominated now by game-show and "reality TV" formats. Sport, too, is increasingly represented through its celebrity figures and the forms of merchandising they generate: David Beckham has trademarked his name for perfumes and toiletries, keyrings, DVDs and computer accessories, watches, posters and calendars, clothing (including football kit), and games – but not for football (Davies 2004: para. 3).

More striking than anything in the literary world has been the promotional apparatus that has, for all intents and purposes, created the canon of contemporary British art. A single figure, Charles Saatchi, has combined patronage on a Renaissance scale with the resources of his advertising agency to define the group of conceptual artists known as Young British Artists (YBAs) as the cutting edge of the art world, with BritArt as its brand name. Its leading figures – Damien Hirst, Tracy Emin, the Chapman brothers – have reproduced the strategies of the great publicity machines of the earlier twentieth-century avant-gardes to create scandal and copy, and reputations that thrive on both.

It is of course true that the production of scandal has been integral to modernist art, writing, and music from Monet, Baudelaire, and Wagner onwards. What has changed over the last couple of decades is perhaps that scandal has come adrift from the work of art – since we are all inured now to aesthetic provocation – and attaches itself more firmly to the person; the very cynicism of and towards the machinery of mass publicity allows it to be seen to be manufacturing controversy without attracting censure, which would in any case only feed it. Fay Weldon's acceptance of an undisclosed payment from the Italian jeweler Bulgari to write a novel (*The Bulgari Connection*) which is entirely an exercise in product placement is of interest less for the predictable condemnation she received than for the widespread acceptance that this step was inevitable, and acceptance, too, of Weldon's portrayal of herself as provocateuse ("They never give me the Booker Prize anyway"); the scandal was that there was no scandal.

If celebrity in the worlds of art, of classical music (Nigel Kennedy, Simon Rattle), and of literature is in important ways different from celebrity in popular culture, it can nevertheless always be defined by the fact that it is largely created outside and beyond the immediate domain of recognition and across a range of secondary media. Just as the Hollywood star was constructed above all in the fanzines, so the construction of literary celebrity takes place in the press and on television. Its specificity resides in the particular media niches where this occurs, and the distinctive modalities it takes. *Hello!* and *OK!* magazines don't care about Martin Amis's teeth; the Sunday broadsheets, continuing a long British tradition of *feuilleton* journalism, do. So does the *South Bank Show*, much of BBC Radio 4, and some of the more high-minded late-night quiz and chat shows which regularly feature the likes of Germaine Greer, Will Self, or Clive James. (None of these, however, give the kind of platform for serious political and social commentary that one could find on Canal Plus, where intellectuals like Bernard-Henri Lévy or Pierre Bourdieu were assumed to have something to say about the world beyond books.)

Yet a peculiarity of the mass market in which literary celebrity flourishes and which it helps to sustain is that it lacks one of the characteristic features of such markets: their impersonality – the fact, that is to say, that sellers and buyers are typically strangers to each other, that an author can never personally know most of his or her readership. Readers, it seems, crave the personal presence of the author; they want to listen to them read or talk, and they want them to sign their books. So it is in the sites of authorial presence – in the book festivals of Hay-on-Wye and Edinburgh and a host of lesser meetings, in bookshop readings by everyone from J. K. Rowling to the local self-published poet – that hundreds of thousands of readers come to listen and talk to the authors whose books they will then buy. Behind the text is the author; if the case of Mark Twain reveals how contemporary mass-cultural celebrity has come to inflect the older regimes of the signature, the reverse is nevertheless also true: the readerly desire for authorial authenticity continues to inflect the branded, quality-controlled seriality of industrialized literary production. The peculiarity of contemporary literary celebrity is, then, that it brings these two modalities together: a notion of authenticity and of personal presence that characterized the Romantic regimes of authoriality, of signature, and of copyright; and a model of seriality that is characteristic of the contemporary culture industries.

The model of the author as brand name is thus never a completely commercial model; it is, rather, a matter of the careful management of a persona which continues to be seen as the source of value, not a figure of the author as, say, commercial entrepreneur, or as an assembly team. One of the flaws in the Romantic model of authorship, however, is that books are not performances of a persona in the way that a film or a song can be taken to be: the figure of the writer does not occupy the stage as that of the performer does, and there are good grounds, particularly perhaps in the case of fiction, to assume that what the text is "about" is the story it tells, not the storyteller. Nevertheless, Romantic authorship requires a persona, and literary texts are, accordingly, read as kinds of performance, the acting out of the inner life of the author. Celebrity, we could say, is the production of persona in secondary performances (on television or radio or in newspaper columns) *as though* they were merely supplements or reflections of the "real" performance of persona in the book. It depends upon the signature effect, the effect of authenticity, and on its careful fostering in the marketplace.

Rather than forming contrasting regimes of value, the aesthetics of the signature and of the brand are successive but complementary orders, where the latter is at once more explicitly commercial in its orientation and yet more openly concerned with the value of the signature (that is, of authorial presence). This is the source of the paradox that informs it: that it constitutes a (further, enhanced) commercialization of something that is, in principle, beyond considerations of commercial value. The authorial brand name, the name as a mark of trade and of quality control, undermines its own first premise (cf. Frow 2002).

The tensions inherent in literary celebrity have to do with these contradictions in the aesthetics of authorial presence that sustains canonical literary value. The figure of the noncommercial author, disinterested and remote from the market, is of course almost entirely a figment of the cultural imagination, although certain writers (Jane Austen, Emily Brontë, even Joyce) can with a bit of stretching be made to fit the outline. Its more realistic version today might be the figure of the *moderately* commercial writer, the craftsperson who chooses the work over the life: a William Trevor, a Timothy Mo, a Penelope Fitzgerald, perhaps – to all of whom a certain anonymity attaches. Yet they too take a part in the game of brand-name creation and maintenance, and have a readership which is loyal to their name.

The celebrity is differentiated from this figure by the degree of public notice they receive, the extent of their presence in the organs of middlebrow taste where fame breeds further fame, and their more acute subjection to the tensions between the value systems of the restricted and the general field of literary production. Ultimately, what is of interest is not so much the figure of the celebrity in itself but what it can tell us about the shifts in the system of literary value that we have been discussing: the emergence of a new relationship between the aesthetics of the signature and the aesthetics of the brand, and the concomitant opening of new ways for celebrity to be deployed, by authors, publishers, journalists, or others, on the literary field.

Celebrity, Values, and Cultural Struggle

These deployments – the strategic uses of celebrity in the contemporary literary "game" – involve, as we observed at the outset, more than simply commercial and aesthetic interests. In describing the shift from signature to signature/brand, we do not mean to suggest that the system of literary value production boils down to a single tension or struggle between the forces of corporate power and those of autonomous aesthetic judgment, or that the scandals attendant on celebrity – which are inherent to its mode of operation – involve no other kinds of ambiguity or crossing over than that between culture and commerce, serious and popular, high and low.

One example will perhaps serve to illustrate the broader system of cultural struggle in which the literary celebrity is implicated. The tremendous scandal of *The Satanic Verses* (1989), which vaulted Rushdie – already a celebrity figure – to the position of best-known and most controversial novelist in the world, was a function of ongoing dispute across not one but several fault lines of power and legitimacy. Most crucially, the *Verses* affair expressed a struggle between literature and religion and their competing claims to political legitimacy. In the decade following publication of his *Midnight's Children* (1981), Rushdie had become the leading literary figure of his generation in Great Britain, widely read, acclaimed by critics, prize juries, and other respected authors, and discussed in numerous scholarly articles, conference papers, and PhD dissertations. By virtue of this apparently seamless legitimacy on the literary field, coupled with his outsized ego and knack for attracting the media, Rushdie had become the most visible representative and spokesman for "Black British" culture, a public intellectual whose newspaper and magazine pieces, appearances on TV or at live colloquia, and so forth, not only advanced a particular vision of Britain's immigrant populations but reinforced the claim of the literary author to a place of special standing or advantage within that vision – and indeed to a uniquely legitimate authority in defining the realities of the immigrant situation and the proper terms of its address. (See, for example, his insistence on the superiority of the narrative artist to the "race industry professional" or social scientist in his 1987 review of the film *Handsworth Songs* (Rushdie 1991).)

By the same token, the challenge to Rushdie (which originated in Britain before being exported to India and eventually appropriated by an opportunistic leadership in Tehran) was a way of disputing this vision of "Black Britain" (with its emphasis on hybridity, translation, in-betweenness, the paradoxes and ambiguities of postcolonial identity), and of resisting, even more strenuously, the authority of its author in respect to individuals and collectivities who themselves had no standing whatsoever on the literary field that had produced him. That Rushdie possessed literary capital in such abundance was one thing; but the attempted conversion of this capital, by means of the whole apparatus of his celebrity, into a special kind of political standing was, from the standpoint of the local religious leaders who first attacked the novel, a threat and an affront. This is why early attempts, on the part of professional critics of postcolonial literature, to diffuse the conflict by offering close readings of offending passages, laying out the critical strategies by means of which the putative offenses might be negated (attending, for example, to the distinct levels of dream and reality within the narrative) only exacerbated hostilities; such specifically literary modes of reading and interpretation (the modes authorized by specifically literary authorities) were precisely what was being rejected.

To be sure, there was a commercial element in the *Verses* affair – and we do not mean simply the predictable marketplace backfiring of attempts to suppress the book (which immediately became the most lucrative *succès de scandale* since *Lolita*). Graham Huggan has argued that Rushdie's emergence in the 1980s as a literary celebrity was at least partly a function of the desire, on the part of publishers, book-sellers, and literary sponsors such as Booker plc (i.e., the forces of commerce) to manage the terrain of postcoloniality so as to establish a flow of neocolonial cultural profits alongside and through contemporary anti-colonial cultural practices: "prizing otherness" in literature precisely to the degree that it might be successfully brought to market as an exotic commodity (Huggan 1994, 1997). Rushdie was thus packaged up as the saleable Other, becoming in the process a lightning rod for controversy. But this does not mean that (genuine, emancipatory) art and (falsifying, imperialistic) commerce were the only axes of Rushdie's celebrity or of the scandal that arose from and augmented it. What was at stake in the *Verses* affair, and in Rushdie as a figure of such resonant celebrity as to warrant the affair, was not just money but symbolic power. And symbolic power is determined by the relative strength or value of all the different kinds of currency that participants bring to a cultural transaction: the currency of academic credentials, political office, religious rank, a jail record; or of bestseller status, good reviews, honors and awards, social connections, street cred, physical attractiveness or photogeneity. Aided and abetted by all the symbolic instruments of the contemporary literary scene, the celebrity – the *cause célèbre* – of Salman Rushdie forced a sudden and intense burst of transactions among these different "forms of capital," with consequent renegotiations of their rates of exchange. (One effect, for example, was a devaluation of strictly secular values within academic postcolonialism and, among left academics, a new and more respectful attention to religious aspects of identity along with the established trio of race, class, and gender.) This indeed is what Rushdie's celebrity, and the apparatus of its production, were always all about: the economics of literature in the broadest sense of that term, the accumulation of literary capital (or power), and its convertibility into or out of other kinds of capital (or power). And in this respect, the phenomenon of literary celebrity well deserves all the attention it has lately been receiving; it has lodged itself so firmly at the heart of the scene that we cannot hope to take the measure either of the stakes or of the balance of forces in contemporary British literature unless we reckon with its unique and still expanding role.

References and Further Reading

Avery, Simon & Maunder, Andrew, (2001). Editorial. *Critical Survey*, special issue on Literature, Fame, and Notoriety in the Nineteenth Century, 13(2), 1–6.

Baker, Thomas N. (1999). *Sentiment and Celebrity: Nathaniel Parker Willis and the trials of literary fame.* New York: Oxford University Press.

Boorstin, Daniel (1992). *The Image: A guide to pseudo-events in America.* New York: Vintage (first published 1961).

Bourdieu, Pierre (1977). *Outline of a Theory of Practice* (trans. Richard Nice). Cambridge: Cambridge University Press.

Bourdieu, Pierre (1986). The forms of capital (trans. Richard Nice). In: John G. Richardson (ed.), *Handbook of Theory and Research for the Sociology of Education* (pp. 241–58). Westport, CT: Greenwood Press.

Bourdieu, Pierre (1993). The field of cultural production, or: the economic world reversed. In: Pierre Bourdieu & Randal Johnson, *The Field of Cultural Production: Essays on art and literature* (pp. 29–73). New York: Columbia University Press.

Bourdieu, Pierre (1996). *The Rules of Art: Genesis and structure of the literary field* (trans. Susan Emanuel). Cambridge: Polity Press.

Braudy, Leo (1997). *The Frenzy of Renown: Fame and its history.* New York: Oxford University Press.

Briggs, Peter M. (1991). Laurence Sterne and literary celebrity in 1760. *The Age of Johnson* 4, 251–73.

Coombe, Rosemary J. (1992). The celebrity image and cultural identity: publicity rights and the subaltern politics of gender. *Discourse,* 14 (spring), 59–88.

Davies, Gillian (2004). The cult of celebrity and trade marks: the next installment. *SCRIPT-ed,* 1(2). Available at: www.law.ed.ac.uk/ahrb/scripted/issue2/celebrity.asp.

Dyer, Richard (1998). *Stars.* London: British Film Institute (originally published 1979).

English, James F. (2004). The literary prize phenomenon in context. In: Brian Shaffer (ed.), *A Companion to the British and Irish Novel 1945–2000* (pp. 160–76). Oxford: Blackwell.

Ferris, Kerry O. (2001). Through a glass, darkly: the dynamics of fan-celebrity encounters. *Symbolic Interaction,* 24, 25–47.

Fiske, John (1989). Madonna. *Reading the Popular* (pp. 95–113). Boston, MA: Unwin Hyman.

Frow, John (2002). Signature and brand. In: Jim Collins (ed.), *High-Pop: Making culture into popular entertainment* (pp. 56–74). Malden, MA: Blackwell.

Gaines, Jane (1991). *Contested Culture: The image, the voice, and the law.* Chapel Hill, NC: University of North Carolina Press.

Glass, Loren (2001). Trademark Twain. *American Literary History,* 13 (winter), 671–93.

Gledhill, Christine, ed. (1991). *Stardom: Industry of desire.* London: Routledge.

Harvey, David (1990). *The Condition of Postmodernity: An inquiry into the conditions of cultural change.* Cambridge, MA: Blackwell.

Huggan, Graham (1994). The postcolonial exotic: Rushdie's Booker of Bookers. *Transition,* 64, 22–9.

Huggan, Graham (1997). Prizing "Otherness": a short history of the Booker. *Studies in the Novel,* 29, 412–33.

Lang, Gladys & Lang, Karl (1998). Recognition and renown: the survival of artistic reputation. *American Journal of Sociology,* 94 (July), 79–109.

Look, Hugh (1999). The author as star. *Publishing Research Quarterly*, 15, 12–29.

McDonald, Paul (1998). Reconceptualizing stardom. In: Richard Dyer, *Stars* (supplementary chapter, pp. 176–211). London: British Film Institute.

Margolis, Stacey (1995). The public life: the discourse of privacy in the age of celebrity. *Arizona Quarterly*, 51 (summer), 81–101.

Marshall, P. David (1997). *Celebrity and Power: Fame in contemporary culture.* Minneapolis, MN: University of Minnesota Press.

Moran, Joe (2000). *Star Authors: Literary celebrity in America.* London: Pluto Press.

Pattanaik, Dipti R. (1998). "The Holy Refusal": A Vedantic interpretation of J. D. Salinger's silence. *MELUS*, 23(2), 113–27.

Radway, Janice (1990). The scandal of the middlebrow: the book-of-the-month club, class fracture, and cultural authority. *South Atlantic Quarterly*, 89, 703–36.

Rein, Irving J., Kotler, Philip, & Stoller, Martin (1997). *High Visibility: The making and marketing of professionals into celebrities.* Chicago, IL: NTC Business Books.

Rubin, Joan Shelley (1992). *The Making of Middlebrow Culture.* Chapel Hill, NC: University of North Carolina Press.

Rushdie, Salman (1981). *Midnight's Children.* London: Jonathan Cape.

Rushdie, Salman (1988). *The Satanic Verses.* London: Viking.

Rushdie, Salman (1991). Handsworth Songs. In: *Imaginary Homelands: Essays and criticism 1981–1991* (pp. 115–17). London: Viking.

Smith, Barbara Herrnstein (1988). *Contingencies of Value: Alternative perspectives for critical theory.* Cambridge, MA: Harvard University Press.

Todd, Richard (1996). *Consuming Fictions: The Booker Prize and fiction in Britain today.* London: Bloomsbury.

Wicke, Jennifer (1998). Celebrity material: materialist feminism and the culture of celebrity. In: Joan B. Landes (ed.), *Feminism, the Public and the Private.* New York: Oxford University Press.

Chapter 3

Fiction and the Film Industry

Andrew Higson

Both literature and the cinema are organized primarily around the creation and marketing of extended narrative fictions. In many ways the relationship between the two media is symbiotic: fictions are transposed from one medium to the other, characters have parallel lives on the page and on the screen, writers move between the two media, publishers and film studios are occasionally owned by the same parent companies. The largest audience for British fiction originating from the printed word is the audience for film adaptations of British novels. This can be a global mass audience, or it can be a more specialized art-house audience – although that niche audience too is generally international. And it is quite likely that the majority of those audiences have not read the novels on which the film adaptations are based. What can this tell us about contemporary British fiction? This chapter responds to this question by exploring the relationship between the contemporary British novel and the cinema, and the different ways in which literature and cinema engage with each other, as businesses and cultures. Has cinema come, over the last century or so, to play an especially powerful role in shaping literary production, the literary canon, and literary culture in Britain? Or is it, as some critics have claimed, that literature and literary culture have tended in contemporary Britain to exert an unusually formative effect on the cinema business?

Literary Adaptation, the English Literary Film, and Literate Cinema

Between 1980 and 2004, some 120 films were adapted from British novels published since the 1970s. Leaving aside around a quarter of those films, since they had no British financial involvement, the adaptations of contemporary novels constitute around 5 percent of the total number of British films produced in that period. Around the same number of British films in this period were adaptations of British novels and other literary material published before the 1970s – so the total proportion of British literary adaptations produced between 1980 and 2004 was still only just over 10 percent. To put it another way, one in every ten British films was an adaptation of British literary source material, and one in every twenty was an adaptation of a *contemporary* British novel. Such statistics depend of course on how one defines British literature and British cinema; I have deliberately not been too finicky in this respect, aiming instead for a general picture of the relationship between these two cultural practices.

It is important to look beyond strict definitions of British cinema in any case, since some 30 or so of the films produced between 1980 and 2004 and adapted from contemporary British novels had no British financial involvement, a key criterion in such definitions. The vast majority of these films were American, including big budget productions of bestselling novels by such prominent mass-market authors as James Herbert, John Le Carré, and Patrick O'Brian, as well as children's writers such as Anne Fine, Dick King-Smith, Roald Dahl, and J. K. Rowling. There were also a few American adaptations of more self-consciously literary authors such as Martin Amis, J. G. Ballard, Pat Barker, William Boyd, and Alex Garland. Oddly, most of the adaptations of contemporary British novels that had neither British nor American financial involvement were of Ruth Rendell's crime fiction, with four French-language adaptations, one German, and one Spanish.

Clearly, then, British cinema is not alone in adapting novels into films. On the contrary, this has long been one of the ways in which the film industry internationally has obtained its stories. And of course some of Hollywood's most successful films of the 1990s were adaptations, with the work of John Grisham, Thomas Harris, and Michael Crichton particularly prominent. Nor would it be fair to conclude from the statistics above that British cinema is overwhelmingly a literary cinema, or that it has depended overly on literary adaptations.

Andrew Higson

When it does tackle canonical literature, British cinema is sometimes berated for the reverence with which it treats the source novel and a reliance on the verbal, the assumption being that cinema is primarily a visual medium. But the richness and diversity of adaptations of contemporary novels, their visual qualities, and the qualities of their performances hardly suggest that reverence is a good description of the process of adaptation. Inevitably, when confronted with an adaptation, many literary critics will worry about how faithful it is to the source novel. And many novelists understandably dislike surrendering control over their work to a filmmaker. But many filmmakers would argue that it is vital that they shape their films according to the needs of film audiences rather than the novelist or his or her readers.

The above notwithstanding, there remains a close and dynamic relationship between the contemporary British novel and the cinema, in both the highbrow and the middlebrow sections of the market. Given the established cultural resonance of "serious literature," quality and prestige in the film business are frequently associated with literariness in one guise or another. For some, this is a betrayal of cinema and all that it is capable of as an aesthetic medium; for others, it is simply an acknowledgment of the pervasive inter-penetration of cultural practices, the extent to which they are constantly feeding off each other. Britain's vibrant literary culture has thus contributed in important ways to British film culture in the 1980s, 1990s, and 2000s and helped consolidate what we might call the English literary cinema (notwithstanding the contributions from a handful of Scottish authors and directors). That cinema has certainly included some commercially and critically successful adaptations – but even if we include adaptations of established classics as well as contemporary novels, this is still only a small section of British cinema as a whole, and there are plenty of equally successful films that have no literary connections.

Another way in which cinema engages with literature, literary culture, and literary readerships as audiences is through the literary biopic. There has been a surprising number of British and American films depicting the lives of prominent writers associated with Britain, and focusing in some way on the process of writing – at least nine since 1994, portraying writers as diverse as Shakespeare and Wilde, J. M. Barrie and C. S. Lewis, Virginia Woolf and Sylvia Plath. But only one such film dealt with a contemporary British author: *Iris* (Richard Eyre 2001), about Iris Murdoch.

Such films form another strand of the English literary cinema. Does that cinema shape literary culture or the literary canon in any significant

60

ways? It certainly boosts sales of the source novels and makes them known to wider readerships. It can also reinforce their status as literary milestones. But even if minor literary novels by little-known novelists can be given a very similar audiovisual treatment to that afforded a Booker Prize winner, it is much more likely that critical reception and literary prizes, rather than a film adaptation, will shape a writing career and establish a novel's cultural status. Some writers have earned enough from adaptations of their work to support their novel writing; some have moved fluidly back and forth between the two media, developing hybrid careers. But such developments have as yet had little impact on literary culture *per se*. While adaptations of successful novels are likely to draw attention to the status of the novel and the author in the marketing of the film, adaptations of little known novels or authors are unlikely to be marketed in the same way, since the names will have little market presence. And a novel with a proven critical or commercial status is likely to attract bigger name directors and casts for the adaptation, thereby increasing the market presence of both novel and film. On the one hand, then, the publishing industry and the film industry frequently work closely together, using each other to maximize the profitability of the cultural products they handle. On the other hand, the hierarchies of status and prestige within literary culture have been little affected by the business of adaptation.

Even so, from the point of view of so-called serious literature, it has to be said that cinema is still often viewed with some disdain, with cinema seen as a corrupter of literary integrity rather than a marker of it. The irony of this is that critics will occasionally invoke the literary as a way of praising "good" cinema and recommending a film to "sophisticated" audiences. Several reviewers described *Howards End* (James Ivory 1992), for instance, as a "literate" film – where literate meant intelligent, subtle, civilized entertainment, as opposed to the "mindless" attractions of mainstream Hollywood cinema (French 1992; Salamon 1992).

Literature may be a source of stories, characters, and cultural status for films – but it does occasionally work the other way around too, with some "serious" writers drawing on films for inspiration. Thus popular cinema figures large in the work of Jonathan Coe, both in his novels, *What a Carve Up!* (1994) and *The House of Sleep* (1997), and in his nonfiction writing, which includes biographies of James Stewart and Humphrey Bogart. In *What a Carve Up!*, for instance, film features as subject matter, as structuring device, and as reference point or intertext. Other writers use what are often seen as filmic devices – swift changes in perspective, for instance, as if editing from one shot to another. Thus Ian McEwan's *Enduring Love* opens with a series of images, starting with what is in effect a close-up of a champagne bottle at a picnic, "cutting" to a point of view shot, complete with sound effects, then cutting again to an aerial shot, looking down from a bird's eye perspective on the unfolding action of a hot-air balloon in trouble. This cinematic quality subsequently emerges in other ways in the novel – at one point, for instance, the narrator ponders the consequences of "the narrative compression of storytelling, especially in the movies" (McEwan 1997: 213).

Authors! Authors!

It is adaptations, however, that dominate the literature/film relationship. Looking at the full range of film adaptations of contemporary British novels, it is surprising to find that some of the biggest mass-market British authors of the period have not seen their work transposed to the big screen. Thus there were no film adaptations of four of the best-selling fiction writers of the 1980s and 1990s, Dick Francis, Jeffrey Archer, Catherine Cookson, and Joanna Trollope. Nor did some of the biggest names in literary fiction find favor with the film industry, including Iris Murdoch and Salman Rushdie – although of course there is the biopic of Murdoch, and Rushdie appears as himself in *Bridget Jones's Diary* (Sharon Maguire 2001). Some authors seem to be preferred by television but overlooked by cinema, including bestsellers such as Archer, Cookson, Jilly Cooper, and Terry Pratchett, and more self-consciously literary figures such as Malcolm Bradbury, David Lodge, and Fay Weldon. But looking at the situation the other way around, it is clear that many of the most commercially and critically successful contemporary British novelists have seen at least one of their novels adapted as a film.

Thus eight Booker Prize-winning novels were adapted between 1980 and 2004, including Kazuo Ishiguro's *The Remains of the Day* (1989/James Ivory 1993), A. S. Byatt's *Possession* (1990/Neil LaBute 2002), and Graham Swift's *Last Orders* (1996/Fred Schepsi 2001); there were also a further six adaptations of novels on the Booker shortlists, and at least 12 winners of other prestigious literary prizes. A good selection of the Young British Novelists listed by *Granta* in 1983, 1993, and 2003 have been adapted, as well as at least seven authors honored with a CBE or an OBE. And at the mass-market end of the spectrum, most of the genres and authors that dominate the bestselling fiction lists have found their way into the cinema too. Thus there are thrillers by the likes of Frederick Forsyth, Ken Follett, Nicci French, and Jack Higgins; crime novels by P. D. James and Ruth Rendell; spy stories by John Le Carré and Len Deighton; historical fiction by Patrick O'Brian; chick lit by Helen Fielding and Kathy Lette; "lad lit" by Nick Hornby; comic fiction by Ben Elton; and horror by Clive Barker. Then of course there is the cult youth market, served by Danny Boyle's adaptations of Irvine Welsh's *Trainspotting* (1993/1996) and Alex Garland's *The Beach* (1996/2000), and another Welsh adaptation, *The Acid House* (1994/Paul McGuigan 1998).

An eclectic list of eighteen writers had at least two novels adapted between 1980 and 2004, but only six of them had more than two novels adapted – and most of those six were associated with particular and well-proven market niches. Thus three of each of James Herbert's horror novels, Le Carré's spy novels, Hornby's "lad lit" novels, and Rowling's Harry Potter novels were made into films, while the most adapted contemporary British writer is Rendell, eight of whose crime novels found their way to the big screen.

The most surprising author in this list is perhaps Ian McEwan, with five adaptations. McEwan makes for an interesting case study. His writing is self-consciously literary and often cerebral, but it also works with popular genre conventions, which has ensured a strong crossover readership with healthy sales, especially latterly. Adaptations of his work have emphasized its eroticism and its thriller elements, and include *The Comfort of Strangers* (1981/Paul Schrader 1990), *The Cement Garden* (1978/Andrew Birkin 1993), *The Innocent* (1990/John Schlesinger 1993), *Enduring Love* (1997/Roger Michell 2004), and *First Love, Last Rites* (1975/1997), adapted from one of his short stories. Surprisingly, despite the provenance of the stories and the reputations of the directors, the scriptwriters, and the casts, none of these films was particularly successful, either critically or commercially.

McEwan's involvement with the cinema has in fact been more extensive than this, and is indicative of other ways in which writers engage with the film world. Thus he adapted his own novel and wrote the screenplay for *The Innocent*, and wrote the stories on which two European films were based. Perhaps more significantly, he also adapted Timothy Mo's Booker-shortlisted *Soursweet* (1982/Mike Newell 1988), and wrote original screenplays for *The Ploughman's Lunch* (Richard Eyre 1983) and *The Good Son* (Joseph Ruben 1993). McEwan's involvement in these films epitomizes some of the ways in which writers seek to make a living from their work, selling the rights to their fictions and working on film and television scripts. Thus William Boyd adapted two of his own novels, *Stars and Bars* (1984/Pat O'Connor 1988) and *A Good Man in Africa* (1981/Bruce Beresford 1994), both American productions; wrote screenplays for several films and television programs; and even directed his own script for *The Trench* (1999). Hanif Kureishi wrote original screenplays for Stephen Frears (*My Beautiful Laundrette*, 1985, and *Sammy and Rosie Get Laid*, 1987) before publishing his first novel, *The Buddha of Suburbia* (1990), which he later adapted as a television series. He then wrote and directed *London Kills Me* (1991) for the cinema; adapted his own short story, *My Son The Fanatic* (1997/Udayan Prasad 1997); and wrote the original screenplay for *The Mother* (Roger Michell 2003). Several people involved in television comedy have moved between media too, writing occasional novels, some of which have been adapted as films, and either writing or directing occasional films, in addition to their television work; such figures include Stephen Fry, Meera Syal, Charlie Higson, and Ben Elton.

Another writer that deserves a case study in his own right is Clive Barker, bestselling author of horror and fantasy stories, several of which have found their way to the screen. After two short stories were handled poorly as films, Barker took on the director's role for *Hellraiser* (1987), adapted from one of his novels (*The Hellbound Heart*, 1987). He has since directed two further films adapted from his own writing, produced several more, and either written or lent his name to screenplays featuring his stories and characters. Both *Hellraiser* and *Candyman* (1986/1992) have seen several sequels, some going straight to video with no theatrical exhibition. Such is his reputation among his fans that many of his films include his name in the title: *Clive Barker's Candyman, Clive Barker's Nightbreed* (1988/Barker 1990), and so on.

Alongside authors who have moved between writing for the screen and writing novels, it is worth noting film directors who have specialized in literary cinema and who frequently work with well-known authors rather than screenplay specialists. Stephen Frears, for instance, prefers to work closely with his writers, who have included Alan Bennett and Hanif Kureishi; he has also directed several adaptations, including novels by Roddy Doyle and Nick Hornby. Roger Michell also worked with Kureishi, in both television and the cinema, and adapted novels by Mary Costello and Ian McEwan, as well as Jane Austen. Mike Newell too has directed several adaptations, including recent novels by Peter Prince, Timothy Mo, and Beryl Bainbridge. Even Steven Spielberg, who favors literary adaptations for his more prestigious projects, directed a film of J. G. Ballard's *Empire of the Sun* (1984/1987).

Themes and Variations

In many ways, cinema and literature seem to run alongside each other – and not surprisingly, some of the same themes and trends can be identified in the two media. One of the key tendencies often identified in recent British literature and which equally finds a place in contemporary British cinema is the exploration of the changing geopolitical landscape of Britain: the forces of devolution, regionalism, and postcolonialism, and the emergence of multicultural and hybrid British identities. The British-Asian experience, for instance, has been explored by Hanif Kureishi, in both his original screenplays and his adaptations, and by Meera Syal, in her adaptation of her own novel, *Anita and Me* (1996/ Metin Hüseyin 2002). The adaptation of Mo's *Soursweet* looks at the Chinese community in Britain. Adaptations of novels by Bruce Chatwin (*On the Black Hill*, 1982/Andrew Grieve 1987), Graham Swift (*Waterland* 1983/Stephen Gyllenhaal 1992, and *Last Orders*), and Helen Cross (*My Summer of Love*, 2001/Pawel Pawlikowski 2004) have focused on very specific local or regional identities. And the film versions of *Trainspotting* and *The Acid House*, as well as A. L. Kennedy's reworking of her own short story in *Stella Does Tricks* (1994/Coky Giedroyc 1996), have addressed the question of what it means to be Scottish.

Women's writing and the exploration of female experience have also been staples of British cinema, in films ranging from the feminist fairy tales of *The Company of Wolves* (1979/Neil Jordan 1984), based on a series of short stories by Angela Carter; to *Dirty Weekend* (1991/ Michael Winner 1993), regarded by some as a feminist vigilante novel, by Helen Zahavi, who co-scripted the film version with Michael Winner; to Tracy Chevalier's period piece about a servant girl in the seventeenth-century Netherlands, *Girl with a Pearl Earring* (2000/ Peter Webber 2003). Some of the most critically acclaimed British female writers of the late twentieth century have seen their work adapted as films, including Doris Lessing (*Memoirs of a Survivor*, 1974/ David Gladwell 1981), Anita Brookner (*Hotel du Lac*, 1984/Giles Foster 1986), A. S. Byatt (*Angels and Insects*, 1992/Philip Haas 1995, and *Possession*), Rose Tremain (*Restoration*, 1989/Michael Hoffman 1995), Pat Barker (*Regeneration*, 1991/Gillies MacKinnon 1997), and Esther Freud (*Hideous Kinky*, 1992/Gillies MacKinnon 1998).

Such films appeal to the film industry because they have the potential to attract a range of different audiences, including both the niche literary audience and the female audience. And if some of this material explores female experience from a self-consciously feminist perspective, there is also the post-feminist chick lit of Kathy Lette's *Mad Cows* (1996/Sara Sugarman 1999), and the immensely successful adaptations of Fielding's *Bridget Jones's Diary* and its sequel, *The Edge of Reason* (2000/Beeban Kidron 2004), which attracted substantial numbers of women cinemagoers of all ages.

Surveys of the contemporary British novel have also frequently commented on the turn toward historical fiction, to memory and the past (see chapter 5 of this volume). The turn to the past has been a prominent feature of contemporary British cinema, as well, especially at the quality end of the market, in what has come to be known as the heritage film (Higson 2003). Some of these films are original screenplays about real or imagined historical characters or events, some are adaptations of nineteenth- and early twentieth-century novels – but a good number are adaptations of more recent novels which engage with the past, and with ideas of heritage. Such adaptations tend to work as tasteful period pieces for the niche art-house market, and where possible for the crossover market (though some in recent years have been targeted more directly at the mainstream).

Several such films were set in nineteenth-century England, including *Angels and Insects*. Rather more were set in the early twentieth century, including low-budget art-house adaptations of Isabel Colegate's *The Shooting Party* (1980/Alan Bridges 1984), J. L. Carr's *A Month in the Country* (1980/Pat O'Connor 1987), and Barker's *Regeneration*. Moving into the middle decades of the twentieth century, Ishiguro's Booker Prize winning *The Remains of the Day* was reworked by the Merchant–Ivory team, specialists in highly tasteful, quality adaptations of prestigious novels with period English settings; also set in this period were versions of Angela Huth's *Land Girls* (1995/David Leland 1998) and Sebastian Faulks's *Charlotte Gray* (1998/Gillian Armstrong 2001). Some of the "historical" novels and their adaptations move between past and present in postmodernist fashion, including John Fowles's *The French Lieutenant's Woman* (1969/Karel Reisz 1981) and Byatt's *Possession*. Some, such as James Fox's *White Mischief* (1980/Michael Radford 1987), deal with the English abroad, a theme also explored by a number of "postcolonial" writers, such as Peter Carey, in *Oscar and Lucinda* (1988/Gillian Armstrong 1997), Michael Ondaatje, in *The English Patient* (1992/Anthony Minghella 1996), and Ruth Prawer Jhabvala, in *Heat and Dust* (1975/James Ivory 1982), all Booker Prize winners successfully remade as films.

It is perhaps here, in the turn to the past, that the English literary cinema has most taken hold, but if many of the films about the past are adaptations, the heritage film has at the same time developed its own filmic conventions, its own ways of embracing heritage. The frequently rich and spectacular visual qualities of these films, their pictorialist use of the image, their strong performances, and their preference for the long take and the medium shot, rather than fast cutting and close-ups, for instance, are all features that owe little to the novel. The literary connections are important, but all of these adaptations work effectively as films in their own right, their artfulness and their cinematic cross-references enabling them to inhabit a world of their own while at the same time benefiting from their literary intertexts.

Might the problem in fact be the obverse? Has the very contemporaneity of contemporary British literature been diminished by the power of the heritage-dominated market for British films? One could certainly argue that the cinema in its dealings with the past makes few distinctions between living and dead writers, or between contemporary and classical literature – or indeed between writers of different nations. Two Merchant–Ivory productions provide interesting examples here. Both *Howards End* and *The Remains of the Day* are tasteful heritage films mainly set in the early twentieth century, in southern England, among fine heritage properties, and both star Anthony Hopkins and Emma Thompson. But one is adapted from a novel by the long-dead English writer E. M. Forster and the other from a novel by the living Anglo-Japanese writer Kazuo Ishiguro. For the film industry, both are marketable products, at the prestige end of the market – and perhaps more to the point, both are presold properties, with a guaranteed core consumer base in the literary audience.

The Remains of the Day also happens to be one of several contemporary British novels reworked as films that involve some form of first-person narration. Nick Hornby's male confessional style; *Bridget Jones's* diaristic form; the perverse narrators of *Remains* and *Enduring Love*; the more straightforward narrators of *A Month in the Country* and *Girl with a Pearl Earring*; the twin narrators of *Chocolat* (Joanne Harris 1999/Lasse Hallström 2002); and the multiple narrators of *Last Orders* and *Trainspotting*: all are variants of first-person storytelling. Feature films, however, have rarely been able to sustain subjective narration, and the adaptations of these films use various devices to overcome this difficulty without losing the spirit of their source novels. In *Girl with a Pearl Earring*, for instance, the camera stays with the eponymous heroine most of the time – but no effort is made actually to render her point of view as the point of view of the film or the spectator. Much the same is true of *Chocolat* and *Trainspotting*, where – apart from brief passages of voice-over – the films again adopt a third-person narrational style that irons out the multiple perspectives of the novels. *Enduring Love*, too, eschews the highly self-conscious first-person storytelling of the novel, although several scenes in the film attempt to create a sense of interiority, of inhabiting a consciousness. In the Bridget Jones films, fragments from the titular diary are occasionally written on the screen – but more as a reminder of the way the novel works than as a consistent style; likewise, scenes featuring the diary are there more to justify the title than to carry any narrational responsibility.

Adaptation and the Marketplace

In market terms, the relationship between a book and its adaptation can be extremely valuable. Adapting a bestseller means working with a product that already has massive visibility to a range of consumers – but the process works round the other way as well. Most adaptations are accompanied by a tie-in edition of the source novel, released by the publishers to capitalize on the new visibility of the title. "Now a major motion picture," it will say on the cover of most of those tie-in publications, over an image from the film version featuring the stars. Film tie-in editions can send books right to the top of the bestseller charts, even if the film itself is not particularly successful. According to figures reported in the *Guardian*, "the two Picador paperback editions of *Bridget Jones's Diary* sold an extra 1,730,535 copies," while the tie-in edition of *Chocolat* "put Joanne Harris up alongside her namesakes Thomas and Robert. Her *Black Swan* paperback, 357,287 last year, is now close on 1,200,000." Even the expensive but critically and commercially disappointing film version of *Captain Corelli's Mandolin* (1994/John Madden 2001) "contributed another 548,148 to Louis de Bernières's sales to make up a total of 2,358,446" (Hamilton 2001).

All of these titles are examples of the publishing and film businesses exploiting new markets in the 1990s and early 2000s: on the one hand, the crossover product, which has the capacity to shift out of a niche market into the mainstream; and on the other hand chick lit, or the "city girl" novel, as represented by the Bridget Jones franchise. Like chick lit's masculine variant, lad lit, these generic categories emerged in the 1990s and were carefully nurtured by publishers and subsequently by film distributors. Behind these relatively new developments is the more established high/low market framework in which both literary and cinematic fictional experiences are produced and sold to consumers – with the high/low distinction routinely upheld by critics.

At one end of this framework there is mass-market genre fiction, the bestseller, the novel as popular culture – what in film terms is now referred to as the multiplex market. This in turn can be further subdivided by genre and consumer base. Thus there are the primarily action-based genres, which tend to be popular with male readers and cinemagoers. And there is women's romance fiction, which has not in recent years been much taken up by the British film industry. Hence the significance of both the chick lit phenomenon and the crossover success of titles by the likes of Joanne Harris, which can work both as serious literature and as romance fiction.

At the other end of the market is the so-called serious novel, self-consciously literary fiction for "middle to highbrow," "discriminating readers" (Hamilton 1999; Sutherland 2002: 166). This is the arena of prize-winning fiction and the "literary novelist," who specializes in slow-moving character studies or novels of ideas rather than in narratives of action. The film business too has its quality fare and its specialized niche market, the art-house cinemas and the festival circuit, with its own system of prizes and awards. As with literary culture, it is a market traditionally defined in terms less of commercial success than of critical impact and reputation, with the reviewing practices of the quality press playing a vital role in this respect. And as with literary culture, the core consumer group is educated and middle-class, and expects certain sorts of production values, moral dilemmas, intellectual enigmas, and aesthetic experiences.

But if mass-market genre fiction and serious literature are traditionally considered as quite distinct, those markets and cultures have increasingly overlapped in recent decades, and the film industry has been quick to exploit this overlap. Booker Prize winners have frequently found their way to the top of the bestseller lists, as in recent years have "serious" novels without that accolade, by the likes of Ian McEwan and Zadie Smith. Little surprise, then, that there have been film adaptations of *Remains of the Day* and *Possession* (and television adaptations of *Hotel du Lac* and *Oranges Are Not the Only Fruit*), all commercially successful Booker winners, as well as *Enduring Love*, one of McEwan's most successful novels (and, on television, Smith's *White Teeth*). Such achievements are rarely coincidental. As publisher Dan Franklin puts it, people in his business are always looking for the "novel that is at once literary and commercial, a book with big ambitions that will appeal to a very wide audience" (Franklin 2002: 275). Franklin also makes it clear that the possibility of securing an advance from a film producer is an important factor at a certain level in the fiction publishing business.

Other fiction is much more self-consciously middlebrow and mid-market from the outset, and this is where the emergent genres of chick lit and lad lit fit in. *Bridget Jones's Diary*, with its Jane Austen subtext indicating its pretensions toward the highbrow, was not initially an obvious bestseller, yet with its sequel and its adaptations, it became a major literary and filmic phenomenon, and attracted readers and audiences well beyond its target female thirtysomethings. The key lad lit author was Nick Hornby, whose novels were again both critically applauded and immensely successful (including in the USA) – with *Fever Pitch* (1992/David Evans 1997), *High Fidelity* (1995/Stephen Frears 2000), and *About a Boy* (1998/Chris and Paul Weitz 2002) all being made into films. Irving Welsh's *Trainspotting* is a rather more hard-edged version of lad lit, and again had its highbrow pretensions, yet it was exploited extremely effectively in the youth market in both print and film versions.

The Harry Potter series can also be seen as crossover fiction, with its adult editions, its prizes, and its success in the American market. The film business clearly likes this sort of bestselling but upmarket genre fiction aimed at either the core family audience or the youth (16–30) markets – especially when it takes on franchise proportions, as it did with the Harry Potter series. But it also likes the crossover fiction that has its feet planted firmly at the "serious literature" end of the market, even if it still plays vibrantly with the conventions of more accessible genre fiction. It is worth noting some overlapping cycles here. In the space of four years, between 2000 and 2004, the British production company Working Title made adaptations of both of the Bridget Jones novels, *High Fidelity*, and *Captain Corelli's Mandolin*, one of the most commercially successful "serious" books of recent years. The American company Miramax, which had made its reputation turning apparently niche market films into major crossover hits, was also involved with *Captain Corelli* and *Bridget Jones: The Edge of Reason*, which were part of its own cycle of mid-market, middlebrow literary adaptations. These included *Mansfield Park* (Jane Austen 1814/Patricia Rozema 1999),

Chocolat, The Hours (Michael Cunningham 1998/Stephen Daldry 2002), and *Cold Mountain* (Charles Frazier 1997/Anthony Minghella 2003) – respectively a racy adaptation of an English literary classic, a contemporary British novel set in France, an American novel in part about an English author, Virginia Woolf, and an adaptation of an American novel directed by a Brit. Precise cultural provenance is an irrelevance in the film business, so long as a market can be identified.

A film adapted from a novel takes the shape it does partly from the source novel, and partly from a whole range of other circumstances. *Captain Corelli* must have seemed an ideal text to work with since it already had a huge market presence, and could be presented as solidly middlebrow fare. On the one hand, it drew on the kudos of serious literature; on the other it had all the attractions of a romantic Mediterranean holiday setting, a gender-inclusive blend of the war film and the romance, and an apparent nostalgia for simpler times. It needs then to be seen alongside other middlebrow literary adaptations of the period, especially those produced by Working Title and Miramax, but also middlebrow material without a strong literary connection, whether produced by those same companies (e.g. *Notting Hill*, Roger Michell 1999) or with similar ingredients (e.g. *Shirley Valentine*, Lewis Gilbert 1989, with its Greek holiday romance). In that context, it is hardly surprising that the trenchant political discourse of de Bernières's source novel all but disappeared from the film.

The Process of Adaptation: *Possession*

There are two main motivations for filmmakers to adapt a novel. First, the novel provides a well-crafted story, carefully drawn characters, narratively meaningful settings, and a world view, a moral and ideological framework – that is, the raw ingredients for fiction, whether in print or on film. Second, to adapt a novel may mean taking on a product that already has a market presence, and that can be further marketed on the basis of that reputation. Working with a presold property in this way may reduce the risk involved in financing the production. Most adaptations combine the two motivations, though some will involve a source novel that has virtually no market presence. To take on a well-known novel, or a novel by a well-known author, may require a third motivation to come into play: the desire to reproduce the novel as faithfully as possible. But that aspiration will always be counterbalanced by the need to create something that

71

will work well as a film, and that will engage both those audiences familiar with the novel and those who are not. The film must be able to play off the reputation of the novel, and summon up sufficiently adequate memories of it for audiences who have read the novel, but it must also work in its own right as a film.

The process of adaptation is necessarily a process of reshaping and repackaging. A written text must become an audiovisual text, and it must have some of the ingredients that will encourage financiers to invest in the project and audiences to watch it. There is almost invariably a process of narrative condensation in adapting novels as films: screenwriters will often pare down the range of events and the number of characters. But at the same time there is a process of opening up, of creating a fuller diegetic effect, filling out the world of the fiction – whether in the settings or in the physical presence and performances of the actors. The film must reshape the source material according to its own conventions, while not losing sight of the novel, if it is well known enough to be marketed on that basis. Events may be re-ordered, narrational material transposed as dialogue. Novels as long as *Possession* and as short as *A Month in the Country* must come out at roughly the same length. And the readily recognizable genre features of *Possession* and *Enduring Love* will often win out over the more philosophical aspects of such self-consciously literary novels, rendering them as much more straightforward narratives. A perversely multi-stranded work like *Captain Corelli* will be turned into a simpler linear narrative with a central romantic couple and not too many distracting characters and stories around them. Even a spy thriller like Le Carré's *The Tailor of Panama* (1996/John Boorman 2001) may find a new, less ambivalent, more conventional happy ending imposed on the film version.

The conventional mythology of literary authorship is that the process of creating a book is entirely the responsibility of the individual author. But of course the publishing business also plays its part, in the guise of editors, marketing people, book designers, and so on, as does the business of criticism, literary reviews, and the like. But when we move to cinema, the business end of things is even more elaborate and multilayered, whether it is the business of creation or the business of the moving image industry as a whole.

Take the film *Possession*, for instance, directed by an American, Neil LaBute, and adapted from Byatt's Booker Prize winning novel of the same name. The screen rights to the novel were purchased by Warner Bros, one of the major American studio-distributors, shortly after the book was published. But it was not until some 10 years later that LaBute and his scriptwriting collaborators produced a screenplay that Warner was happy with (LaBute 2003). The credits for the finished film in fact list *three* screenwriters, adding that the screenplay was "based on the novel by A. S. Byatt," while the cinema trailer made no bones about the fact that this was an adaptation, of the *"best-selling"* novel by Byatt. The film itself plays intertextually with the source novel, but neither flaunts that relationship too openly, nor makes too bold claims about the fidelity of the adaptation.

Byatt's *Possession* is subtitled *A Romance*. And indeed it is, but it is also a novel of ideas, an imaginative and erudite exploration of literary history, and an intelligent and witty satire about the modern academic enterprise. The film retains some of this narrational richness. It is still decidedly a romance, but the details of academic research become something closer to a detective thriller, albeit one that retains an academic veneer. The film also lacks the novel's intellectual pretensions. The basic outline of the story and some of the key characters and events remain the same. But other material that is vital to the novel must make do in the film with a passing visual reference or a suggestive moment of dialogue.

The plot concerns a group of academics piecing together the story of a love affair between two Victorian poets. One of the main changes is that, in the novel, we only know the Victorians through their letters, poems, diaries, and journals, and through academics reconstructing their lives. In the film, this archival past is brought to life, audio-visualized, with the characters taking on a flesh-and-blood existence that is as real on the screen as the academics in the present. These are then two quite distinct modes of narration, one reworking in post-modernist fashion the conventions of the epistolary novel, the other adopting throughout the familiar present historic tense and third-person narration of the classical story film. In fact, it is not quite as simple as this. The film, for instance, moves enigmatically between present and past, often in the same shot, interweaving its two sets of characters in a richly suggestive manner. It also in various ways absorbs extracts from the letters, poems, and diaries by various aural and visual means. And the novel not only adopts a familiar third-person narrational style for the present-day events, but adopts the same style for three brief passages set in the past. Nevertheless, the peculiar obscurity and constructedness of the past, continually underscored in the novel, is given much less play in the film – as is Byatt's unrelenting irony, which LaBute has mostly expunged.

Adaptations of self-consciously literary novels will often include scenes of people reading or writing, in an effort to regain something of the literate quality of the word. This wordiness will sometimes attract criticism, since it is felt not to do justice to the "essentially visual" quality of cinema. Such criticism seems misplaced if the point is precisely to establish overtly literary reference points. In the case of *Possession*, it seems entirely appropriate to adapt a sometimes epistolary novel about two poets, and the effort to know them through contemporary written archival material, by including scenes of people reading or reciting poetry, or extracts from journals and diaries. Sometimes the recitation is in voice-over, sometimes it is delivered on screen, sometimes we see the author writing something, which we also hear spoken both in their own voice and in the voice of one of the present-day detective-academics. These are highly conventional strategies of the literary adaptation. Another familiar strategy is to refigure as character dialogue in the film material that is given as authorial commentary in the novel – something that is done in the final scene of *Possession*, where Jeremy Northam, in the role of Ash, strolls through a summer field reciting, rather incongruously, Byatt's self-reflexive authorial observations from her Postscript.

There are other changes at the level of the script, three of which LaBute himself has commented on, noting that the changes were designed to improve the dramatic structure of the film as a film, rather than as an obsessively faithful adaptation (LaBute 2003). First, the number of present-day academics centrally involved in the story is reduced to two, with some being cut altogether and others playing bit parts that are quite different to the much fuller development they receive in the novel. Second, one of those two characters, Roland, is transformed from an Englishman to an American, ostensibly to create a greater dramatic tension with his (English) counterpart, Maud, as they work out their own romantic relationship. (Ironically, Maud is played by American actress Gwyneth Paltrow.) LaBute claims that the refiguring of an Englishman as an American was "not [done] as a way to reach a wider American audience," but it will certainly have helped in that respect. Third, another of the academics, Cropper, who plays a large part in the novel but is reduced to a much smaller character in the film, is at the same time asked to take on the role of evil antagonist, in effect a mere cipher of a felt dramatic requirement, to act as a foil to the two central protagonists.

These changes were made at the scripting stage. The screenplay, however, is by no means the end of the process of adaptation. As

LaBute puts it, "You make [the film] one time when you write it and you make it again when you shoot it and you make it a third time when you edit it" (LaBute 2003). Each time, a different set of creative workers is involved. Actors, and especially stars, must be cast to play the characters; they must be dressed by the costume designer, and must inhabit buildings and landscapes created or chosen by the production designer; and all of this must be filmed by the director of photography and his or her team. The director will interact with each of these co-workers to produce the look or feel for which they are aiming.

One of the effects of envisaging the past in the film, filling out the diegesis of the Victorian period, is to give the film a generic texture that is not there in the novel. For part of its screen-time, the film thus adopts the conventions of the period costume drama, the English heritage film. With actors such as Jeremy Northam and Jennifer Ehle, rich mid-Victorian costumes, interior designs, and forms of transport, ancient buildings and stately homes set in rolling green parkland – all familiar from a host of other heritage films – a whole new dimension of intertextuality is brought into play. Even the shooting style, with its frequent long takes and ornate tableau shots, is reminiscent of other heritage films. The problem of adaptation is in one sense about the degree and type of intertextuality that is allowed or encouraged – and in some cases unexpectedly made possible by historical circumstances beyond the control of the filmmakers. For the literary faithful, the intertextual references should be limited to a strong sense of resemblance between the source novel and the film adaptation. But for others, it is recognized that the film must have a life of its own, that its dramatic structure, its audiovisual design, and the interplay of its characters must work in their own right, without spectators feeling they have to read the novel to make sense of the film.

This is not to suggest for a moment that the film operates in a vacuum, but that the source novel is far from its only intertext. In fact, each new ingredient introduced to the film will make its own aesthetic and cultural demands on the shape and feel of that film. Casting any star brings with it memories of the star's previous roles and invokes the star's public image above and beyond any particular roles. Casting Paltrow as Maud, for instance, enabled the film to benefit from several other films of the period in which Paltrow played refined English characters (*Emma*, Douglas McGrath 1996; *Shakespeare in Love*, John Madden 1998; *Sliding Doors*, Peter Howitt 1998). On the other hand, it also exploited her presence as an American star of a particular type, and LaBute (2003) notes that he consciously modeled her first entrance in the film on that of Grace Kelly in *Rear Window* (Alfred Hitchcock 1954).

Finally, there is the post-production stage, where the material that has been shot must be edited into shape, and often a music track added. There is no music in Byatt's *Possession*, of course, but the events in the film are insistently overlain with a romantic music track which plays a large part in coloring the way that audiences respond to particular scenes and characters. At the editing stage, story material may well be reorganized, or scenes and even whole characters cut out.

Possession the film is then very different to *Possession* the novel. The latter was a *tour-de-force*, both critically and commercially. The adaptation endeavored to exploit that cultural presence and to find a means of reproducing the novel in a way that would work for cinema audiences. As such, it can be seen as an example of the English literary cinema, a distinct niche within contemporary British cinema – albeit a British cinema very much under the sway of Hollywood. Those involved with the production clearly hoped that its middlebrow qualities as a film would enable it to bridge the gulf between the mass market and the art-house, in the same way that Byatt's novel had evidently crossed over from the serious literature market to become a bestseller. But while the film was marketed in part on the strength of the novel's sales, and the filmmakers sought to gain from its cultural status, it would be difficult to say that the film had any impact on the status of the book: by the time the film came out, the achievement of the novel was already well established. In other words, money aside, the film had far more to gain in this instance than the novel – even if the film did not in the end fare very well at the box office.

As the case of *Possession* illustrates, literature and cinema remain distinct media, yet feed off and are colored by each other in a variety of ways. What the chapter as a whole surely demonstrates is the depth and breadth and sheer intricacy of the film/novel relation in contemporary Britain. As businesses, publishing and the film industry frequently engage with each other, to their mutual benefit. The English literary cinema and the wider field of literary adaptations have also undoubtedly made their mark on British film culture – though not as indelibly as some have claimed. The cultural status of "serious literature" has certainly helped shape a particular strand of British cinema, its audiences and its apologists – but there are many other strands to consider, both historically and on the contemporary scene. Nor is that shaping necessarily to the detriment of cinema as a cultural practice.

One might say the same more generally about the role of adaptations within contemporary cinema, while noting further that mainstream Hollywood filmmakers have found it as productive as those at the more specialized, niche end of the market to work with literary sources.

Contemporary British novelists have also engaged with cinema in a variety of productive ways, but there is little evidence that cinema has played a *major* role in shaping literary production, the literary canon, or literary culture in Britain in recent decades. Novelists have occasionally adopted what some see as cinematic devices in their writing – and in some cases have written specifically for the cinema. And publishers have seen the profit to be had from selling a novel to a film producer. But there is little to support the view that literary culture is being eroded or debased by its contact with the cinema.

Acknowledgments

I am grateful to Jon Stubbs for research assistance. The statistical information about adaptations of British novels draws on *Monthly Film Bulletin, Sight and Sound*, and the Internet Movie Database (www.imdb.com). Statistics on British film production are from the British Film Institute website at www.bfi.org.uk. Information about bestselling fiction draws on Sutherland (2002), the website of *The Bookseller* (www.thebookseller.com), Alex Hamilton's annual "Fast-sellers" survey in the *Guardian* (see below for examples), and Cader Books' US bestsellers website (www.caderbooks.com/best80.html).

References and Further Reading

NONFICTION

Ashby, Justine & Higson, Andrew (eds.) (2000). *British Cinema, Past and Present.* London: Routledge.
Cartmell, Deborah, Hunter, I. Q., Kaye, Heidi, & Whelehan, Imelda (eds.) (1996). *Pulping Fictions: Consuming culture across the literature/media divide.* London: Pluto Press.
Cartmell, Deborah & Whelehan, Imelda (eds.) (1999). *Adaptations: From text to screen, screen to text.* London: Routledge.
Franklin, Dan (2002). Commissioning and editing modern fiction. In: Zachary Leader (ed.), *On Modern British Fiction* (pp. 270–83). Oxford: Oxford University Press.

French, P. (1992). Be-all and end-all for triumph. *The Observer*, 3 May, 52.

Hamilton, Alex (1999). Fastsellers of 1998. *The Guardian*, 9 January, 10.

Hamilton, Alex (2000). Fastsellers '99. *The Guardian*, 8 January, 10.

Hamilton, Alex (2001). Fastsellers 2001: hot paperbacks. *The Guardian*, 29 December. Available at: books.guardian.co.uk/news/articles/0,6109, 625340,00.html.

Higson, Andrew (2003). *English Heritage, English Cinema: Costume drama since 1980*. Oxford: Oxford University Press.

Hill, John (1999). *British Cinema in the 1980s: Issues and themes*. Oxford: Clarendon Press.

LaBute, Neil (2003). Commentary by Director Neil LaBute, special feature on *Possession*, Warner Home Video (DVD Z1 22264).

McFarlane, Brian (1996). *Novel to Film: An introduction to the theory of adaptation*. Oxford: Clarendon Press.

Murphy, Robert (ed.) (1997). *The British Cinema Book*. London: British Film Institute.

Murphy, Robert (ed.) (2000). *British Cinema of the 90s*. London: British Film Institute.

Salamon, Julie (1992). Film: Merchant Ivory's "Howards End." *Wall Street Journal*, March 12.

Stam, Robert (2004). *Literature through Film: Realism, magic and the art of adaptation*. Oxford: Blackwell.

Stam, Robert & Raengo, Alessandra (eds.) (2004). *A Companion to Literature and Film*. Oxford: Blackwell.

Stam, Robert & Raengo, Alessandra (eds.) (2004). *Literature and Film: A guide to the theory and practice of film adaptation*. Oxford: Blackwell.

Street, Sarah (1997). *British National Cinema*. London: Routledge.

Sutherland, John (2002). *Reading the Decades: Fifty years of the nation's bestselling books*. London: BBC.

FICTION

Ballard, J. G. (1984). *Empire of the Sun*. London: Victor Gollancz.

Barker, Clive (1987). *The Hellbound Heart*. London: Century.

Barker, Pat (1991). *Regeneration*. London: Viking.

Boyd, William (1981). *A Good Man in Africa*. London: Hamish Hamilton.

Boyd, William (1984). *Stars and Bars*. London: Hamish Hamilton.

Brookner, Anita (1984). *Hotel Du Lac*. London: Jonathan Cape.

Byatt, A. S. (1989). *Possession: A romance*. London: Chatto & Windus.

Byatt, A. S. (1992). *Angels and Insects*. London: Chatto & Windus.

Carey, Peter (1988). *Oscar and Lucinda*. London: HarperCollins.

Carr, James Lloyd (1980). *A Month in the Country*. London: Harvester.

Chatwin, Bruce (1982). *On the Black Hill*. London: Jonathan Cape.

Chevalier, Tracy (1999). *Girl with a Pearl Earring*. London: HarperCollins.

Coe, Jonathan (1994). *What a Carve Up!* London: Viking.

Coe, Jonathan (1997). *The House of Sleep*. London: Viking.
Colegate, Isabel (1980). *The Shooting Party*. London: Hamish Hamilton.
Cross, Helen (2001). *My Summer of Love*. London: Bloomsbury.
Cunningham, Michael (1998). *The Hours*. New York: Farrar Straus Giroux.
de Bernières, Louis (1994). *Captain Corelli's Mandolin*. London: Secker & Warburg.
Faulks, Sebastian (1998). *Charlotte Gray*. London: Hutchinson.
Fielding, Helen (1996). *Bridget Jones's Diary*. London: Picador.
Fox, James (1982). *White Mischief*. London: Jonathan Cape.
Frazier, Charles (1997). *Cold Mountain*. London: Sceptre.
Freud, Esther (1992). *Hideous Kinky*. London: Hamish Hamilton.
Garland, Alex (1996). *The Beach*. London: Viking.
Harris, Joanne (1999). *Chocolat*. London: Viking.
Hornby, Nick (1992). *Fever Pitch*. London: Victor Gollancz.
Hornby, Nick (1995). *High Fidelity*. London: Victor Gollancz.
Hornby, Nick (1998). *About a Boy*. London: Victor Gollancz.
Huth, Angela (1993). *Land Girls*. London: Sinclair Stevenson.
Ishiguro, Kazuo (1989). *The Remains of the Day*. London: Faber.
Jhabvala, Ruth Prawer (1975). *Heat and Dust*. London: John Murray.
Kureishi, Hanif (1990). *The Buddha of Suburbia*. London: Faber.
Le Carré, John (1996). *The Tailor of Panama*. London: Knopf.
Lessing, Doris (1974). *Memoirs of a Survivor*. London: Octagon.
Lette, Kathy (1996). *Mad Cows*. London: Picador.
McEwan, Ian (1975). *First Love, Last Rites*. London: Jonathan Cape.
McEwan, Ian (1978). *The Cement Garden*. London: Jonathan Cape.
McEwan, Ian (1981). *The Comfort of Strangers*. London: Jonathan Cape.
McEwan, Ian (1990). *The Innocent*. London: Jonathan Cape.
McEwan, Ian (1997). *Enduring Love*. London: Jonathan Cape.
Mo, Timothy (1982). *Scoursweet*. London: Andre Deutsch.
Ondaatje, Michael (1992). *The English Patient*. London: Bloomsbury.
Swift, Graham (1983). *Waterland*. London: Heinemann.
Swift, Graham (1996). *Last Orders*. London: Picador.
Tremain, Rose (1989). *Restoration*. London: Hamish Hamilton.
Welsh, Irvine (1993). *Trainspotting*. London: Secker & Warburg.
Welsh, Irvine (1994). *The Acid House*. London: Jonathan Cape.
Zahavi, Helen (1991). *Dirty Weekend*. London: Macmillan.

Part II

Elaborations of Empire

Chapter 4

Tropicalizing London: British Fiction and the Discipline of Postcolonialism

Nico Israel

He was hovering high over London! – Haha, they couldn't touch him now, the devils rushing upon him in that Pandemonium! – He looked down upon the city and saw the English. The trouble with the English was that they were English: damn cold fish! – Living underwater most of the year, in days the colour of night! "City," he cried, and his voice rolled over the metropolis like thunder, "I am going to tropicalize you."

Salman Rushdie, *The Satanic Verses*

In this exuberant scene from Salman Rushdie's 1988 novel *The Satanic Verses*, Gibreel Farishta, a famous Indian actor, his head full of grandiosity and invective, floats in the sky above the heart of the metropolis, former center of the empire on which the sun never set (though on whose own territory it never seemed to rise) and, imagining himself as the archangel Gabriel poised to announce the coming of the apocalypse, vows to bring light and warmth to a cold, dark, heartless country. It is a passage that also announces, in its own droll, contradictory way, the enigmatic arrival of postcolonial theory on the British literary scene.

Anti-colonialism and Postcolonial Theory

Almost from the very beginning of modern colonialism – which dates back at least to the later eighteenth century – there was organized resistance to it among the colonized. Anti-colonial political movements gained force beginning with the Sepoy Rebellion in India in 1857, and later, at the turn of the twentieth century, with the so-called Boxer Rebellion in China and the Boer War in South Africa – each of which outbreak was successfully put down by the relevant colonial administrations. But, after two bloody world wars sapped the European powers' will (and economic wherewithal) for sustained military engagement, and the increased mobilization of colonized subjects made them a formidable political and potential military force (just two of many factors that contributed to a complex historical process) the quarter century after 1945 saw the rapid decolonization of much of the globe. To speak only of former British colonies, by way of example: India became independent in 1947 (and was immediately partitioned from Pakistan, which itself split into two states with the secession of Bangladesh in the early 1970s); Malaya won its sovereignty in 1957, as did Ghana; while Kenya, Nigeria, Uganda, and most other British-controlled African states achieved independence in the 1960s (along with Jamaica, Trinidad, and several Caribbean nations). White-minority-ruled Rhodesia finally became independent Zimbabwe in 1980, and Hong Kong was returned to China in 1997.

Just as modern colonialism was a global condition, so the anti-colonial movement was a global force, sometimes operating under the banner of the "third world," a term which itself initially signified those nations unaligned to either the United States or the Soviet Union (at the time, the world's two superpowers), but which came to mean "formerly colonized," "underdeveloped" (or, more optimistically, "developing"), or simply "poor." But it is important to bear in mind that while decolonization struggles were sometimes legitimized, both in the colonized countries and in Europe, as part of a universal historical phenomenon – liberation of the wretched of the earth from the yoke of domination – most independence movements were *national* in scope, extending only to the limits of (frequently arbitrary) borders that themselves were drawn up in the colonial period. And, at least at the outset, the idea of achieving Algerian, Ugandan, or Indian sovereignty was more a product of resistance to colonialism than an autochthonous phenomenon linked to a deeply ingrained notion of national identity in any individual colony. Eventually, however, these acts of resistance often led to an increased effort to assert a cohesive national identity, which in turn became a key aspect of the way decolonization was portrayed in the literature of these new nation states.

To the extent that "third world" anti-colonial struggles were successful in making the dominant powers cede both the reins of government and a military presence in the colonized countries, they were less adept at ridding the new states of colonialism's economic and ideological residues. The rhetoric of progress and democracy (derived in part from the European Enlightenment) that subtended African, Asian, and Caribbean independence movements was frequently belied by inefficiency, corruption, and inequality in the new nation states, and a growing indigenous upper-middle-class frequently took the place (and even the former residences of) the colonizers, while watching the overall standard of living of the majority of the population decline, especially after the 1970s. Moreover, with the reliance of many "developing" countries on the International Monetary Fund and World Bank for funding of large-scale projects (and, in some cases, on nongovernmental organizations for food aid), early postcolonial dreams of economic self-determination seem to have morphed into a debt-ridden, corrupt nightmare. This has led some critics of the IMF and World Bank to speak of a "neocolonialism" that has never allowed postcolonial societies to develop according to their own terms.

Of course, anti-colonial theory throughout the twentieth century was instrumental in helping to shape resistance to colonialist domination. Some of the most influential political theorists to support this movement were not "native" peoples at all, but such European theorists as Marx, Engels, and Lenin, and, of the generations that preceded them, Hegel, Rousseau, and Locke. Nevertheless, a tradition of indigenous leaders, beginning with Mohandas Gandhi (who took his law degree in England) and Mao Zedong, with their polar-opposite tactics for ending colonial domination (non-violent and ultra-violent, respectively), began, especially in the post-World War II period, to exert wide influence as well. Particularly influential thinkers included the Tunisian Jew (and sometime novelist) Albert Memmi, whose celebrated study *The Colonizer and the Colonized* powerfully portrayed the oppressive core of colonialism. As was the case with Memmi, many later-twentieth-century anti-colonial theorists were highly familiar with, and influenced by, literary traditions of the West. Leopold Senghor, the poet who eventually became leader of Senegal, was associated with the "negritude" movement which drew on surrealist and Sartrean notions of identity and otherness to trumpet the liberationist potential of the putatively soulful, bodily African; Senghor, like many Francophonic early postcolonial leaders, was educated in Paris.

Certainly one of the most significant theorists of anti-colonial struggle was Frantz Fanon, who was born in the Caribbean island of Martinique and educated in part in France, after which time he served as a psychiatrist for the French Army in Algeria. Fanon wrote three impassioned books, two of which, translated as *Black Skin, White Masks* (1952) and *The Wretched of the Earth* (1961) – focusing respectively on the psychical harms of colonialism and the necessarily national and militant character of African independence – had a profound impact on the eventual directions of postcolonial theory. (Not incidentally, Jean-Paul Sartre, in the early 1960s the most recognized philosopher in Europe, wrote the militant preface to *The Wretched of the Earth*, whose title comes from the Socialist anthem, the *Internationale*.) When Rushdie's Gibreel Farishta hovers over London in the passage excerpted above, Fanonian theory – "The native is an oppressed person whose permanent dream is to become the persecutor" (Rushdie 1992: 353) – runs willy-nilly through his head.

While anti-colonial theory gained force throughout the 1950s and 1960s, what is typically called "postcolonial theory" was written after the initial period of decolonization was finished, which is to say, beginning in the late 1970s, and most of its most influential texts have been written by intellectuals of "third world" origin but educated in universities in Britain and/or the United States. Just as anti-colonial theory, like colonialism itself, derived in part from an engagement with a European political and philosophical tradition, so the emergence of postcolonial theory in the United States and Britain owes much to an encounter with then-prevalent poststructuralist theory (sometimes imprecisely called "postmodern theory"), which was itself associated with an anti-foundationalist critique of the history of Western metaphysics and the "white mythologies" that such metaphysics relied on and produced, even if they were trying, as in the case of structuralist anthropology, to critique ethnocentrism. For example, Palestinian-born American literary and social critic Edward Said, whose massively influential book *Orientalism* (1978) helped put postcolonial theory on the academic map, drew liberally on the idea of "archive" as articulated in French theorist Michel Foucault's early work in order to demonstrate how the Western academy's notion of the "Orient" linked apparently neutral notions of knowledge to the exercise of political power and control. Calcutta-born Gayatri Chakravorty Spivak, the self-described "Marxist-Feminist-Deconstructive" critic whose works dominated discussions of postcolonialism in the 1980s, derived much of her analysis of subalternity, marginality, and racial "difference" (and even her circular, interrogative writing style) from Jacques Derrida, one of whose most important works, *De La Grammatologie*, she herself had translated. Jamaica-born Stuart Hall, the pre-eminent black "cultural studies" critic in Britain in the 1980s, whose writings, sometimes called postcolonial, were always more directly engaged with a British sociological tradition, nevertheless also drew on a tradition of French poststructuralism to describe concepts of racial difference in the British national context.

In the late 1980s and early 1990s, as postcolonial studies courses began to appear with increasing frequency on US and British college campuses, scholars refined and challenged these earlier critical positions. Homi K. Bhabha, imbued in theories of Derrida, Foucault, and Jacques Lacan (and, through them, the philosopher Martin Heidegger), and drawing on the Fanon of *Black Skin, White Masks*, endorsed a psychoanalytic mode of theory that moved away from the nationalist, "third worldist" rhetoric of Said – despite its novelty, Said's "archival" method still relied on earlier models of liberation – and sought to account for productive impasses in what Bhabha called the "colonial encounter." Paul Gilroy, drawing on the "rhizomatic" analysis of Gilles Deleuze and Felix Guattari and the notion of "counterculture" associated with sociologist Zygmunt Bauman, suggested an approach to the "Black Atlantic" (the former slave-trade routes between Europe, Africa, and the New World) that accounted for cultural flows among nations. Sara Suleri, raised in Pakistan and influenced by deconstructive critic Paul de Man's ideas concerning "rhetorical" reading, argued in her book *The Rhetoric of English India* for an acknowledgment of the complicated eroticism inherent in the Anglo-Indian colonial project, an eroticism that called into question the predominant imperialism-as-rape narrative. These more recent advocates of postcolonial theory – and younger critics following in their footsteps – have argued that postcolonial analysis disturbs the very foundation of the distinction between West and East (or North and South), colonizer and colonized, metropole and periphery, by showing their historical, political, and cultural imbrication; and they frequently have viewed the condition of migrants from the formerly colonized countries now living in Europe (and particularly Britain) equally worthy of their intellectual attention.

(Because of these theorists' apparent abandonment of a connection to militancy, such Marxist critics as Aijaz Ahmad, writing from India, have in turn inveighed against "postcolonialism"'s insufficient sense of collective politics.)

Notwithstanding the important political legacy of the term, and in spite of the fact that some postcolonial critics can be found in the fields of anthropology (notably Arjun Appadurai, whose theoretical account of global media flows has had wide influence), history (e.g. Arif Dirlik, who has attracted much notice in his writings about the "Pacific rim"), and so-called area studies, postcolonialism as a subject has found a home mostly in literature (and especially English literature) departments, at least in the US and Britain. There the rubric "postcolonial literature" – as with the term "Commonwealth literature" before it (described in greater detail below) – has tended to refer less frequently to the kinds of recent international-oriented work outlined above and more often to a sort of cordoned-off zone in which imaginative writers from South Asia, Africa, and, occasionally, the Caribbean could be explored as if they were part of their own self-generating tradition. In any case, the development of the phenomenon of "postcolonial literature" in the US must be understood as having emerged in relation to political concerns over gender, race, and ethnic identity as they flowered on college campuses in the "culture wars" of the late 1980s and 1990s. There, the "multicultural" demand for inclusion in the literary canon of more works by women writers and writers of color (including those from formerly colonized countries) had the apparently contradictory effect of linking a grounded, identity-political notion of gender and race with the anti-essentialist critique of identity that, through its filiations with poststructuralist thought, then dominated postcolonial theory. As postcolonialism has become more disciplinarily endorsed, this discursive tension remains unresolved. In Britain, the study of postcolonialism was less institutionally oriented, and linked more closely to the politics of "Black Britain," a movement of South Asians and West Indians (including but not limited to academics) that arose in response to Thatcherism, and especially to the Conservative government's repressive response to the so-called "race riots" in Brixton and Toxteth in the early 1980s. Although that perceived convergence of interests under the rubric of "blackness," as well as the sense of solidarity between academics and community activists, began to unravel around the time of the *Satanic Verses* affair, these were clearly the conditions out of which a specifically British postcolonial studies emerged.

From "Commonwealth Literature" to "Postcolonial Literature"

These were some of the political, theoretical, and institutional contexts in which postcolonial literature of the 1980s and 1990s, particularly literature produced by "third world" writers educated in the West, emerged. But the literature itself rarely responded directly to the theory; more frequently, authors of works that fit the description "postcolonial" were responding primarily to other imaginative writers, as writers arguably have always done. Rewinding to the early twentieth century for a moment: the arch-modernist James Joyce, born and raised in colonized Ireland, before leaving it forever, is perhaps the most extreme example of a colonized writer – although he would certainly have rejected the term – who sought to address the whole history of British writing as a means of extending its artistic achievements but subverting its political power. Also writing in the modernist period, though in some ways not a modernist at all, was Rabindranath Tagore of Calcutta, one of the first non-Western writers to be celebrated in the West. Tagore's decidedly local poems and stories, all but a few of which were written in his native language of Bengali, were greatly influenced by British Romanticism (and they in turn influenced contemporary European writers, most notably W. B. Yeats). Undoubtedly the most important imaginative texts for early non-Western postcolonial writers describing colonized lands (at least in the English language) were not written by "natives" but rather by such colonial authors as Rudyard Kipling, Joseph Conrad, and E. M. Forster, whose powerful depictions of India and Africa have left an imprint on all later writing about those regions, even if the later writing seeks to dispute with, revise, or overturn the earlier.

Before there was "postcolonial" literature in English, though, there was "Commonwealth" literature, under whose ambivalent rubric anglophone writers from such formerly colonized countries as Canada, Australia, New Zealand, and, later, India and other South Asian, and Caribbean and African countries were studied (and also marketed and published, by such imprints as Heinemann in its African Writers series). But, beginning in the 1980s, the term seemed too capacious and decidedly apolitical (or, worse, reiterative of the old imperial lines): after all, what contexts linked such authors from "settler" colonies as Nadine Gordimer (South Africa) and Margaret Atwood (Canada) to authors from "native"-dominated colonies such as Chinua Achebe

(Nigeria) and Derek Walcott (St Lucia) besides their use of the English language and the fact that they were not born British or American? Between the mid-1960s and the late 1970s, the best-known and most frequently taught non-white "Commonwealth" writer was probably the Trinidad-born V. S. Naipaul, who won the Booker Prize in 1971, and in 2001 was awarded the Nobel Prize. (Incidentally, as Graham Huggan has shown, the Booker Prize – now the "Man Booker" – has long been and remains the single most important means of generating an audience for Commonwealth and postcolonial literary texts, from 1975's *Heat and Dust*, German–English author Ruth Prawer Jhabvala's account of India in the late colonial period, to such recent winners as *The God of Small Things* (1997) by India's Arundhati Roy, which explores the postcolonial history of Southern Indian villages against the backdrop of the massive social changes of the early 1990s.)

Naipaul's acutely observed, dyspeptic, and sometimes scathing novels and travelogues such as *A House for Mr Biswas* (1961), *The Mimic Men* (1967), *In a Free State* (1971), and *Guerillas* (1973) portrayed former colonies in Africa, the Caribbean, and the Indian subcontinent as landscapes degraded by poverty, stupidity, political corruption, and a ruling class doing a very poor imitation of Englishness. While Naipaul, whose clipped, deeply ironic prose demonstrates a clear affinity to Conrad's, was often admired for his laconic wit and his elegant style, and praised, particularly by British journalists, for his lack of sentimentality, he was also excoriated, notably by Edward Said, for reaffirming stereotypes of the "third world" and for perhaps unconsciously suggesting that times were better under colonialism.

It is partly out of resistance to this anti-anti-colonial tendency in Commonwealth literature that one can locate the emergence, in English-language writing, at least, of recognizably "postcolonial" literature. Beginning in the early 1980s, with the publication of Salman Rushdie's *Midnight's Children* (also a Booker Prize winner) in 1981, a number of texts that reviewed the history of postcolonial societies from a perspective more critical of colonial domination and somewhat more sympathetic to the potentialities of political newness began to attract notice. Rushdie, born in Bombay and educated in England at Cambridge University – he took a degree in history – drew on the disorienting, nonlinear narrative techniques of "magic realism" (in which official and unofficial national histories are woven through grandiose allegory) characteristic of such South American writers as Gabriel García Márquez, and in boisterous, Bombay-accented English portrayed the subcontinent in the twentieth century as subject both to perpetual crisis and to transformative possibility. (Magic realism itself, like the negritude movement, owed much to surrealist notions of the "authentic" non-Western exoticism of other places, which Rushdie seemed at once to endorse and disavow.) In *Midnight's Children*, Saleem Sinai, born at the mystical hour of India's independence (and simultaneous separation from Pakistan) reflects, in his own rapidly decomposing, high-metabolism body, India's own bloody colonial legacy and disaster-prone postcolonial history from Partition to Indira Gandhi's State of Emergency. Also concerned with the corrupting experience of a dying colonialism and the painful transition to early postcolonialism was Anita Desai, born in Delhi to parents of Indian and German heritage. Her early novel *Clear Light of Day* (1980) recounts more local, less pyrotechnically political situations than do Rushdie's, but through a family narrative nevertheless also addresses some of the same crises and resistances in, as well as promises of, postcolonial societies.

While these "early" postcolonial novels thus mainly were set in formerly colonized countries – no doubt part of their appeal to Western readers was a residue of the tradition, in colonial literature, of the perceived exoticism of the East – frequently taught in disciplinarily nascent "postcolonial literature" classes were texts which focused on the migrants from these countries into Britain. (These migrants' numbers, visibility, and cultural impact increased dramatically from the 1980s on: one can chart this impact simply by considering the television images of London's citizenry during the 1982 wedding of Prince Charles and Lady Diana, and then, 15 years later, of the mourners for Diana Spencer after her death; during that time London had become, even in its celebration of royal rule, a strikingly more "multicultural" city.) As is clear in the passage excerpted at the beginning of this essay, much of Rushdie's *The Satanic Verses* explored migrants' traumas of displacement while also celebrating the new London that was being shaped by immigrants. But of course this element of the text was eclipsed by the novel's portrayal of the humanity of the Islamic prophet Muhammad and the furor over the subsequent death sentence declared by the Iranian Ayatollah Ruhollah Khomeini (which *fatwa* itself generated recognition and galvanized support for Rushdie and in part helped elevate the status of "postcolonial" literature). Meanwhile, Hanif Kureishi, born and raised in Bromley (UK) and author of the screenplay for Stephen Frears's film *My Beautiful Laundrette* (about a young Pakistani man and his gay relationship with his white working-class lover), published his first novel, *The Buddha of Suburbia*, in 1990; it explores the travails of a young bisexual man, half-Indian and half-English, growing up in a London suburb. In significant ways, *The Buddha of Suburbia* followed an American tradition of children-of-immigrant assimilation-and-resistance stories, one which nevertheless operates in different registers in Britain, owing to the lasting legacy of colonialism and the relatively recent histories of postcolonial migration.

These two tendencies – "exotic" novels and stories set in former colonies on the one hand, "domestic" literature charting the lives of immigrants on the other – and, especially, the filiations between the "exotic" and the "domestic," shaped the development of postcolonial literature in the 1990s and early 2000s. As the term became established as an academic discipline, that decade-and-a-half witnessed an explosion of celebrated "postcolonial" texts, such as Ben Okri's *The Famished Road* (1991), which weaves Yoruba myths into a portrayal of politically and economically stagnant pre-postcolonial Nigeria, Vikram Seth's *A Suitable Boy* (1993), a marriage romance set in early postcolonial India, and, more recently, Hari Kunzru's *The Impressionist* (2002), an exuberant and sexually explicit restaging of Kipling's *Kim*, set in the era of the dying Raj. On the "domestic" front, Zadie Smith's *White Teeth* (2000), heavily indebted to Rushdie, explores the life of various migrants – West Indians, South Asians, Jews – amid the politics of 1990s London, while Monica Ali's recent *Brick Lane* (2003) delicately charts the story of two Bangladeshi sisters, one settling in London's East End while the other remains in her native country.

Postcolonial Literature and Postcolonial Theory

In 1990, Homi Bhabha (then a lecturer at Sussex University in Falmer, UK, now an endowed professor at Harvard) published a collection of essays he edited called *Nation and Narration*. In his own densely written contribution, "DissemiNation," whose title Bhabha acknowledges was inspired by the "wit and wisdom" of Jacques Derrida, Bhabha asserts the necessity of being "alive to the *metaphoricity* of the people of imagined communities, migrant or metropolitan" (1990: 141, emphasis in text). Stressing the importance of how such metaphoricity dislodges static, essentialist ideas of national identity, Bhabha suggests, emphatically, that "we need another time of *writing* that will be able to inscribe the ambivalent and chiasmatic intersections of time and place that constitute the problematic 'modern' experience of the Western nation" (p. 141, emphasis in text). At the end of the essay, as if to substantiate his claim, Bhabha offers an abbreviated but powerful reading of Rushdie's then recently published *Satanic Verses*, in which Bhabha claims that the text "attempts to redefine the boundaries of the Western nation, so that the 'foreignness of languages' becomes the inescapable cultural condition for the enunciation of the mother-tongue" (p. 166).

A few years later, writing in hiding under the peculiar conditions of Khomeini's bounty-bolstered *fatwa*, Rushdie seemed to respond directly, if a bit snarkily, to Bhabha's thesis, when, in his novel *The Moor's Last Sigh*, he has a Bombay Parsi academic character named Zeenat Vakil (Bhabha is from a well-known Bombay Parsi, or Zoroastrian, family) write a book called "Imperso-Nation and Dis/Semi/ Nation: Dialogics of Eclecticism and Interrogations of Authenticity . . ." (Rushdie 1995: 329). The parodic title humorously suggests that Rushdie was aware of, but did not necessarily endorse, the way that his earlier novel (in which Zeenat Vakil first appeared) had participated in the shaping of academic postcolonial theory, and, perhaps, demonstrates his unwillingness to become fodder for jargon-laden theoretical speculation.

Already by 1989, "postcolonial theory" was recognized as a discipline in literary study for which there was a potential market in academic publishing. *The Empire Writes Back: Theory and practice in post-colonial literatures* by Australian critics Bill Ashcroft, Gareth Griffiths, and Helen Tiffin was the first of several widely circulated anthologies of criticism to appear over the subsequent half dozen years (including Ashcroft et al.'s *Post-Colonial Studies Reader* in 1995). Significantly, it was not until 1996 that anthologies of creative writing grouped under the "postcolonial" rubric began to appear: first among them was *The Arnold Anthology of Post-colonial Literatures in English*, published by Oxford University Press. The order of publication clearly demonstrates that the discipline *preceded* the literature – at least in anthologized form, packaged for the classroom – even if this belated construction of a "postcolonial literature" involved retroactive designation of much earlier works such as Achebe's 1958 novel *Things Fall Apart*.

It is difficult to assess the extent to which non-white anglophone writers of the 1980s and 1990s were influenced by postcolonial theoretical writing, as "influence" appears to be at once too general and too restrictive a term. The earlier generation of "Commonwealth" writers was certainly more familiar with anti-colonial political tradition; many such writers living in the United States (e.g. Achebe and Ngugi wa Thiong'o) wrote both literature and theoretically inclined criticism. The more recently published young British writers, such as Kunzru, Smith, and Ali, were likely to have at least encountered the seminal postcolonial theoretical texts as university students: Kunzru and Ali attended Oxford, and Smith, Cambridge (and one might casually observe from this list that race *per se* seems less an obstacle to literary success in Britain than does educational class status; there are relatively few Booker Prize winning writers from the UK who do not have Oxbridge credentials).

If it is hard to pinpoint ways in which writing coming out of Britain and its former colonies itself directly responded to postcolonial theory, what seems an easier case to make is that postcolonial theory has helped to provide a disciplinary frame for the *reception* of literature – what gets read and how it gets read. It may be the case that both the literary and theoretical writing are responding to the same material and cultural contexts, which is to say, the emerging "New World Order," but it is surely significant that some of the central themes of recognizably postcolonial literature – diaspora, hybridity, migrancy, mimicry, hyphenated identity, magic, colonizer/colonized relations – have also been extensively theorized by postcolonial scholars (based in part on their readings of poststructuralist theory), and that these themes with a few notable exceptions have proven more commercially successful and pedagogically amenable than, say, representations of local struggles in postcolonies portrayed in direct "realist" idiom. To be sure, this was also true of formally innovative "British" modernist literature as well – Joyce and Eliot demand close reading and consequently tend to "teach" better than John Galsworthy or Arnold Bennett – but the extent to which postcolonial literature thereby extends the presumptions of modernist criteria of difficulty and transnational identity (spiced up with racialized notions of the persistence of "magic" in the "East") and thereby excludes an effective recognition of or engagement with the local politics of the formerly colonized (or racially different) is open to question.

In any case, while Rushdie, Okri, Smith, and Ali seem ambivalently to have embraced the rubric of "postcolonial," other "minority-identified" British writers have adamantly rejected it, not for the reasons cited above – that is, for its inadequate political scope – but because they feel it exerts excessive political demands that do not reflect their own local realities or literary priorities. For example, Kazuo Ishiguro, author of the celebrated novel *The Remains of the Day* (1989), has bristled at being called a "postcolonial" or even an "Asian" writer, given that his Japanese ethnicity is hardly reflective of a collective immigrant narrative in Britain, and his works have rarely directly addressed the Asian immigrant experience, whether collective or individual.

Impasses in Postcolonial Theory

The case of Ishiguro raises analogous thorny questions concerning identity and representation that have gnawed at the foundations of postcolonial theory since its inception. Does the rubric "postcolonial literature" in some way hinge on the racial or ethnic identification of the author, thereby extending segregated categories produced in the discourse of colonialism itself? If so, does the demand for representation of a collective "minority" experience restrict and further ghettoize non-white writing, neutralizing its political efficacy? Or should any writer who depicts the colonial or postcolonial experience be considered a producer of "postcolonial" literature? In the former case, we might consider Kureishi's recent novel *Intimacy* (1998), about the demise of the marriage of a well-known London writer, in which the issue of race or migration is rarely if ever mentioned; the novel has far more in common with works by non-immigrant British writers like Martin Amis than it does with those of Rushdie or Zadie Smith, and yet it has been promoted as a "postcolonial" text and taught in postcolonial literature courses in the US. In the latter case, we might consider whether a white South African writer such as J. M. Coetzee – who, with nebulous allegoricity but stunning acuteness, stages the ethical dilemmas of apartheid as part of a broader investigation of cruelty and complicity – ought by virtue of his subject matter to be considered postcolonial, or, extending this logic, whether the rubric applies to texts written by white Englishmen – *Brazzaville Beach* (1995) by William Boyd, *Last King of Scotland* (1999) by Giles Foden – whose authors, well aware of the contemporary critiques of colonialism and imperialism, portray African history and contemporary African life with empathy and political sensitivity. It might be argued, after all, that all of these writers inhabit a postcolonial world.

To put even more pressure on the rubric "postcolonial," one might consider the case of Irish or Scottish writers. It is undeniable that Ireland, in particular, colonized since the twelfth century, was a cultural and administrative test case for later British incursions in Africa, South Asia, and the New World, and that Irish people suffered terribly under the yoke of colonial domination, economic dependency, cultural imperialism, and racism. An Irish poet like Seamus Heaney, whose poetry everywhere dredges up this history, and attempts to make English speak a sort of Irish idiom, might fairly be said critically to stage colonizer/colonized relations. Concerning Scottish literature, to what extent ought such recent novelists as James Kelman – whose *How Late It Was, How Late* relates the tale of a drunken shoplifting ex-con who wakes to a world gone black, with Beckettian narrative techniques rendered in Glaswegian slang – to be considered "postcolonial"?

Perhaps because postcolonial literature owes its emergence in part to real political transformations, the issue of agency and responsibility is seen by some critics to be paramount: recognizably postcolonial literature, often written by middle-class and upper-middle-class immigrants – and it is not hard to notice the relative overrepresentation of Indian writers in comparison to African or Afro-Caribbean writers – is *expected*, in a residue of vanguardism no longer demanded of most literature by white writers, to address the plight of the wretched of the earth, either in the third world or in immigrant communities. But others argue that emphasizing the dominant metaphors of postcolonialism – diaspora, hybridity, and transversality among them – tends to exclude major writers from former colonies who, sometimes writing in their own languages about local experiences, are much less frequently encountered in postcolonial literature courses in the US or Britain – such writers as Pius Ngandu Nkashama, Calixthe Beyala, T. Janakiraman, Werewere Liking, and the late Ken Saro-Wiwa.

In response to these vexing problems, it may fairly be claimed that postcolonial theory, following the poststructuralist credo "the death of the author," emphasizes not the perceived "identity" of the writer but the effect of the writing, and that what is to be pursued in the analysis of these works need not bear any biographical connection to their creator. If this is the case, it must be acknowledged that the teaching and marketing of literature, as with the gallery/art-history system in contemporary art, still relies on the myth of the Maker, however theoretically outmoded the figure may be. Another response might be simply that, as with the discourse of colonialism, postcolonialism now *exists*: it is not merely a question of accepting or rejecting a disciplinary term. Such writers as Ishiguro, Kureishi, and Timothy Mo may feel constrained by the rubric, but the apparent alternative – to embrace a universal, belletristic notion of "Literature" – would be to reduce a cultural product to a banality. One must be nominative, the argument goes, and, despite the term's insufficiencies – which after all, are no greater than those of "Romanticism" or "British modernism"

– "postcolonialism" at least allows for a recognition of a conflictual history and the possibility of critical opposition.

Destinations of Postcolonial Theory and Literature

Beginning in the early 1990s but especially since the publication of Michael Hardt and Antonio Negri's controversial book *Empire* in 2000, a good deal of critical heat has been generated by the term "globalization." Hardt and Negri argue that the world has entered a new era: no longer are we subject to "modern sovereignty" in which the nation is the central form of political expression or force; we are now in a realm of "empire," in which extra-national structures – multinational corporations, the World Bank, the IMF, the UN, but also the hazily defined "multitude" – express and exert power. Consequently, "empire," according to Hardt and Negri, is to be distinguished from nineteenth- and twentieth-century imperialism: given the mobility of labor and radically transformed distribution networks, domination no longer works as directly or obviously as it did in the past. For this reason, Hardt and Negri are keen to distinguish between postcolonial theory and globalization theory. "Postcolonialist theorists," they write, "in general give a very confused view of this passage [between modern sovereignty and empire] because they remain fixed on attacking an old form of power and propose a strategy of liberation that could be effective only on that old terrain" (2000: 145–6). Extending the polemic, they assert that "postcolonialist theory [is] a very productive tool for rereading history, but it is entirely insufficient for theorizing contemporary global power" (p. 146).

Postcolonial theorists have responded to this provocation by attacking globalization theory's inadequate emphasis on racial and ethnic difference, and by asserting that, as was made clear after the US-led invasion of Iraq in 2003, old-style imperialism had by no means disappeared (Balakrishnan 2003). Moreover, they have argued – in a way that perhaps unconsciously restages debates within poststructuralism of the 1970s and 1980s between Derridean deconstruction and Deleuzian rhizomatics – that one *must* "reread history" in order to understand the structures of domination and possibilities for liberation; it is not a question of turning the page of history and assuming one has arrived at "contemporaneity," especially in a world which everywhere shows the effects of colonialism and racism.

The extent to which such globalization theory (or its transnationalist and regionalist offshoots) will eclipse postcolonial studies or create some new disciplinary variant remains to be seen. One aspect immediately worth noticing is that the disciplinary surfacing of postcolonial studies – which, as discussed above, I locate around 1988–9 – coincides almost precisely with the emergence of what some theorists of globalization assert is the global era, coming after the fall of the Berlin Wall in 1989, the end of the Cold War, and the stark entrance of the "New World Order." (Other influential globalization theorists set the starting point of contemporary globalization back to the early 1970s; of course, whether globalization was "born" in 1989 or even in 1972, it would be necessary to admit that its gestation period lasted hundreds, if not thousands, of years.) This is not to suggest that postcolonial theory is merely a *symptom* or subset of globalization, but rather to indicate that the two positions – "globalization" and "postcolonialism" – are not necessarily inherently antagonistic. In fact, their genealogies are entwined: both terms were coined in the 1950s in similar political contexts (among them the rise of the "third world" as a force to oppose the two superpowers).

How these issues pertain to the production and reception of literature is still to be determined. It is easy enough to conceive how globalization has affected the *business* of literature – its "production" in the commercial sense. As detailed by Richard Todd in chapter 1 of this volume, the last 15 years – years in which postcolonial literature established itself as a force in British publishing, with its star authors occasionally earning huge advances – have seen a remarkable consolidation of the publishing industry, with multinational conglomerates (e.g., AOL-Time Warner, Viacom, News Corp, the Bertelsmann Group, Disney) acquiring controlling stakes in formerly family-owned literary publishing houses. (Most theoretical texts are put out by university presses, but many are published by Routledge, now a subsidiary of the Thompson conglomerate; Hardt and Negri's recent book *Multitude* (2004), which seeks to refine *Empire*'s theorization of liberation and acknowledges the benefits of postcolonial theory's emphasis on racial and ethnic differences, has been published by venerable Penguin, owned by the Viking Group, in turn presently owned by the multinational giant Pearson.) At the same time, the expansion of the World Wide Web and the success of online booksellers such as Amazon have allowed for an exponential extension of the reach of literature, exposing buyers in remote areas of the world (at least those who have access to electricity and computers) to an ever wider range of texts, while also increasingly putting local bookshops, with their owners' sometimes idiosyncratic affinities, out of business.

Meanwhile, globalization as a *theme* of contemporary literature has, not surprisingly, been pervasive. Even in the "postcolonial" *Satanic Verses*, Salman Rushdie has his half-mad character Gibreel Farishta sing a little patriotic ditty, translated from the Hindi: "O, my shoes are Japanese/These trousers English, if you please/On my head, red Russian hat – /My heart's Indian for all that" (1992: 5). If we are at all attentive to the allegorical inflections in Gibreel's tune, we would recognize that even before its recent wholehearted embrace of economic globalization (outsourcing, high-tech training and entrepreneurship, and so on), postcolonial India was already politically and culturally intimately linked to the outside "modern" world, yet it also maintained a recognizably separate, national (and even local) identity. The challenge for postcolonial theory and literature in the increasingly globalized world is to account at once for the external contours of global flows – how shoes, trousers, hats, people, *texts* cross borders – and for the persistence of something as nebulous, differential, local, and potentially dark, as the "heart."

References and Further Reading

NONFICTION

Ahmad, Aijaz (1992). *In Theory: Classes, nations, literatures*. London: Verso.
Appadurai, Arjun (1996). *Modernity at Large: Cultural dimensions of globalization*. Minneapolis, MN: University of Minnesota Press.
Ashcroft, Bill, Griffiths, Gareth, & Tiffin, Helen (eds.) (1989). *The Empire Writes Back: Theory and practice in post-colonial literatures*. London: Routledge.
Ashcroft, Bill, Griffiths, Gareth, & Tiffin, Helen (eds.) (1995). *The Post-Colonial Studies Reader*. London: Routledge.
Balakrishnan, Gopal (ed.) (2003). *Debating Empire* (New Left Review Debates). London: Verso.
Bhabha, Homi K. (ed.) (1990). *Nation and Narration*. London: Routledge.
Bhabha, Homi K. (1994). *The Location of Culture*. London: Routledge.
Dirlik, Arif (2000). *Postmodernity's Histories: The past as legacy and project*. Lanham, MD: Rowman & Littlefield.
Gilroy, Paul (1993). *The Black Atlantic: Modernity and double consciousness*. Cambridge, MA: Harvard University Press.
Hall, Stuart (1993). *Modernity and its Futures: Understanding modern societies*. London: Polity.
Hardt, Michael & Negri, Antonio (2000). *Empire*. Cambridge, MA: Harvard University Press.

Hardt, Michael & Negri, Antonio (2004). *Multitude*. Harmondsworth: Penguin.
Huggan, Graham (2001). *The Postcolonial Exotic: Marketing the margins*. London: Routledge.
Memmi, Albert (1991). *The Colonizer and the Colonized* (trans. Howard Greenfield). Boston, MA: Beacon (first published 1957).
Said, Edward (1978). *Orientalism*. London: Vintage.
Said, Edward (1994). *Culture and Imperialism*. London: Vintage.
Spivak, Gayatri Chakravorty, Landry, Donna, & MacLean, Gerald M. (eds.) (1996). *The Spivak Reader: Selected works of Gayatri Chakravorty Spivak*. London: Routledge.
Suleri, Sara (1992). *The Rhetoric of English India*. Chicago, IL: University of Chicago Press.
Thieme, John (ed.) (1996). *The Arnold Anthology of Post-Colonial Literatures in English*. Oxford: Oxford University Press.
Williams, Patrick & Crisman, Laura (eds.) (1994). *Colonial Discourse and Post-Colonial Theory: A reader*. New York: Columbia University Press.

FICTION

Ali, Monica (2003). *Brick Lane*. London: Doubleday.
Boyd, William (1990). *Brazzaville Beach*. London: Sinclair Stevenson.
Desai, Anita (1980). *Clear Light of Day*. London: HarperCollins.
Fanon, Frantz (1991). *Black Skin, White Masks* (trans. Charles Lam Markmann). New York: Grove (first published 1952).
Fanon, Frantz (1991). *The Wretched of the Earth* (trans. Constance Farrington, with Preface by Jean-Paul Sartre). New York: Grove (first published 1961).
Foden, Giles (1999). *The Last King of Scotland*. London: Faber.
Ishiguro, Kazuo (1989). *The Remains of the Day*. London: Faber.
Jhabvala, Ruth Prawer (1975). *Heat and Dust*. London: John Murray.
Kelman, James (1994). *How Late it Was, How Late*. London: Secker & Warburg.
Kunzru, Hari (2002). *The Impressionist*. London: Hamish Hamilton.
Kureishi, Hanif (1990). *The Buddha of Suburbia*. London: Faber.
Kureishi, Hanif (1998). *Intimacy*. London: Faber.
Naipaul, V. S. (1961). *A House for Mr Biswas*. New York: McGraw Hill.
Naipaul, V. S. (1967). *The Mimic Men*. New York: Macmillan.
Naipaul, V. S. (1971). *In a Free State*. London: Andre Deutsch.
Naipaul, V. S. (1973). *Guerillas*. London: Andre Deutsch.
Okri, Ben (1991). *The Famished Road*. London: Jonathan Cape.
Roy, Arundhati (1997). *The God of Small Things*. London: Flamingo.
Rushdie, Salman (1981). *Midnight's Children*. London: Jonathan Cape.
Rushdie, Salman (1992). *The Satanic Verses*. Dover, DE: Consortium (first published 1988).
Rushdie, Salman (1995). *The Moor's Last Sigh*. New York: Pantheon (first published 1994).
Seth, Vikram (1993). *A Suitable Boy*. London: HarperCollins.
Smith, Zadie (2000). *White Teeth*. Harmondsworth: Penguin.

Chapter 5

New Ethnicities, the Novel, and the Burdens of Representation

James Procter

In January 1989, Muslims across Britain gathered in the northern industrial city of Bradford to protest against the publication of Salman Rushdie's *The Satanic Verses* (1988). Some members of the community perceived it to be a work of obscene blasphemy. It renamed the Prophet Muhammad "Mahound" (meaning false prophet); it questioned the historical provenance of the Qur'an; it appeared to re-cast the wives of the Prophet as whores. The demonstration in Bradford, which culminated in the burning of the book outside City Hall, came to represent the most dramatic reception of a fictional text ever witnessed. Repeatedly disseminated by the national and international media, the flaming cover of *The Satanic Verses* became an iconic image of the late 1980s and, subsequently, a key intertext in novels such as Hanif Kureishi's *The Black Album* (1995) and Zadie Smith's *White Teeth* (2000).

In the month after the Bradford book burning, the Ayatollah Khomeini issued a *fatwa*, or death sentence, on Rushdie, driving the author of *The Satanic Verses* into hiding for nearly a decade. The novel was banned in 45 Islamic countries and its Japanese translator was killed. What became known as "the Rushdie affair" was generally understood as highlighting certain irreconcilable differences between a rational West and a fanatical East, between the values of censorship and free speech, fundamentalist religious intolerance and secular, liberal tolerance. What such binarisms failed to register, however, were the *internal* tensions and divisions exposed by the Bradford book burning. Not only did the Bradford protest expose the fragile state of the supposedly homogeneous national community under Mrs Thatcher (British Prime Minister, 1979–90); it also pointed to the breakdown of traditional alliances within and between Britain's various non-white communities.

The emphatic rejection of *The Satanic Verses*, by the very communities it appeared to represent, highlighted a crisis of representation which has been a recurring feature of the reception of black and British Asian fiction since the late 1980s. Hanif Kureishi's writing and films have been repeatedly attacked for their "negative" portrayal of the Asian community. Accusations of misogyny and stereotyping have been directed at Victor Headley's cult black British crime novel *Yardie* (1992). More recently, and shadowing the success stories of Zadie Smith's *White Teeth* and Monica Ali's *Brick Lane* (2003), there has been an increasingly prominent debate concerning the "representative" status of the two novels. *Brick Lane* found itself being compared with *The Satanic Verses* by some residents of east London, who regarded it as an "insulting and shameful" depiction of their community. Meanwhile, Zadie Smith defended herself against the tendency of reviewers to locate her novel in a black literary tradition, which she felt reduced her to the role of spokesperson on issues of race and ethnicity:

> Do you go to Don DeLillo and say, "He doesn't represent middle-class white people enough"? . . . No. You give him complete freedom. Why would you limit writers of any ethnicity or gender to be a sex or class politician and give freedom to white writers to write about absolutely anybody? (Jones 2000)

To reduce writers to the role of representatives who are expected to delegate, or speak on behalf of a particular community, is to curb their artistic freedom, Smith suggests. Her comments foreground an important tension between representation as a process of fictional depiction and representation as an act of political delegation that has become increasingly apparent since the late 1980s. This essay will explore the ongoing crisis of representation in contemporary British fiction in relation to the shifting discourses of race and ethnicity from the late 1970s to the present.

At stake in this crisis is more than a simple conflict between a white literary establishment and the African, Caribbean, and Asian communities depicted in contemporary multicultural fictions. What is striking about all of the writers listed above is the extent to which they have been both celebrated and condemned in almost equal measure by white *and* South Asian/African-Caribbean commentators. Rather than taking sides, or seeking a "balanced" account of these discrepant responses, this essay will suggest that the conflict over the issue of representation (as an act of delegation) is itself valuable to an understanding of the shifting modes of representation (as an act of artistic depiction) adopted within contemporary black and British Asian fiction over the past 25 years.

Cheering Fictions

In his influential essay "New ethnicities" (1988), Stuart Hall identifies a shift between two dominant "moments" of representation in the 1980s. In the first moment, black artists tend to contest negative media stereotypes with positive representations, and correct racist stereotypes in order to produce what Hanif Kureishi terms "cheering fictions." In seeking to depict a true or authentic black experience, these artists privilege the aesthetic values of realism. The second moment of representation typically refuses "a simple set of reversals" (for example, replacing negative depictions of blacks with positive ones) by working "with and through difference" (Procter 2000: 268–9). Differences (for example, of ethnicity, gender, generation, and sexuality) that were subordinate to dominant black identity formations in the first moment, flourish in the second. The second moment is characterized by a shift from the notion of representation as mimetic, to a recognition that representation plays a formative, constitutive role. Black experience is not something that exists outside culture, something whose essence or nature it is the task of representation simply to "capture." Rather "'black' is essentially a politically and culturally *constructed* category, which cannot be grounded in a set of fixed trans-cultural or transcendental racial categories and which therefore has no guarantees in nature" (Procter 2000: 268).

Published in the same year as *The Satanic Verses* and in response to a dispute among black and Asian intellectuals over the critical evaluation of Black British film (see Procter 2000: 261–5), "New ethnicities" emerged at a particular conjuncture in the late 1980s, as "black" ceased to operate as a unifying collective category. The two moments of Hall's essay do not emerge out of the blue then, but in conjunction with specific historical shifts taking place in postwar British society. During the 1970s and early 1980s, on the rare occasions that blacks were depicted in the media, they were overwhelmingly represented as the bearers of a crisis in British society, as criminals, thieves, and muggers requiring authoritarian state intervention (see Hall 1978). Such representations were used by Margaret Thatcher's Conservative government to legitimize the intrusive policing of black neighborhoods. These tactics sparked numerous riots and protests in places like Southall (1979), Brixton (1981), and Broadwater (1985). While they had different causes, these uprisings were commonly diagnosed as symptomatic of a lack of access to dominant regimes of representation: political, journalistic, and artistic. As Lord Scarman, who conducted the official enquiry into the Brixton Riots of 1981, put it, "the limited opportunities of airing their grievances at national level in British society encourage them to protest in the streets" (Scarman 1982: 35).

The lack of access to dominant modes of representation in the 1970s and early 1980s did not just have an impact in the streets, it also placed what Hall and others have termed a "burden of representation" (a play on the imperialist notion of "the white man's burden") on those exceptional black British artists who *did* gain access. Hall associates the need to speak for the whole community in the first moment, with the emergence of "black" as an organizing, hegemonic category referencing unity and alliance between very different ethnic groups (African, Caribbean, and Asian).

This burden of representation was tangible in the late 1970s, when the state identified multiculturalism as a key initiative in educational reform; a potential solution to the growing racial tensions in Britain outlined above. As Hazel Carby notes in her seminal essay "Multicultural fictions" (1979), literature, and fiction in particular, was identified in this period as an "expressive" medium capable of inculcating multicultural values. Carby uses Robert Jeffcoate (an educational theorist) and his arguments in the tellingly titled *Positive Image, Towards a Multicultural Curriculum* (1979) to exemplify some of the limitations of this approach:

> Multicultural fiction becomes important in reflecting the multicultural nature of society. Robert Jeffcoate cites the importance of minority race pupils encountering "people like themselves" in fiction. This type of "reflective" theory can be subjected to a number of serious criticisms. With regard to the presentation of other races, Robert Jeffcoate's approach is to assume that books with Black people in them reflect them "as they are" in a "real world" outside of the text. (Carby 1979: 23)

In short, multicultural fiction was felt to offer a means of *reflecting* a more democratic, or *representative* society. Read within the context of the multicultural discourses described by Carby, the generic and thematic preoccupation with education in Black British fiction during the 1970s and early 1980s would appear to be circumscribed by a burden of representation. Specifically, the pressure to create a more democratic or representative curriculum suggests that the prominence of education as a theme in novels of this period has a compensatory function, countering an absence in representations of black and Asian experience in schools and about schooling.

Farrukh Dhondy was one of the most prolific and successful authors of children's fiction in the late 1970s and early 1980s, publishing collections of short stories such as *East End At Your Feet* (1976), *Come to Mecca* (1978), *Siege of Babylon* (1978), and *Trip Trap* (1982). Dhondy migrated from India to London in the mid-1960s and subsequently joined the Black Panther Movement and the Caribbean-run Race Today Collective, affiliations that testify to the significance of "black" as a unifying, collective category for diverse ethnicities in this period. Dhondy was also a schoolteacher, and many of his texts take schooling as a major theme.

Dhondy's short story collection *Come to Mecca* (1978) is typical of many multicultural fictions published in this period and is primarily focused on encounters with racism in the classroom, at the workplace, and on the street. If Carby is right to note that such "multicultural fictions" were valued by educationalists for their ability to *reflect* the black British experience, then it is worth noting that this is not just registered in terms of the issue-driven contents of *Come to Mecca*, but in the ways it has been labeled and classified. The text is still typically housed under Sociology in British libraries, while the book's cover advertises it as part of the "Collins/Fontana Books for multi-ethnic Britain" series. Moreover, the collection itself takes on a *representative* burden in terms of speaking for the whole "black" community, in that the stories it gathers articulate both the South Asian and the African-Caribbean experience in Britain.

"Come to Mecca," the eponymous opening story of the collection, concerns the plight of Shahid and his Bengali co-workers as they walk out on their "guv'nor" at "Nu-Look Fashions," a garment factory exploiting their cheap labor. As with other stories in the collection, this core narrative is framed within a broader narrative concerning the issue of representation. Betty, a white socialist and journalist, tries to intervene and politicize the Bengali strikers by representing their cause in the press. She takes pictures of them holding placards ("even though we didn't want to be in the photograph" (p. 16)), and the next day meets them in a Brick Lane café to show them the press coverage. The headline, which runs "Workers Fight Blacklegs in Sweat-shops" (p. 17) is misread by Shahid, who responds: " 'No blacks in that factory . . . only Bengalis' " (p. 17). Shahid's response emerges as one of a series of misunderstandings, characterizing a more general communicative breakdown between Betty and Shahid and his friends. (The title of the story refers to one of these incidents, when Shahid, who develops a crush on Betty, asks her to "Come to Mecca" – the name of a dance hall – and Betty wrongly assumes he means the religious city of the same name.) During the course of the story, Betty represents the Bengali boys in political speeches, press reports, and discussions, as, variously, "working-class," "Asians," and "comrades" in a way that is clearly perceived by them as misrepresenting their Bengali-ness. The story ends with Shahid and the narrator distribut-ing socialist newspapers for Betty in central London. On reaching Tower Bridge, Shahid throws the whole pile into the River Thames.

In a strikingly similar story, "Iqbal Café," a white, well-meaning, liberal reporter called Clive documents the growing racial tensions in Brick Lane. Like Betty, Clive is regarded with increasing suspicion by the Bengali community he claims to represent. Clive's stories come from the inarticulate Bengali youths who gather at Iqbal Café, and his name, with its imperialist echoes of Clive of India (Robert Clive, 1725–74, was a British soldier and administrator who established British rule in India), suggests his parasitic relationship to those who provide the raw materials for his career. At the end of the story, and following a riot in the vicinity, Clive enters the café to cover the story only to be confronted by a wall of silence. The youths now speak to him in Bengali and refuse to answer his questions. Rafiq, who is the leader of the group and, significantly, illiterate, eventually dismisses Clive with the words "You are writing story in the newspaper. We are knowing for living" (p. 59).

Both Clive's dismissal and the dumping of Betty's newspapers in the River Thames amount to unequivocal rejections, by the local Bengali community, of the dominant white regimes of representation. As such, they assertively articulate the first moment of represention, refusing to be spoken for by white modes of mediation. Dhondy's *Come to Mecca* signals the presence of what the title of one story in the collec-tion terms "Two Kinda Truth": black/Bengali and white. The central event of "Two Kinda Truth" concerns Bonny, a West Indian boy who reads one of his poems in class, beginning: "All across the nation/ Black man suffer aggravation/Babylon face us with iration/Man must reach some desperation./It have to be iron, brothers y'all, it have to be iron, my sisters" (p. 38). The poem is criticized by his white school teacher (nicknamed, significantly, Mr Wordsworth), who promotes canonical white poetry in the classroom and who feels: "The poem is too much of a slogan; to be poetry it has to have the sound, not of propaganda but of, well, how shall we put it, of *truth*" (p. 39). Bonny, whose verses are clearly influenced by Black British protest poetry of the 1970s, leaves the class after stating "there's *two* kinda truth" (p. 40). Bonny's positive assertion of another kind of truth here becomes a reality when he goes on to become a successful performance poet in the local community. While summaries such as this neglect the nuances of Dhondy's short stories (in which, for all their negative associations, Betty, Clive and Mr Wordsworth are presented as well-meaning characters), the stories are nevertheless firmly of the first moment in terms of their suspicion of false representations of the black community and their investment in more positive, *truthful* articulations by that community itself.

The Second Moment

When viewed from the perspective of the first moment of representation, the dramatic reception of Salman Rushdie's *The Satanic Verses* becomes clearer. On one level, this novel marks a radical departure from the horizons of expectation installed by earlier modes of representation in the 1970s and early 1980s, helping to explain the seemingly disproportionate reaction to it. Rushdie has said of the book's notorious title that it strives for "the sort of affirmation that, in the United States, transformed the word black from the standard term of racist abuse into a 'beautiful' expression of cultural pride" (Rushdie 1991: 403). This is an interesting statement that links the novel to the first moment of representation when black still functioned as a relatively stable, hegemonic signifier. Yet the novel itself ultimately avoids the binaristic shift implied in the rearticulation of the negative term "black" as a positive, affirmative sign: "black is beautiful." In place of simple reversals (which ultimately maintain the binary divide established by racism), Rushdie prefers metaphors of ongoing metamorphosis; mobile notions of becoming instead of established notions of being.

The novel opens 29,002 feet above sea level, as its protagonists, Gibreel Farishta and Saladin Chamcha, tumble through the skies, high above London. Far from causing their deaths, however, Gibreel and Saladin's violent expulsion from an exploded airplane is imagined as a rebirth, a new beginning. Shortly after landing on a beach in Hastings, these two Indian actors begin to metamorphose into angelic and devilish forms.

Through its fragmented, fantastical opening, *The Satanic Verses* abandons the transparent immediacy of realism in favor of magic realism. The opening pages are punctuated with metafictional asides and questions – "Which was the miracle worker?/Of what type – angelic, satanic – was Farishta's song?/Who am I?" (p. 10) – that serve both to highlight the self-conscious artifice of the narrative and to undermine any authority or certainty we might invest in it. Where in the first moment of representation, binary differences are inverted, in *The Satanic Verses* there is no such thing as pure, essential difference. If at first glance Gibreel and Saladin appear to be opposing characters, then during their fall they also conjoin and cartwheel through the air as "Gibreelsaladin Farishtachamcha" (p. 5) so that it is no longer clear where one character begins and the other ends.

In one of the central scenes of the novel, a riot takes place outside the Hot Wax Club in the fictional east London location of Brickhall. With its connotations of Brick Lane, Southall, and Brixton (key areas of Black and Asian struggle in the 1970s and early 1980s), this imaginary setting signals a distance from the referential realism of Dhondy's fiction. Meanwhile, the riot itself is devoid of the transparency and immediacy associated with rioting/living in *Come to Mecca*, a fact that is highlighted by the narrative, which presents the scene from the distant and indirect perspective of the attendant television cameras:

> This is what the camera sees: less gifted than the human eye, its night vision is limited to what klieg lights will show. A helicopter hovers over the nightclub, urinating light in long streams; the camera understands this image. The machine of state bearing down on its enemies. – And now there's a camera in the sky; a news editor somewhere has sanctioned the cost of aerial photography, and from another helicopter a news team is *shooting down*. (p. 454)

Like Dhondy's stories, *The Satanic Verses* demonstrates how the dominant regimes of white representation do violence (the metaphor of the news team "shooting down" is not innocent) to the migrant communities they depict. Just as in Dhondy's fiction Clive and Betty's ways of seeing were questioned, so here are the limitations of the camera's technology (which is "less gifted than the human eye"). However, where Dhondy's fiction hints at the realities of the black and Bengali experience beyond mediation in a way that suggests "two kinda truth," Rushdie's points to the inevitable constructedness of "experience," which "has no guarantees in nature." Saladin and Gibreel offer no promise of a true, authentic or essential Asian-ness: as actors, migrants, and mimic men, they are *essentially* hybrids, changing characters playing out roles as suits the occasion.

Of course, it would be a mistake to suggest that *The Satanic Verses* marks an absolute break between two moments of representation. Hall takes great pains in "New ethnicities" not to chronologize these moments, describing them as uneven and unstable *tendencies* within cultural representation and ruling out any wholesale, progressive "break" between one and the other. His prime example of the second moment, Frears and Kureishi's 1986 film *My Beautiful Laundrette*, is seen as a work that emerged from an ongoing struggle over representational modes, rather than one that launched a decisively new and more advanced artistic movement. Indeed, Kureishi's first novel, *The Buddha of Suburbia* (1990), is a work of far more conventional realism than were his screenplays of the mid-1980s, and in this respect it certainly seems closer to Dhondy than to the Rushdie of *The Satanic Verses*. Having said this, Kureishi shares Rushdie's preoccupation with tropes of acting and performance in a way that foregrounds identity as something that is *staged* rather than authentic or essential. *The Buddha of Suburbia* centers on Karim and his father Haroon as they act out a variety of "Indian" roles in suburban and central London. Haroon is asked to perform the role of mystic Buddha for Eva and her white middle-class friends in a living room in Chislehurst, while Karim, an aspiring actor, first takes to the stage as Mowgli in an adaptation of Kipling's *The Jungle Book*. Haroon and Karim are chosen for these roles as authentic Indians.

The problem is that Karim has never been to India, while his father, in spite of his protestations to the contrary, is now very much of the suburbs. Haroon's performances as Buddha are not drawn from lived experiences of a religious life on the subcontinent, but from what he has read in books acquired at "the Oriental bookshop in Cecil Court, off Charing Cross" (p. 5). While Karim replies "yes" when asked whether his father meditates and chants in the mornings, it is the sheer ordinariness of his daily life in semi-detached suburbia that is most clearly impressed on the reader: "Dad running around the kitchen looking for olive oil to put on his hair; my brother and I wrestling over the *Daily Mirror*; my mother complaining about having to go to work in the shoe shop" (p. 14). Such moments in the novel do more than comically disrupt notions of authentic ethnicity, they also reveal how characters like Haroon and Karim inventively exploit such notions for their own ends, displacing the victims of racism and representation that populate fictions of the first moment.

At one point in the novel, Karim is asked by a director to create a "black" character; "someone of your own background," as he puts it. Karim's response distances him from the unifying notion of black experience in the first moment; he does not know any blacks "though I'd been to school with a Nigerian" (p. 170). The comic deflation of Karim's aside here, which satirizes race rather than taking it seriously, registers a more general refusal in Kureishi's work to delegate or speak for a "right-on" black British experience. Indeed, many of Kureishi's more recent novels and short stories do not represent (non-white) race or ethnicity at all, a fact which has frustrated and bewildered many critics and readers but which powerfully disrupts the notion of the "ethnic writer" as representative of a particular community. As we have seen in relation to *The Buddha of Suburbia*, even those of his fictions that do deal with the British Asian experience are perhaps more productively read as critiques of the way ethnicity is conventionally represented than as faithful attempts to capture "the Asian experience."

In the concluding paragraphs of "New ethnicities," Hall argues that the importance of Kureishi's work has to do with its refusal "to represent the black experience in Britain as monolithic, self-contained, sexually stabilized and always 'right-on' – in a word, always and only 'positive'" (Procter 2000: 274). The essay goes on to cite Kureishi's critique of "the writer as public relations officer, as hired liar. If there is to be a serious attempt to understand Britain today, with its mix of races and colours, its hysteria and despair, then, writing about it has to be complex. It can't apologise or idealize. It can't sentimentalize and it can't represent only one group as having a monopoly on virtue" (Procter 2000: 274).

Kureishi's critique of the writer as "public relations officer" anticipates Zadie Smith's attack on the writer as "sex or class politician" mentioned earlier in this essay. Such criticisms have laid the foundation for new, innovative forms of fiction since the late 1980s. However, it would be a mistake to see Kureishi and others as simply debunking earlier modes of representation in the first moment, or as suggesting writers before the late 1980s were somehow naive or simplistic cheerleaders of the black community. On the contrary, "New ethnicities" suggests that positive black cultural representations of the first moment played a vital political role as *necessary* fictions that contested the dominant regimes of white racist representation in the 1970s and early 1980s, regimes from which black artists were largely denied access. The burden of speaking for the entire black community was part of a political intervention on the part of Britain's African, Caribbean, and Asian communities in the 1970s and early 1980s, a means of creating an imagined unity or front to tackle the forces of white racism.

Difference, Inc.?

Accounts of contemporary British fiction since the millennium have been dominated by media coverage of two debut novels: Zadie Smith's *White Teeth* (2000) and Monica Ali's *Brick Lane* (2003). Both attracted ebullient reviews for their depictions of modern, "multicultural" London; both won major literary prizes and secured headline grabbing advances from leading publishing houses; both authors were selected by *Granta* as "Best Young British Novelists" of 2003. While I shall suggest below that *White Teeth* and *Brick Line* satirize multiculturalism and are in certain ways resistant to issue- or race-based readings, their critical acclaim and their mainstream popularity are undeniably bound up with issues of race and ethnicity. One review asked whether Zadie Smith was "the Tiger Woods of literature." Three years later, Monica Ali was heralded as the "new Zadie Smith" and *Brick Lane* was reviewed in the *Guardian* as a story that "bites"; an unacknowledged allusion to the structuring motif of *White Teeth* and Rushdie's review of it. Such critical responses have the effect of positioning these texts within a racialized genealogy that the novels seem both to disavow and to flirt with.

The early reception of both books hints at a broader fascination with African, Caribbean, and South Asian culture in Britain in recent years. As Meera Syal, the co-producer of the hit British comedy programme *Goodness Gracious Me!* (first televised in 1998), put it within the context of British Asian culture:

> *Goodness Gracious Me*'s phenomenal success, with its cross-over audience appeal and refreshingly non-PC humour, coincided with a thriving Asian comedy scene, when ten years ago, Asians and Funny was a paradox. Artists appeared like Anish Kapoor and Chila Kumari Burman, musicians

111

> like Nitin Sawhney, Talvin Singh and Black Star Liner, the fusion-
> wallahs coexisting with the ever thriving Bhangra and Dub scenes.
> Asian fashions swept the catwalk; every North London home sported
> Rajasthani cushion covers and Tibetan wall hangings. Madonna did
> Mehndi and yoga, Jemima Khan became Pakistani aristocracy, Indian
> women kept sweeping the board at beauty competitions and any clubber
> worth their salt flocked to Asian fusion nights in London's hippest
> venues, wearing their bindis with pride. (Syal 2003: 33)

Such developments mark a significant shift from the early 1980s, when Britain's African, Caribbean, and Asian communities were better known for rioting than writing and when Black British fiction was a minority rather than a mainstream interest. In line with the shifting politics of representation outlined above, Syal suggests that part of the newness of recent British Asian representation is its "refreshingly non PC humour," that is, its refusal to be politically correct, "right-on," or responsible in terms of how it represents race and ethnicity. It remains to be seen, however, whether these developments are superficial or substantive. The high-profile murder of black teenager Stephen Lawrence; the persistence of institutional racism in the police force; the election of BNP (British National Party) candidates in the north of England; and the current war on refugees and asylum seekers in Britain are also important, contradictory contexts against which the celebrated fictions of Smith and Ali need to be read. Is the current interest in the work of writers like Smith and Ali merely skin deep?

Graham Huggan's *The Postcolonial Exotic* (2001) represents one of the most ambitious attempts so far to understand the contradictory significance and success of writers like Smith and Ali in relation to the "global commodification of cultural difference" (p. vii). According to Huggan, books like *Brick Lane* and *White Teeth* might be said to have "capitalized on [their] perceived marginality while helping to turn marginality itself into a valuable cultural commodity" (p. viii). For example, the cover illustrations for the British first editions of *White Teeth* and *Brick Lane* combine brightly colored fabrics, textiles, and patterns in ways that plainly market cultural difference, while the inner sleeve of Smith's novel refers to it as "a sparkling comic epic of multicultural Britain." The value, or cultural capital, accrued by such representations cannot be detached from the exoticist discourses they generate, Huggan suggests.

These issues concerning the commodification of difference suggest the need to update the second moment of representation outlined in Hall's "New ethnicities." Difference provided a vital vocabulary for cultural criticism in the late 1980s, an alternative to Thatcherism and its xenophobic distrust of alterity. Since the mid-1990s however, and, as Hall himself has observed in connection with Blairism, difference has also become incorporated into New Labour's hegemonic vision, as part of the "cool" in "that transient New Labour phenomenon," "cool Britannia" (Hall 2000: 2). As difference gets incorporated, reworked, and pieced out according to the logic of late global capitalism, it is worth asking whether (ethnic) difference is still capable of making a difference.

Huggan's response to such a question would be "yes and no." He argues that novels such as Kureishi's *The Buddha of Suburbia* are not simply the passive victims of contemporary patterns of "ethnic" consumption. The acts and performances of characters like Haroon and Karim outlined earlier signal a "staging" of marginality that amounts to what Huggan calls "strategic exoticism." Strategic exoticism describes the process whereby texts negotiate their incorporation into the cultural mainstream by commenting on, critiquing or satirizing the very exoticist discourses they are bound up in. While *The Buddha of Suburbia* might be read as an exoticist commodity, the way the novel satirizes Eva's exoticization of Haroon, and the director's of Karim, suggests a certain critical distance from the commodification of difference in contemporary culture.

Similarly, while *White Teeth* and *Brick Lane* have been celebrated by the media for their embrace of diversity and difference in multicultural Britain, both texts carefully narrate the past in ways that historicize and challenge the forms of exoticist multiculturalism that prevail in the present. Though both books have been largely reviewed as *zeitgeist* fictions that capture the new spirit of Britain at the millennial threshold, they are also in fact historical novels, which move from the 1970s and 1980s to the present day (*White Teeth* also moves further back in time to 1857, 1907, and 1945). The chronologies of the two texts invite us to reflect critically on certain continuities and transformations within British society between then and now.

White Teeth

In the middle sections of *White Teeth* we move from the early 1980s to the end of the decade through references to the Falklands/Malvinas war (1982), the "Rushdie Affair" and the burning of *The Satanic Verses* in Bradford (1989), and the fall of the Berlin Wall (1989). The decade is captured in the excremental vision of *White Teeth* as a time when "all the shit of the eighties – Irish bombs, English riots, transatlantic stalemates" was "spewed out" on television and "everyone [was] weeping for themselves and their children, for what the terrible eighties were doing to them both ... A distance was establishing itself, not simply between *fathersons, oldyoung, bornthere-bornhere*, but between those who stayed indoors and those who ran riot outside" (pp. 187, 190). The violent divisions of the 1980s appear distinct from the postcolonial present of *White Teeth*, which centers on the intimate relationships between three families living in North London at the close of the century: the Joneses, the Iqbals, and the Chalfens. Respectively British/Jamaican, Bangladeshi, and Jewish, these families would appear representatives of a new, interactive multiculture.

Nevertheless, the historical narrative of *White Teeth* is not simply one of linear progress toward a celebratory multiculturalism. In a novel where "past is prologue" (the book's epigraph), the advance of history is repeatedly questioned. If the fall of the Berlin Wall signals borders coming down and the freeing up of movement and migration between east and west, then it is positioned in the text alongside an account of the burning of Rushdie's *The Satanic Verses*, a text that inflamed racial tensions within Britain's multicultural cities and highlighted certain divisions between east and west, sacred and secular communities.

In a section of the novel set in 1984, *White Teeth* satirically evokes the early multicultural discourses of education described earlier. Samad Iqbal, the father of twins Millat and Majit, has been invited to become a parent-governor at his children's school. At his first meeting, Samad puts forward 13 motions to the school governors, the last of which is a call for the harvest festival to be removed from the school calendar. When the chairwoman, Katie Miniver, sees Samad's hand in the air for the thirteenth time, she begins to worry whether she has been "undemocratic, or worse still *racist* (but she had read *Colour Blind*, a seminal leaflet from the Rainbow Coalition, she had scored well on the self-test)" (p. 110). Here *White Teeth* satirizes political correctness as it is enshrined within multicultural thinking. Ms Miniver defends the inclusion of the Harvest Festival in terms of its place in the school's broader commitment to multicultural representativeness:

> Mr Iqbal, we have been through the matter of religious festivals quite thoroughly in the autumn review. As I am sure you are aware, the school already recognizes a great variety of religious and secular events:

amongst them, Christmas, Ramadan, Chinese New Year, Diwali, Yom Kippur, Hanukkah, the birthday of Haile Selassie, and the death of Martin Luther King. The Harvest Festival is part of the school's ongoing commitment to religious diversity, Mr Iqbal. (p. 112)

However Samad Iqbal, whose very presence as a parent-governor at the meeting is part of the school's commitment to multicultural diversity, persists:

"It is very simple. The Christian calendar has thirty-seven religious events. *Thirty-seven*. The Muslim calendar has *nine*. Only nine. And they are squeezed out by this incredible rash of Christian festivals. Now my motion is simple. If we removed all the pagan festivals from the Christian calendar, there would be an average of" – Samad paused to look at his clipboard – "of twenty days freed up in which the children could celebrate Lailat-ul-Qadr in December, Eid-ul-Fitr in January and Eid-ul-Adha in April for example." (p. 113)

Samad and his reply here are not intended to "correct" or right the wrongs of Katie Miniver. With his clipboard and his pedantry, Samad is an equal target of Smith's satire. If fiction of the first moment of representation encouraged us to take sides, "putting in the place of the bad old essential white subject, the new essentially good black subject" (Procter 2000: 268), the second moment offers no easy binaries in relation to which readers can position themselves. Samad's public performance as the devout, principled Muslim is contradicted after the meeting, as he flirts with (and subsequently dates) the young and attractive music teacher, Poppy Burt-Jones. Poppy describes Indian culture in exotic terms as "colourful," compares Samad with Omar Sharif, and is disappointed when he points out: "I'm not actually *from* India, you know" (p. 116). The reference to Omar Sharif is historically plausible here, given that *The Far Pavilions* (in which Sharif starred) was screened on British television in 1984. One of a number of Raj adaptations to appear in the early 1980s, films like *The Far Pavilions* were criticized at the time by Salman Rushdie and others for generating a form of exoticism linked to imperialist nostalgia under Mrs Thatcher around the time of the Falklands crisis.

For all its historical veracity, this scene is as much a comment on the multicultural present of the novel as it is on the recent past. It is this historical perspective, made available in the gap between past and present, that allows the narrative to satirize the *representative* rhetoric of the first moment and strategically distance itself from the very

exoticism the novel flirts with elsewhere. For the most part, multiculture no longer appears exotic in the contemporary scenes of *White Teeth*.
It is something that appears taken for granted, ordinary, mundane
even. The emergence of what Laura Moss calls "everyday hybridity"
in *White Teeth* is stressed through the historical shifts between past
and present in the novel: "This has been the century of strangers,
brown, yellow and white . . . It is only this late in the day that you
can walk into a playground and find Isaac Leung by the fish pond,
Danny Rahman in the football cage, Quang O'Rourke bouncing a
basketball . . ." (p. 281).

Brick Lane

Unfolding in east London between 1985 and 2002, the central narrative
of *Brick Lane* evokes similar transformations in British society as we
follow the changing fate of the novel's passive protagonist, Nazneen.
Dutifully entering into an arranged marriage at the age of eighteen,
Nazneen finds herself migrating from Bangladesh to live in London
with her husband, Chanu. Lonely and isolated in a cramped flat in
Tower Hamlets, one of Nazneen's early rebellions against her husband
involves taking a walk, alone and unattended, through the streets of
London. She wanders into Brick Lane, an area of concentrated Bengali
settlement, to find silent streets filled with piles of filthy rubbish. It is
the mid-1980s and Margaret Thatcher's public spending cuts (which
we are told jeopardize Chanu's chances of promotion within the local
council) contribute to the air of neglect and deprivation associated
with their rented council flat and the surrounding area. Lost in London,
Nazneen stumbles from the dirty streets of Brick Lane into the glis-
tening central business district of the capital. In this post-industrial
landscape of towering glass buildings and streets full of white professionals with perms, power suits, and puffed out shoulder pads, we
encounter something of the racialized divisions and inequalities of
London in the 1980s.

As the novel shifts to the early years of the twenty-first century,
the urban landscape appears transformed. Walking down Brick Lane
with her husband in 2001, Nazneen notes how:

> The bright green and red pendants that fluttered from the lamp-posts
> advertised Bangla colours and basmati rice. In the restaurant windows
> were clippings from newspapers and magazines with the name of the

restaurant highlighted in yellow or pink. There were smart places with starched white tablecloths and multitudes of shining silver cutlery. In these places the newspaper clippings were framed. The tables were far apart and there was an absence of decoration that Nazneen knew to be style. In the other restaurants the greeters and waiters wore white, oil-marked shirts. But in the smart ones they wore black. A very large potted fern or a blue and white mosaic at the entrance indicated ultra-smart. (p. 208)

The neglected facades of Brick Lane in the 1980s are being gradually tidied up and refurbished. The capital that had previously been reserved for the center now appears to be flowing through the streets of east London. The area of the city that was once described as "visible but unseen" in Rushdie's *The Satanic Verses* is now on prominent display.

Yet this is no utopian image of multicultural development. The minimalist architecture, starched linen, and carefully framed newspaper clippings are suggestive of a less intimate, more formal and sanitized local community. Further down the street, a camerawoman turns her telescopic lens from a restaurant façade and points it at Nazneen, who is seemingly objectified as part of the locale's multicultural furniture and its tourist landscape. Ethnicity appears to signify primarily as surface style or fashion in this new version of multicultural London. The derelict streets around Brick Lane have been gentrified, the old three-story houses renovated: "There were shutters in dark creams, pale greys and dusty blues. The doors were large and important. The window boxes matched the shutters. Inside there were gleaming kitchens, rich dark walls, shelves lined with books, but never any people" (p. 209). The community of Brick Lane has been de-localized as the city's wealthy commuters move in – attracted, presumably, by the taste of difference, the encounters with exoticism on offer here.

Brick Lane's implied critique of such transformations in the multicultural city ultimately refuses any easy opposition between essentially bad white consumers of multicultural difference and a good Bengali community being consumed. Nazneen is not just positioned at the end of the white media's camera lens, she is also an object of desire, first for her husband Chanu and then for her lover, Karim. The locus of this desire is not her feminine beauty, but her perceived exoticism as a migrant from Bangladesh. For both Chanu and Karim, Nazneen's desirability resides, as they put it, in her "authenticity." As the text proceeds, this authenticity is repeatedly called into question. Far from being the "right-on" subject of this fiction, Nazneen is in many ways a conservative character who prefers the derivative eighties pop music

117

of Shakin Stevens to Bhangra and whose passion for ice skaters Torvill and Dean contrasts with her apparent boredom with Chanu's lectures on race and ethnicity.

Brick Lane refuses to present characters as mouthpieces for a political vision. Paying an impromptu visit to Dr Azad's house, Nazneen and Chanu are surprised by the irreverence of Mrs Azad as she drinks beer in a short skirt, proudly proclaims she can't cook, and challenges Chanu's account of the immigrant tragedy:

> "Why do you make it so complicated?" said the doctor's wife. "Assimilation this, alienation that! Let me tell you a few simple facts. Fact: we live in a Western society. Fact: our children will act more and more like Westerners. Fact: that's no bad thing. My daughter is free to come and go. Do I wish I had enjoyed myself like her when I was young? Yes!" (p. 93)

Mrs Azad's lines are controversial, both within the novel where it silences the other characters and for the reader hoping to find a classic race relations discourse reflected within it. If her unsympathetic account of Bangladesh and unassimilated migrants might be regarded as problematic, and deliberately designed to generate discomfort within and outside the narrative, the novel itself does not condemn or condone it. Nazneen herself feels "something like affection" for Mrs Azad following her outburst. Of course, as the protagonist and heroine of the novel, Nazneen carries an inordinate burden of representation. Yet she is repeatedly presented articulating reactionary as well as progressive, "incorrect" and "correct" political statements. By the end of the novel, Nazneen has acquired an empowering degree of agency, yet it is not channeled in an obviously "positive" manner. In the closing pages it emerges that she is working in partnership with Fusion Fashions, a trendy white-run clothes store that plies the kind of fashionable ethnic chic the novel elsewhere appears to deprecate.

This would appear an odd kind of emancipatory ending for the text. What kind of political alternative does it represent? It clearly disrupts certain conventional ways of representing race, racism, and identity in productive ways, decoupling identity from essentialist statements that repeat, in reverse form, the negative stereotypes of racist discourse. It insists on a more complex, unguarded understanding of black representation and subjectivity. But while it rejects the consolatory narrative of political unity and correctness, it has little to offer in the way of political alternatives.

Indeed, fictions of the second moment are notable for their skepticism regarding communal forms of action and resistance. In *The Buddha of Suburbia*, Karim ultimately disengages from the political alternatives offered him as Asian protester or Marxist. In *White Teeth*, the decision of Millat and his gang to journey to Bradford to join the protest against Rushdie's *The Satanic Verses* is clearly confused and ill motivated, while the use of acronyms like FATE and KEVIN for organized political groups in the novel renders them ridiculous. Meanwhile, the Bengali Tigers of *Brick Lane* are characterized by an egotistical in-fighting and organizational impotence that is finally rejected by Nazneen.

At the same time, the taken-for-grantedness of multiculture in these novels, their everyday indifference to difference, perhaps also registers what Paul Gilroy has recently termed "aspects of Britain's spontaneous, convivial culture," the "ability to live with alterity without becoming anxious, fearful, or violent" (Gilroy 2004: xi). The refusal to worry about "race" in these novels, or to invest in insurrectionary forms of violence as progressive alternatives, is not necessarily a retreat from politics, a sign of the margins' incorporation into a commodified mainstream. It also registers a new, if inevitably contradictory, politics of conviviality in which, as Gilroy argues:

> the processes of cohabitation and interaction . . . have made multiculture an ordinary feature of social life in Britain's urban areas and in postcolonial cities elsewhere. I hope an interest in the workings of conviviality will take off from the point where "multiculturalism" broke down. It does not describe the absence of racism or the triumph of tolerance. Instead, it suggests a different setting for their empty, interpersonal rituals, which, I suggest, have started to mean different things in the absence of any strong belief in absolute or integral races. (Gilroy 2004: xi)

References and Further Reading

NONFICTION

Ball, J. (2004). *Imagining London*. Toronto: University of Toronto Press.
Carby, Hazel (1979). Multicultural fictions, paper no. 58. Birmingham: Centre for Contemporary Cultural Studies.
Donnell, Alison, ed. (2002). *Companion to Contemporary Black British Culture*. London: Routledge.
Hall, Stuart et al. (1978). *Policing the Crisis: Mugging, the state, and law and order*. London: Macmillan.

Hall, Stuart (1996). New ethnicities. In: David Morley & Kuan-Hsing Chen (eds.), *Stuart Hall: Critical dialogues in cultural studies*. London: Routledge (first published 1988).

Hall, Stuart (2000). The multicultural question. The Political Economy Research Centre Annual Lecture, delivered May 4, 2000, Firth Hall Sheffield. Available at: www.shef.ac.uk/uni/academic/N-Q/perc/lectures/halltext.pdf.

Huggan, Graham (2001). *The Post-Colonial Exotic: Marketing the margins*. London: Routledge.

Gilroy, Paul (2004). *After Empire, Melancholia or Convivial Culture?* London: Routledge.

Jones, Vanessa E. (2000). Zadie Smith's grinding her teeth. *Boston Globe*, 13 June.

McLeod, John (2004). *Postcolonial London: Rewriting the metropolis*. London and New York: Routledge.

Moss, Laura (2003). The politics of everyday hybridity: Zadie Smith's *White Teeth*. *Wasafiri*, 39.

Nasta, Susheila (2002). *Home Truths: Fictions of the South Asian diaspora in Britain*. Houndmills: Palgrave.

Procter, James (ed.) (2000). *Writing Black Britain, 1948–1998*. Manchester: Manchester University Press.

Procter, James (2003). *Dwelling Places: Postwar Black British writing*. Manchester: Manchester University Press.

Rushdie, Salman (1991). *Imaginary Homelands: Essays and criticism 1981–1991*. London: Viking.

Scarman, Lord (1982). *The Scarman Report – The Brixton Disorders 10–12 April 1981*. Harmondsworth: Pelican.

Stein, Mark (2004). *Black British Literature: Novels of transformation*. Columbus, OH: Ohio State University Press.

Syal, Meera (2003). Last laugh. *Cultural Breakthrough*. London: Voluntary Service Overseas. Available at www.vso.org.uk/Images/culturalbreakthrough_essays_tcm8-2848.pdf.

FICTION

Ali, Monica (2003). *Brick Lane*. London: Doubleday.
Dhondy, Farrukh (1976). *East End at your Feet*. Basingstoke: Macmillan.
Dhondy, Farrukh (1978). *Come to Mecca*. London: Macmillan.
Dhondy, Farrukh (1978). *The Siege of Babylon*. London: Macmillan.
Dhondy, Farrukh (1982). *Trip Trap*. London: Gollancz.
Headley, Victor (1992). *Yardie*. London: X Press.
Kureishi, Hanif (1990). *The Buddha of Suburbia*. London: Faber.
Kureishi, Hanif (1995). *The Black Album*. New York: Scribner.
Rushdie, Salman (1988). *The Satanic Verses*. Harmondsworth: Penguin.
Smith, Zadie (2000). *White Teeth*. Harmondsworth: Penguin.

Chapter 6

Devolving the Scottish Novel

Cairns Craig

Scottish Nationalism and the Politics of Devolution

When Francis Russell Hart's study of *The Scottish Novel* was published in 1978, campaigning had already begun on the proposals put forward by James Callaghan's Labour Government to establish a devolved parliament in Scotland. Since 1707, when the Union between England and Scotland created the United Kingdom as a new nation state, Scotland had been governed from the Westminster parliament in London. Despite the fact that the two nations were, theoretically, equal partners in the United Kingdom, Scottish representation at Westminster was based on the populations of the two countries, so that Scotland had only one tenth of the parliamentary representatives of its "partner." Scottish opinion was, therefore, in a permanent minority within the UK. As long as Scottish politics divided along roughly the same lines as English politics, however, this had no serious constitutional implications, and the imbalance was to some extent ameliorated by the fact that Scottish politicians played disproportionately prominent roles in all of the major political parties.

From the mid-nineteenth century, however, under pressure from Irish nationalists, "home rule" – the re-establishment of parliaments in Dublin and Edinburgh – had become a recurrent issue in British politics. A Bill to establish "home rule" was stopped by the outbreak of World War I in 1914, leading directly to the Easter Rising in Dublin in 1916, and the founding of an independent Irish Republic in 1922. Ulster, however, in the North of Ireland, insisted on remaining within the United Kingdom and, since Ulster had originally been settled largely by Scots in the seventeenth century, Scottish sentiment tended to support Ulster and to refuse the "separatism" of the Irish Republic. Theoretically, "home rule" for Scotland remained the policy of the Labour and Liberal parties, but constitutional issues were of little consequence in the economic depression of the 1930s or during World War II that followed it. In the aftermath of the War, however, the depth of Scottish sentiment about the inequality of its status within the Union was expressed in the Scottish Covenant movement, which organized a mass petition in support of home rule in 1949, and by sporadic acts of violence inspired by anger that Queen Elizabeth was crowned Queen Elizabeth II in 1953, when, in fact, she was the first Queen Elizabeth of the United Kingdom. The Scottish National Party, which had been founded in 1928, began to attract a steadily increasing support, culminating in major electoral gains in the late 1960s. The Labour Party, which held a substantial majority in Scotland, was forced to contemplate some kind of "devolution" of government from Westminster to a Scottish parliament in order to placate a nationalist sentiment that it feared would undermine not only its position in Scotland but its likelihood of keeping office in London, where its majority was dependent on the large number of seats it held in Scotland. The Labour party's proposals for a Scottish parliament – a parliament whose powers were far less than those of German länder or Canadian provinces, but sufficient, Labour leaders hoped, to defuse the appeal of the Scottish Nationalist Party's demand for full independence from England – were eventually put to the Scottish people in a referendum in March 1979.

These political developments were accompanied by increasingly vigorous assertions of Scotland's distinctive cultural identity. From the folk-song revival of the 1950s, led by Hamish Henderson and Ewan MacColl, through the new poetry of Norman MacCaig, Iain Crichton Smith, and Edwin Morgan in the 1960s, to the resurgence of a self-consciously Scottish drama in the 1970s, Scottish art increasingly declared its divergence from the traditions of English – and, indeed, of British – cultural identity. It was as though, with the "End of Empire" and the decay of Scotland's imperial role, an older identity re-emerged, driving forward a nationalist claim for independence that had not been a serious part of Scottish political life since the Jacobite uprising of 1745.

The paradox of this resurgent nationalism, however, was that it was based not on the confident assertion of Scotland's distinctive traditions, but on the belief that Scotland was a *failed* nation. Unlike the many newly independent countries of the British Commonwealth, Scotland had not reclaimed its place as a sovereign state with a seat at the United Nations: the consequence, according to Nationalists, was that Scotland was failing in every aspect of its economic and cultural life. Scotland was a country of chronic unemployment, of deep-seated poverty, of declining industries that had to be kept haphazardly alive by London subsidies. If Scotland's economy was dominated by the long, slow collapse of its traditional industries in mining and ship-building, then its culture was equally blighted by parochialism and disfigured by religious bigotry. Many opponents of the nationalists shared this sense of collective failure, but insisted that only the Union with England could save Scotland from descending into the kind of inter-communal violence between Protestants and Catholics which had erupted in 1968 in Northern Ireland in the wake of the civil rights movement.

The tension between an optimistic cultural revivalism and the pessimistic expectation of continuing national decline was vividly focused in a series of enormously successful theatrical works written by John McGrath for the 7:84 company: *The Cheviot, the Stag and the Black, Black Oil* and *The Game's a Bogey*. These presented Scotland not as a partner in Empire but as itself a colonized country, a case which had been argued by Michael Hechter in his study of the United Kingdom as an instance of *Internal Colonialism* (Hechter 1975). McGrath's answer to Scotland's problems was a call for a renewed international socialism, but his plays presented Scottish iconography and distinctively Scottish theatrical traditions in ways that made their message, for many, one of nationalist resistance rather than socialist solidarity. Was the recovery of Scotland's unique past the basis for its future renewal? Or would Scotland be saved by some international revolution of the proletariat? The contradictions between socialist and nationalist resistance to external oppression were to be replicated across the political spectrum during the Referendum campaign, in which social-ists refused to back a socialist government because its proposals were too nationalist, in which nationalists refused to support a separate Scottish parliament because it would not be separate enough, and in which Conservatives absurdly claimed that they would implement a better form of devolution if elected. The uncertain outcome of the 1979 Referendum – which produced a tiny majority in favor of the establishment of a Scottish parliament but not the 40 percent "yes" vote required by Westminster – led to the Scottish Nationalists withdrawing support from the Labour government, and paving the way for the victorious and aggressive certainties of "Thatcherism." Labour in Scotland never forgave the Nationalists for opening that door; the Nationalists never forgave Labour for not having shut it promptly by delivering devolution. A bitter conflict in Scottish politics was made the more bitter by the fact that for the next 17 years, Scotland was to be ruled by a Conservative government that had no mandate from the Scottish people.

The Predicament of the Scottish Novel

Hart's *Scottish Novel* was written in North America, but it was suffused with these cultural and political uncertainties. On the one hand, his claim that there *was* a distinctive tradition of the Scottish novel, one worthy of academic study, aligned him with the cultural revivalism that had led to the establishment of the School of Scottish Studies in Edinburgh in 1951 and the first Department of Scottish Literature in Glasgow in 1971. To claim that the Scottish novel had a history quite different from that of the English novel was not only to challenge traditional academic histories of the novel in Britain – in which Scottish novelists were simply regional versions of the development of the English novel – it was to make the more menacing claim that Scotland had not, through the years of Union, been successfully integrated into a unified British culture, and to project, therefore, its continuing potential for separate development. At the same time, however, the fear that Scottish values, stripped of the bulwark of English history and culture, would prove inadequate – if not, indeed, illusory – is reflected in the fact that Hart's study ends not by celebrating the achievements of the Scottish novel but by analyzing the problems which had always constrained and continued to hamper its development. "There is," he concludes, "still much truth in Edwin Muir's gloomy diagnosis of the novel in Scotland" (p. 407) – a diagnosis that found in Walter Scott's fiction the symptoms of a failed nation and a failed culture, since Scott "spent most of his days in a hiatus, in a country, that is to say, which was neither a nation nor a province, and had, instead of a centre, a blank, an Edinburgh, in the middle of it" (Muir 1936: 12). There *is* a Scottish tradition, and it is distinctively different from the English tradition, but it is a tradition of unresolved, and largely unsolvable, problems. It is a tradition defined not by its successes but by the typical nature of its failures. This version of Scottishness was to find its most eloquent exposition in Tom Nairn's *The Break-up of Britain* (1977), which, having asserted that "Scotland has its own unmistakable 'identity,'" immediately went on to ask, "Is it right to refuse 'identity' to a hopeless neurotic because he is different from others and unhappy about the fact?" (pp. 172–3). The paradox of Scotland's devolutionary cultural politics in the 1970s was that Scottish identity had to be asserted only in order that it could be properly deplored.

In a review of *The Scottish Novel*, Allan Massie – himself one of the leading younger generation of Scottish novelists – summed up what he saw as the mutually destructive embrace of the Scottish novel and Scottish society:

> it is clear that 19th-century Scots novelists either only found them-selves competent to deal with scenes of rural life or were attracted to Romance as it appeared in a more glamorous Past. It is not . . . unfair to see this as a failure of both nerve and imagination . . . And this posed a real problem which nobody in Scotland has answered satisfactorily. How do you write about a second-hand society? (Massie, 96)

The failure of devolution in 1979 left Scotland's novelists apparently condemned to charting the dwindling, amnesiac self of a "second-hand society" which was a "hopeless neurotic." As a now much-quoted passage in Alasdair Gray's *Lanark* (1981) insists,

> "Glasgow is a magnificent city," said McAlpin. "Why do we hardly ever notice that?" "Because nobody imagines living here," said Thaw. McAlpin lit a cigarette and said, "If you want to explain that I'll certainly listen."
>
> "Then think of Florence, Paris, London, New York. Nobody visiting them for the first time is a stranger because he's already visited them in paintings, novels, history books and films. But if a city hasn't been used by an artist not even the inhabitants live there imaginatively. What is Glasgow to most of us? A house, the place we work, a football park or golf course, some pubs and connecting streets. That's all. No, I'm wrong, there's also the cinema and library. And when our imagination needs exercise we use these to visit London, Paris, Rome under the Caesars, the American West at the turn of the century, anywhere but here and now. Imaginatively Glasgow exists as a music-hall song and a few bad novels. That's all we've given to the world outside. It's all we've given to ourselves." (p. 243)

It is no accident, then, that so many novels of the 1980s and 1990s in Scotland have, as their central character, someone who has lost his or her memory. The most significant is *Lanark* itself, which was published in the immediate aftermath of the Referendum failure. The eponymous hero (of half of the novel), names himself Lanark after arriving by rail in an unknown city, with no memory of who he is or where he has come from: "The earliest name I could remember had been printed under a brown photograph of spires and trees on a hilltop on the compartment wall. I had seen it as I took down the knapsack. I told him my name was Lanark" (p. 20). The amnesia which afflicts Lanark is repeated in Iain Banks's *The Bridge* (1986) and in Irvine Welsh's *Marabou Stork Nightmares* (1995), in both of which the central character is lying unconscious in a hospital ward, the narrative consisting largely of the fantasy projection of their unconscious memories. Jennifer, the central character of A. L. Kennedy's *So I am Glad* (1995), is typical of these protagonists in that she can only describe herself as an absence:

> As I write this, I can see extremely clearly that nothing terribly bad has ever happened to me. I can't recall a single moment of damage that could have turned me out to be who I am today. I can dig down as deep as there is to dig inside me and there truly is nothing there, not a squeak. For no good, no reason at all, I am empty. (pp. 6–7)

Typical of the Scottish novel of this period are narratives in which the central character suddenly comes to consciousness in circumstances which negate his or her past identity – as happens in Alan Warner's *Morvern Callar* (1995), whose life begins for us when she discovers that "He'd cut His throat with the knife. He'd near chopped off His hand with the meat cleaver" (p. 1) – or comes to consciousness with no memory of how they reached their current condition, as is the case with James Kelman's Sammy Samuels in *How Late It Was, How Late*:

> Where in the name of fuck . . .
> He was here, he was leaning against auld rusty palings, with pointed spikes, some missing or broke off. And he looked again and saw it was a wee bed of grassy weeds, that was what he was sitting on. His feet were back in view. He studied them; he was wearing an auld pair of trainer shoes for fuck sake where had they come from he had never seen them afore man auld fucking trainer shoes. (p. 1)

Not knowing where you are, not recognizing the place, not remembering the past, not knowing how you got here – the failed politics of the nation resonates at the personal level in lives that have lost the connection between the narrative of their past and the possible narratives of the future. It is a condition in which the requirements of the traditional novel seem impossible. Instead of being able to reveal the growing complexity and depth of a character's life, it is as though narrative progression is possible only at the cost of etiolation of personality.

In A. L. Kennedy's *Looking for the Possible Dance* (1993), for instance, we are told that, "As Margaret grew her character seemed to shrink and by the time she was Gus's age she had almost forgotten what she was like" (p. 85); or, as Frank Kuppner puts it in the symptomatically entitled *A Concussed History of Scotland*:

> Chapter 279
>   Yet I have always had the keen suspicion throughout my life that
> I was the hidden person sleeping on the other side of a locked door.
> Of course, I often wake up – but frequently only because of the noise
> which someone leaving makes in slamming it shut. (p. 124)

In the concussed world of Scotland's failed politics after month "2" of '79, only a numb absence remains as an imitation of life. Indeed, the title of Kuppner's novel of 1994, *Something Very Like Murder*, might stand as epigraph to the post-devolution period in Scotland, since Thatcherism led directly to the final extinction of Scottish coalmining and to the destruction, in only three years, of much of Scotland's traditional industries.

Declaring Independence: A Devolution of the Word

The bleak and depressing worlds inhabited by these typical characters of post-devolutionary Scotland are, however, represented in novelistic styles that are radically innovative and energetically ambitious. They are styles which do not set out to *avoid* the problems that Hart had identified in the tradition of the Scottish novel – rather, they adopt and exploit the very contradictions which he claimed to be the limitations of the tradition. Hart identified three crucial problems that were, for him, an index of the underdevelopment of the Scottish

127

novel, but in an almost programmatic way the Scottish novel after 1979 set out to reclaim these as fundamental expressions of the differences that underpinned a distinctive Scottish tradition of the novel. First, Hart detected a conflict between the desire to maintain local realism and the attempt to shape the local in terms of some universal paradigm: too often, in the Scottish novel, "fidelity to local truth" is combined with a contradictory "intention to represent national types and whole cultural epochs," and to both are added "an impetus to transcendent meaning" (p. 406) which undermines the "fidelity to local truth" from which the novel begins. These conflicts between "the nominalist historian, the social theorist, and the absolutist theologian" led to formal instabilities in Scottish novels that fractured their aesthetic unity. Second, the Scottish novel necessarily reflected the problem of Scotland's divided history and culture, which had produced a "dissociation of sensibility" – a lack of balance between emotion and reason, between heart and head. This in turn led directly to the oft-cited "Caledonian antisyzygy," the combination of apparently contradictory genres and styles within a single work: "romance repeatedly undercut by irony; austere realism jostling with fantasy" (p. 406). And, third, there was the problem of how an English-writing narrator related to a community of Scots-speaking characters. The linguistic disjunction between narrator and character led to a pervasively "uncertain narrative voice" (p. 407), in which, by "his evident foreignness" to the community, the narrator either became "an accomplice" to those who were engaged in subverting that local community or succumbed to "sentimentality or exploitation" in his presentation of it. What happened in the aftermath of 1979 was that these perceived weaknesses of the Scottish tradition, as viewed through the lens of the more "standard" development of the English novel, were adapted and exploited by Scottish novelists in what, retrospectively, appears as a deliberate act of artistic devolution – if not, indeed, as a declaration of cultural independence.

Thus, Hart's initial problem – how to combine "fidelity to local truth" with "an intention to represent national types and whole cultural epochs" – was to be extravagantly adopted as the very medium of Gray's *Lanark*, probably the most influential Scottish novel of the period. *Lanark* consists of two "books" which recount the life of Duncan Thaw, aspiring Glaswegian artist, with precise "fidelity to local truth," but then counterpoints that narrative with two other "books" in which Thaw is translated into the figure of Lanark, who journeys through fantasy worlds that "represent national types and whole cultural epochs." The complex interaction of realism and fantasy is compounded by the fact that we start the novel in the fantasy world of Book 3, return to the realist world of Books 1 and 2, and conclude – after an "Epilogue" – in the fantasy of Book 4 – a structure designed to challenge the possibility of aesthetic unity. In the fantasy sections of the novel, Lanark encounters characters whose names – such as Monboddo – deliberately invoke national types (Lord Monboddo was a luminary of the Enlightenment), as well as representing, in himself, "whole cultural epochs" as he moves from the sunless, decaying post-industrial world of Unthank to the Enlightenment city of Provan. More significantly, however, the fantasy sections reflect back upon the realist narrative to reveal that they too suffuse their "local truth" with "national types and whole cultural epochs." Thaw lives at the end of Glasgow's industrial era, and Chapter 25 begins with an account, from the 1875 *Imperial Gazetteer of Scotland*, of the Monkland Canal, designed by James Watt: in the same chapter, Thaw is confronted by his art teacher, Mr Watt, who asks him to leave his class because he is a disruptive influence. Also in this chapter, Thaw verbally assaults a statue of Thomas Carlyle and converses with Kenneth McAlpin, who bears the name of the Dalriadic king whose reign established the political territory of Scotland. One of Thaw's other fellow students is named MacBeth, a name which casts an allusive glow on Thaw's first name – Duncan. Thaw, in other words, moves among characters who gesture toward "national types and whole cultural epochs" just as insistently as the narratives into which his *alter ego*, Lanark, will be translated. And Lanark himself invokes those "whole cultural epochs" by having a name that links him with "New Lanark," the site of Robert Owen's experiments in cooperative industry, experiments that failed to "thaw" the destructive effects of the capitalism which blights Duncan's life.

Implicity, Gray has accepted Hart's definition of the contradictions of the Scottish novel, but he glories in their potentialities rather than retreating in embarrassment from their deficiencies. Similarly, Gray accepts and exaggerates the effects of the "Caledonian antisyzygy," combining apparently contradictory genres and styles within his work, and deliberately producing a "romance repeatedly undercut by irony; austere realism jostling with fantasy." Such strategies were to be adopted by a generation of Scottish novelists seeking to come to terms with the blighted world of Thatcherism. Iain Banks's *The Wasp Factory* (1984), for instance, combines a black comedy about a boy who has murdered several of his relatives with a reworking of the Frankenstein myth. The same author's *Walking on Glass* (1985) combines three narratives and three different genres: a modern romance, a study of a mind beset by paranoia, and a science fiction fantasy, each convinced of its own reality and each undermining the other in a deliberate revelation of the novel's own artifice. A. L. Kennedy's *So I am Glad* presents the narrative of a female radio broadcaster, Jennifer, "whose job involves being completely invisible" (p. 10). Her relationship with a down-and-out drug addict who suddenly appears in her house is deployed in terms of "local realism." However, her visitor claims to be – and appears in the novel to be – Cyrano de Bergerac, the French renaissance poet. The first-person narrator confides in us, before the revelation of the identity of her visitor: "A little advice here. If you find what I tell you now rather difficult to believe, please treat it as fiction. I won't be offended" (p. 12). But the narrative turns the "appearance" of Cyrano into a reality in which they can travel together to Paris, a Paris where she "walked in a double city, listening to the past shimmer under the present" (p. 261). The meeting of human beings from different historical eras transforms the contemporary narrative into an archetypal and epochal encounter, parodically imaged when Cyrano deliberately insinuates himself into the photographs of tourists in Paris, so that their pictures will "represent an honourable part of the Paris of history." Jennifer delights in the fact that there are "slides and videos and snapshots in the homes of all nations, each containing a small impossible addition, beaming selflessly in the background" (p. 262). Post-1979, the Scottish novel delights in adding to its bleak realist narrative a "small impossible addition" that disrupts the traditions of realism and reinforces those Gothic traditions of the Scottish novel that celebrate the supernatural and the magical.

Such narratives, with their play of different ontological levels and their self-conscious presentation of novelistic artifice, have inclined some critics to think of them as being Scottish contributions to postmodernism. From being a marginal, eccentric, neurotic nation, Scotland appeared to have been transformed into the very model of a postmodern society: in the words of its leading sociologist, David McCrone, "Scotland stands at the forefront of sociological concerns in the late twentieth century. Rather than being an awkward, ill-fitting case, it is at the centre of the discipline's post-modern dilemma" (McCrone 1992: 1). This rereading of the Scottish condition was applied retrospectively, too, to Scottish literature, which, in the light of contemporary developments, began to look presciently "postmodern" rather than problematically engaged in failing the requirements of realism. James Hogg's *Private Memoirs and Confessions of a Justified Sinner* (1824), George MacDonald's *Phantastes* (1858) and *Lilith* (1895), Robert Louis Stevenson's *Dr Jekyll and Mr Hyde* (1886) and *The Master of Ballantrae* (1889), J. M. Barrie's *Peter Pan* (1906), were reshaped as the central texts of a Scottish tradition which played with precisely those aspects of the novel that postmodernism had thrown into focus. Hogg's *Confessions*, in particular, provided a model not only for self-consuming narrative strategies but also for that desire, expressed by James Kelman, to "obliterate the narrator, get rid of the artist, so all that's left is the story" (McLean 1995: 123). Hogg's novel, already a significant presence in several works by Muriel Spark and Robin Jenkins, was to provide the structural devices for William Boyd's *The New Confessions* (1987), Emma Tennant's *The Bad Sister* (1978), Iain Banks's *Complicity* (1993), and James Robertson's *The Fanatic* (2000). This creative re-reading of the Scottish tradition culminated in 1999 when Jerome McGann announced Walter Scott's "romantic post-modernity" (McGann 2004), dwelling on precisely the similarities between Scott's narrative strategies – with their framing discussions of the nature of history, their self-reflexive ironies, their deliberate references to their own artifice – and works such as *Lanark*. It was a reading which, in many respects, had been anticipated in Allan Massie's novel of Scott's life, *The Ragged Lion* (1994), told through a rediscovered diary in which Scott accounts for the supernatural obsessions in his "realist" fiction. The Scottish tradition, which had seemed, from the perspective of that "realist" mainstream of the English novel, to be marginal, if not deeply flawed, becomes, from a postmodern perspective, at one with an alternative but no less central tradition of the novel, the one that Robert Alter describes as "partial magic," combining apparently incompatible genres as part of its display of its own artifice.

The Devolution of the Word

If Hart's concerns about generic instability were turned inside out by these novelistic tactics, his third concern, about the nature of narrative voice, was to be unceremoniously cast aside by a generation of Scottish writers who promptly adopted Scots not simply as the language of their characters but as the very medium of their narratives.

Through the 1960s and 1970s, Scots had been increasingly used by Scottish poets – such as Ian Hamilton Finlay and Tom Leonard – and by Scottish dramatists – such as Bill Bryden and John Byrne – and had begun to figure more prominently in the dialogue of novelists such as Willam McIlvanney, as, for instance in *Docherty* (1975), his novel of working-class lives at the time of World War I.

But it was James Kelman's *The Busconductor Hines* (1984) and *A Disaffection* (1989) which overthrew the traditional critical view that a Scottish vernacular voice could not be the narrative center of the novel. Just as Gray accepted and extended the interaction of realism and fantasy that Hart had deplored, so Kelman adopted the conflict of standard and vernacular speech as the very identity of his characters. Moving back and forth between third-person narrative, free indirect discourse, dialogue, and interior monologue, but with no typographic markers to distinguish them, Kelman created a style in which it seems as if the character is narrating himself in the third person while commenting on that narration in the first person:

> Why in the name of Christ had he come up. He could have continued down the hill. He could have waited on and maybe gone to the broo with Griff. No. He was to be here and staying to listen to rumours concerning the housing situation in Glasgow of more than quarter of a century ago.
>
> Come on mammy get to the present. No. She is to ramble. People need to reiterate their facts. It makes them feel agents of a verified set, whose clear-eyed vision of the world is justly recognised by one and all. On you go, hen your wee first-born's listening quite the thing, an ever-increasing belief in your continued integrity. No.
>
> Stop the shite. (p. 132)

Is the last sentence spoken or unspoken; directed at the mother or at Hines himself; or directed by the author at himself or at the reader? The undermining of linguistic boundaries in Kelman's work leads not only to an acceptance of the vernacular as integral to the narrative style of the novel but to a radical decontextualizing of meaning that transforms Kelman's apparent "realism" into something equivalent to Hart's "impetus to transcendent meaning." The versatility of a language that can move effortlessly between the highly literary and the demotic is also a language that undermines the stability of both, opening up potentialities of meaning that cross over between standard and dialect speech, between the written and the spoken, as in this passage from *A Disaffection*:

He parked the car. He shut fast the door and locked it, glancing up to see if anybody was out on the veranda. The flats all had these verandas which were ideal for parties to dive from. Excellent for the district's twelve-year-olds. He patted the car bonnet en route to the pavement where he proceeded to traverse the flagstones up the stairs and into the closemouth. Traversed the flagstones up the stair and into the bloody closemouth. Is this fucking Mars! Traversed the fucking bastarn flagstones onto the planet fucking Vulcan for christ sake

except that it no longer exists. That poor old nonentity Vulcan, being once thought to exist, and then being discovered not to. Imagine being discovered not to exist! That's even worse than being declared fucking redundant, irrelevant, which was the fate of ether upon the advent of Einstein. Whether it existed or not it had become irrelevant to the issues. Fuck sake. Ether. (p. 252)

The second sentence plays between the meaning of "parties" in standard speech – pleasurable social events – and "parties" in the vernacular – "persons." The verandas, precisely *not* being "ideal for parties," are "ideal for parties to dive from." The inflated rhetoric of "traversed the flagstones" reveals a world entirely "unreal" from the perspective of the demotic, but an unreality which we are then invited to imagine – "Imagine being discovered not to exist!" – as though the being who is discovered not to exist is the speaker himself – who has, of course, to exist in order to imagine his own nonexistence. Either he exists or he doesn't but the opposition is false – the either/or occludes the fact that something may simply be "declared fucking redundant, irrelevant." "Either," of course, is pronounced "eether" in Scots so that "ether" itself becomes a homophone of the "either" which negates it but cannot help reinstating it at the same time. Demotic and standard language in *A Disaffection* actively undermine and reinstate one another in exactly this fashion, as though each inspires the other to tease fantasy out of realism, or realism out of fantasy, in acknowledgment of the impossibility, in the Scottish context, of escaping from either/ether of them.

Kelman's early works transfused the Scottish novel with a new energy and unleashed a torrent of writing both about and in the language of the Scottish working classes. Early examples, such as Agnes Owens's *Gentlemen of the West* (1984) or Jeff Torrington's *Swing Hammer Swing!* (1992), might have kept to traditional contexts for the use of dialect, but by the 1990s works such as Andrew Greig's *Electric Brae* (1992) were adopting Scots into mainstream narration and Iain Banks's *Feersum Endjinn* (1994) even took it into a science fiction environment. The success of crime writers such as Ian Rankin and Christopher Brookmyre carried these achievements into genre fiction, and in works such as James Robertson's *Joseph Knight* (2002), the Scottish novel returned to its roots in Walter Scott's historical fiction with renewed confidence in its ability to present a real world of Scots speakers.

If the significance of Kelman's breakthrough was officially recognized (if a little half-heartedly, given its repudiation by one of the judges) with the award of the Booker prize for *How Late It Was, How Late* in 1994, then the international acknowledgment of the acceptability of vernacular Scots was underlined by the enormous popular success of Irvine Welsh's *Trainspotting* (1993). Welsh's phonetic transcription of Edinburgh vernacular not only challenged traditional conceptions of the Scottish capital, but provided the sense of a lingua franca for "the chemical generation" by dramatizing a community of users and speakers, each of whom has his or her own unique orthography. And like Kelman, Welsh parodically invokes and negates the "high speech" of traditional conceptions of the human subject to which the novel was assumed to aspire:

> Ah did learn a few things though, based oan Forbes's disclosures and ma ain researches into psychoanalysis and how ma behaviour should be interpreted. Ah have an unresolved relationship wi ma deid brother, Davie, as ah huv been unable tae work oot or express ma feelings about his catatonic life and subsequent death. Ah have Oedipal feelings towards ma mother and an attendant unresolved jealousy towards ma faither. Ma junk behaviour is anal in concept, attention-seeking, yes, but instead of withholding the faeces tae rebel against parental author-ity, ah'm pittin smack intae ma body tae claim power over it vis-à-vis society in general. Radge, eh? (p. 185)

The abstract specialist vocabulary in standard English is undermined by the demotic by which it is encased: standard language cannot come near the truth because it cannot see that it is itself the problem:

> Why is it that because ye use hard drugs every cunt feels that they have a right tae dissect and analyse ye?
> Once ye accept that they huv that right, ye'll join them in the search for this holy grail, this thing that makes ye tick; Ye'll then defer tae them, allowin yersel tae be conned intae believing any biscuit-ersed theory ay behaviour they choose tae attach tae ye. Then yir theirs, no yir ain; the dependency shifts from the drug to them. (p. 187)

As throughout the history of non-Gaelic Scottish literature, from its inception in the Wars of Independence of the fourteenth century, vernacular speech is the medium of resistance to incorporation by more powerful forces – the assertion of independence over dependence, no matter how limited that independence may be.

The paradox of this "renaissance" of writing in Scots is that these are novels largely concerned with individuals in crisis, who replicate the nation's amnesiac inability to understand the relation between its past and its future. And yet, out of this condition, comes a language which asserts at the level of culture an independence that the character has yet to learn to match in his or her own life. The explosion of writing in Scots after 1984 was effectively a devolution of the word, asserting at the level of culture an independence as yet unachieved at the level of politics. In the period leading up to actual political devolution, such assertions of stylistic autonomy came to be typical of the Scottish novel. As Jock McLeish discovers in Alasdair Gray's *1982, Janine*, characters necessarily carry a responsibility for the burdens of their failed nation:

> But if a country is not just a tract of land but a whole people then clearly Scotland has been fucked. I mean that word in the vulgar sense of *misused to give satisfaction or advantage to another*. Scotland has been fucked and I am one of the fuckers who fucked her and I REFUSE TO FEEL BITTER OR GUILTY ABOUT THIS. I am not a gigantically horrible fucker, I'm an ordinary fucker. (Gray 1984: 136–7)

The capital letters convey the hysteria of Jock's refusal of his guilt, which will lead to his attempted suicide before his gradual recovery of the memory that reconnects him to both his and the nation's past. Jock's story, however, is presented in pages that have a running commentary in their margins. Page 137 is headlined "BREAKING A COUNTRY"; page 138, "BUILDING WEALTH." The effect of these running heads is to gesture toward a higher, controlling power than Jock himself, one who has designed the pages such that this novel can never be produced in anything other than the form in which it has first appeared, since the pagination has to be fixed if these running heads are to synchronize with the narrative. This authorial control is then extravagantly invoked in a section in which the running heads proclaim "THE MINISTRY OF VOICES," and in which the page is divided between six different typographies, some upside-down, some in italics, some in italic capitals, each in geometric shapes that *untoil a thick black whip and say, "Momma I am gonna help you strip oh my oh my oh my oh my oh my oh my oh my oh my oh my HONEYMOOOOOOOOOOOOOOOOOOONMUM*

A ge silky milky silky milky silky milky silky milky silky milkyCH
netic milky silky milky silky milky silky milky silky milkyCH
ist fel milky silky milky silky milky silky milky silky milkyCH
la told milky silky milky silky milky silky milky silky milkyCH
me milky silky milky silky milky silky milky silky milkyCH
humans silky milky silky milky silky milky silky milky silky ACH
differ fr round full cheeks chin soft smooth shoulders breasts ACH
on othe bellyfolds thighs labia and buttocks overlapping AACH
t hen br caressing cuddling completing each other how AACH
hen not thirs else but by vile force can I get back into and AAACH
y eating w among warm soft mild eternal you? I want AAAACH
king all round th to fill up and enclose you becoming your AAAACH
e calendar regard tampon and your corset your core and AAAAACH
less of climate and your rind your furniture your walls AAAAACH
torturing and killi the youshaped basket with the big AAAAAACH
ng helpless creatur spike holding and piercing you AAAAAAACH
es of our own kind the boa constrictor entwining AAAAAAAACH
in plain language w you up inside I want to AAAAAAAAACH
have an inborn cap be much too much for AAAAAAAAAACH
ability for intoxicat you whole absolute AAAAAAAAAAACH
on, greed, lust, cruel overwhelming and AAAAAAAAAAAACH
ty and murder i fact inescapable o o AAAAAAAAAAAAACH
which your thinking mo this is hell AAAAAAAAAAAAAACH
ralist will always find mo hell o please AAAAAAAAAAAAAAACH

WHO IS THIS DAPPER CHAP APPROACHING, **help o God** WITH MODEST ARCHANGELIC SMIRK

I am o I

am I

SUFFUFFUFFUFFUFFUCKFUCKFUCKUCKATING

floating in your endless OOOOOOCH
blue blue blue blue blue OOOOOOCH
the morning star shining in OOOOOCH
your black vacuum a solitary OOOOOCH
baton rapping order order order OOOOOCH
into your roaring symphonic chaos OOOOOCH
God folks that is not how it is or FUCKEAS
ever can be when these highbrows get EFULDEA
sexy they go right over the top you're THFUCK
a lot safer with me lady my demands are CEASIN
all external and ritualistic so shake those GONMI
know it is no good because out snakes my cruel TWIT
big black whip with stinging crack splits creamy HINO
linen across your plump hip and at last oh at last PAIN
you feel the trap bite trap bite trap bite trap bite THIS
whipstattoosleatherLochgellytawspricksscuntsjeans ISF
bikinisfishnetstockingsblousesthreepiece UCKIN
suitscollarstiesdungareesoverallsex GMURDE
surveillancealarmdefencetrap RHELIPOLI
securefamilysalarytrap CEMUMMYDA
lovesecuritysex DDYMUMMYDA
happiness DDYMUMMYDADD
trap YMUMMYDADDYMUM

BOAK BOAK BOAK BOAK BOAK
BOAK BOAK BOAK BO y AK BOAK BOAK
BOAK BOAK BOAK BO e AK BOAK BOAK
BOAK BOAK BOAK BO u AK BOAK BOAK
BOAK BOAK BOAK y BOAK BOAK BOAK
BOAK BOAK BOAK BO a AK BOAK BOAK
BOAK BOAK BOAK BO u AK BOAK BOAK
BOAK BOAK BOAK y BOAK BOAK BOAK
BOAK BOAK BOAK BO a AK BOAK BOAK
BOAK BOAK BOAK BO u AK BOAK BOAK
BOAK BOAK BOAK ç BOAK BOAK BOAK
BOAK BOAK BOAK BO a AK BOAK BOAK
BOAK BOAK BOAK BO a AK BOAK BOAK
BOAK BOAK BOAK BO a AK BOAK BOAK
BOAK BOAK BOAK : BOAK BOAK BOAK
BOAK... BOA...
BOA. BOA.

When
last
mid
gro
is I
nine
per
cer
no
will
very
from
least
all
self.
I
Join
me be
free as

at
our
dle
und
found
am
ty
cent
tain
body
be
be far
it,
of
my
Here
stand.
me.

Figure 1 Pages from Alasdair Gray's 1982, *Janine* (Edinburgh: Canongate Books, 2003). First published in Great Britain by Canongate Books Ltd, 14 High Street, Edinburgh EH1 1TE.

divide the single column of the standard novel page into a series of asymmetric "columns" of text (see Figure 1). The body of the text becomes as fragmented as the psyche of its protagonist. Yet the control that that visual fragmentation attests to in the author's handling of his medium becomes the symbol of an autonomy to which the character cannot yet aspire but which he must reach if he and the nation he represents are to stop being "misused to give satisfaction or advantage to another."

Typographic intervention, whether in the orthography of speech or in the shape of the page, comes to represent a devolution of authorial power that prefigures the devolution which was to be achieved in the second referendum of 1997. In Janice Galloway's *The Trick is to Keep Breathing*, for instance, the breakdown of the central character is expressed through a wide range of typographic devices, from mimicry of women's magazines to the visual markers – three "o"s, left aligned – that separate sections of the text, to the representation of dialogue in playscripts. The narrative even begins to invade the margins of the page, first by writing text into them (as though the marginal voice of the character can only exist in the margin) and then by deleting the page numbers of particular pages (as though the reader, like the character, has lost the place in the textual world). On the one hand, these represent the increasing fragmentation of the central character's consciousness, her reduction to a set of discourses which speak through her; on the other hand, they are testimony to an authorial control which can defy the normal conventions of typography and which can invade those spaces of the page that do not normally belong to the author, let alone the character. Such typographical control points in two directions: first, it underlines that the protagonist is not allowed to speak within the normal discourses of a "patriarchal" society – she can, like Scottish society in Thatcherite Britain, only exist in the margins beyond the "body" of the text; on the other hand, it asserts, on the part of the author, an independence of the conventions of publishing and a control over her creative environment that sets a model for what the character lacks. *The Trick is to Keep Breathing* focuses the double perspective of the devolutionary process of the Scottish novel. On the one hand, like many of the novels mentioned above, it is a book about how to survive a future betrayed: "The thing is you can spend so much time in this fantasy future you miss what the hell is going on under your nose ie The Present" (p. 193). On the other, it is a novel about taking back control: "The trick is not to think. Just act dammit. Act" (p. 205). In a world where political action may seem to have become impossible, the assertion of the centrality of the vernacular voice, the assertion of the typographic power of the author, become the actions by which the nation knows itself still to exist, and still to be capable of action.

In the years of Thatcherism there developed in Scotland what was known as the "Doomsday Scenario" – a political and cultural obliteration of Scotland's differentiating features, its forcible incorporation into a Union which was no longer a partnership between nations but the Scottish nation's final submersion in English culture. With each victory of a Conservative government apparently oblivious to Scotland's separate history and identity, the apocalyptic expectations grew more intense. But as the devolutionary period turned into the inter-devolutionary period, and then finally into the post-devolutionary period with the opening of the Scottish parliament in 1999, the radical assertion of authorial control evidenced in works such as *1982, Janine* or *The Trick is to Keep Breathing* disappeared, along with the amnesiac and dislocated individuals whom they had encased. A new trope gradually emerged which focused on the acceptance by an individual or by a family of a child whose paternity was unknown, or whose paternity had to be ignored. Alan Warner's *Morvern Callar* (1995) ends with the titular protagonist's return to Scotland from Spain bearing the "child of the raves" (p. 229), and its sequel, *These Demented Lands*, is the tale not only of the birth of her (illegitimate) daughter but of the struggle as to who will be its surrogate father; Andrew Greig's *Electric Brae* (1992) ends with the protagonist's acceptance of responsibility for the child his schizophrenic lover has borne to his best friend; Jackie Kay's *Trumpet* (1998) ends with the reconciliation between an adopted son and the mother whom he discovers to have lived in a lesbian relationship with the woman – a black woman – he thought was his father; and Anne Donovan's *Buddha Da* (2003) concludes with the father's adoption of the child his wife has borne to another man. In this most recent wave of Scottish fiction, the recovery of creativity is made possible by the acceptance of illegitimate or adopted identity: recollecting of the nation's *impurity* is the beginning of recovery from the nation's amnesia.

References and Further Reading

NONFICTION

Alter, Robert (1975). *Partial Magic: The novel as a self-conscious genre*. Berkeley, CA: University of California Press.

Craig, Cairns (ed.) (1987–89). *The History of Scottish Literature*, 4 vols. Aberdeen: Aberdeen University Press.

Craig, Cairns (1999). *The Modern Scottish Novel*. Edinburgh: Edinburgh University Press.

Hart, Francis Russell (1978). *The Scottish Novel: A critical survey*. London: John Murray.

Hechter, Michael (1975). *Internal colonialism: The Celtic fringe in British national development, 1536–1966*. Berkeley, CA: University of California Press.

Massie, Allan (1979). Tartan Armies. *The London Magazine*, October, 92–6.

McCrone, David (1992). *Understanding Scotland: The sociology of a stateless nation*. London: Routledge.

McGann, Jerome (2004). Walter Scott's romantic postmodernity. In: Leith Davis, Ian Duncan, & Janet Sorensen (eds.), *Scotland and the Borders of Romanticism* (pp. 113–29). Cambridge: Cambridge University Press.

McLean, Duncan (1995). James Kelman interviewed. In: Murdo MacDonald (ed.), *Nothing is Altogether Trivial: An anthology of writing from the Edinburgh Review* (pp. 100–23). Edinburgh: Edinburgh University Press.

Muir, Edwin (1936). *Scott and Scotland: The predicament of the Scottish writer*. London: Routledge.

Nairn, Tom (1981). *The Break-up of Britain: Crisis and neo-nationalism*. London: Verso.

FICTION

Banks, Iain (1984). *The Wasp Factory*. London: Macmillan.

Banks, Iain (1985). *Walking on Glass* London: Macmillan.

Banks, Iain (1986). *The Bridge*. London: Macmillan.

Banks, Iain (1993). *Complicity*. London: Little, Brown & Company.

Banks, Iain (1994). *Feersum Endjinn*. London: Orbit.

Boyd, William (1987). *The New Confessions*. London: Hamish Hamilton.

Donovan, Anne (2003). *Buddha Da*. Edinburgh: Canongate.

Galloway, Janice (1989). *The Trick is to Keep Breathing*. Edinburgh: Polygon.

Gray, Alasdair (1981). *Lanark: A life in four books*. Edinburgh: Canongate.

Gray, Alasdair (1984). *1982, Janine*. London: Jonathan Cape.

Grieg, Andrew (1992). *Electric Brae: A modern romance*. Edinburgh: Canongate.

Kay, Jackie (1998). *Trumpet*. London: Picador.

Kelman, James (1984). *The Busconductor Hines*. Edinburgh: Polygon.

Kelman, James (1989). *A Disaffection*. London: Secker & Warburg.

Kelman, James (1994). *How Late It Was, How Late*. London: Secker & Warburg.
Kennedy, A. L. (1993). *Looking for the Possible Dance*. London: Secker & Warburg.
Kennedy, A. L. (1995). *So I am Glad*. London: Jonathan Cape.
Kuppner, Frank (1990). *A Concussed History of Scotland*. Edinburgh: Polygon.
Kuppner, Frank (1994). *Something Very Like Murder*. Edinburgh: Polygon.
Massie, Allan (1979). *The Ragged Lion*. London: Hutchinson.
McIlvanney, William (1975). *Docherty*. London: Allen & Unwin.
Owens, Agnes (1984). *Gentlemen of the West*. Edinburgh: Polygon.
Robertson, James (2000). *The Fanatic*. London: Fourth Estate.
Robertson, James (2002). *Joseph Knight*. London: Fourth Estate.
Tennant, Emma (1978). *The Bad Sister*. London: Victor Gollancz.
Torrington, Jeff (1992). *Swing Hammer Swing!* London: Secker & Warburg.
Warner, Alan (1995). *Morvern Callar*. London: Jonathan Cape.
Warner, Alan (1997). *These Demented Lands*. London: Jonathan Cape.
Welsh, Irvine (1993). *Trainspotting*. London: Secker & Warburg.
Welsh, Irvine (1995). *Marabou Stork Nightmares*. London: Jonathan Cape.

Chapter 7

Northern Irish Fiction: Provisionals and Pataphysicians

John Brannigan

In *Eureka Street*, Robert McLiam Wilson imagines Belfast as a city of disproportionate significance: "When you considered that it was the underpopulated capital of a minor province, the world seemed to know it excessively well. Nobody needed to be told the reasons for this needless fame . . . Belfast was only big because Belfast was bad" (Wilson 1998: 14). The same might be said for Northern Ireland as a whole (assuming, for the moment, that we can take it for a whole): that it has become an essential part of a global iconography of terrorism and atavistic, tribal war. If the world knows it, then Northern Ireland signifies sectarian murder, urban terror, an atrophied politics in which divided communities locked together in hatred wage violence upon one another for the sake of stale national allegiances, and, latterly, a long, precarious "peace process," of stops and starts, threats and quibbles, demands and suspensions. As I write this (and it is a necessary convention of every critical commentary on Northern Irish culture to include some such phrase indicating the provisional nature of what is to follow), the two political parties most bitterly opposed to each other over recent decades, Ian Paisley's Democratic Unionist Party (DUP) and Gerry Adams's Sinn Fein Party, have become the majority parties in Northern Ireland, and are attempting to recommence negotiations about the region's political future. These negotiations may yet include reconsideration of the historic Belfast Agreement of 1998 (of which the DUP was not a signatory), so that not even the provisional arrangements for devolved government and intercultural affiliations envisioned in that agreement are necessarily part of the future of Northern Ireland. Like its devolved assembly, Northern Ireland remains, politically and culturally, in a state of suspension, between the "bad," dark notoriety of the past, and the precarious and tentative visions of an infinitely abortive future.

This state of suspension has been analyzed by Richard Kirkland in Gramscian terms as the condition of the interregnum, in which, to quote Gramsci, "The crisis consists precisely in the fact that the old is dying and the new cannot be born; in this interregnum a great variety of morbid symptoms appear" (Gramsci 1971: 276). Yet, Kirkland points out, for all the morbid symptoms, Gramsci finds that "the disruptive energies of the interregnum in social relations have more positive than troubling aspects" (Kirkland 1996: 8). In Northern Ireland, the interregnum consists of a paradoxical condition of temporal suspension, in which despite the acknowledged necessity to move forward into new (and as yet unimaginable) narratives of political identity, a stasis of continually deferred negotiation continues to obtain. To procrastinate in such conditions is, as Zygmunt Bauman argues, an elemental feature of modernity, which requires an understanding of history as teleology, and of the present as meaningless until "evaluated and given sense by the *noch-nicht-geworden*, by what does not yet exist" (Bauman 2000: 156). Suspension and deferral are the *sine qua non* of the interregnum, the necessary strategies of temporarily arresting the movement of history, of delaying what Kirkland calls the "desire to return to 'Year One again,' to foreclose the confusion of the past through the establishment of a new calendar" (Kirkland 1996: 10). It is precisely such dreams of new beginnings, whether a utopian United Ireland or a province "as British as Finchley," which have produced the murderous conflicts and deep social divisions of the past. For now, therefore, suspension can seem the best means of avoiding repetition.

The fear that "progress" may turn out to be reversal or repetition, which has underlain the tentative moves within the peace process since its inception, is also, of course, a curiously postmodern phenomenon. It suggests the notion of history as trauma, as the unfolding of moments of recurrence. As the late Jacques Derrida argues, the passage from trauma to promise is a perilous negotiation of "keeping speech 'alive,' without forgetting the traumatism totally and without letting itself be totally annihilated by it" (Derrida 1995: 382). In this case, it is the passage itself, the process of negotiation, which remains critical to evading the repetition of trauma. The promise might, of necessity, be always a promise, and never delivered, in the manner perhaps in which "postmodern" signals an end to modern or enlightenment dreams of the utopian resolution of politics in an ideal state. Is it possible, in this light, to see the drive toward the much-feted Belfast agreement as part of what Jean Baudrillard characterized as the millennial desire "to produce . . . in a burst of paranoia a perfect set of accounts" (Baudrillard 1994: 12)? Against the grim tally of victims, the brokers of peace sought to evince the counterweight of a promise that the future would be different, that the future would accommodate difference, and cherish multiplicity. Baudrillard, however, critiques such millennial fantasies as "illusions of the end," one more of the phantasms produced in the acceleration toward a fictional closure of history.

Equally, however, Bauman's conception of a liquid or light modernity is germane here. Bauman argues that "explosive communities," of a kind analogous to Northern Ireland or the former Yugoslavia, far from being atavistic recurrences of pre-modern tribal conflicts, are "at home in the era of liquefied modernity" (Bauman 2000: 198). Whereas the nation-building era of solid modernity consisted of territorial acquisition, this "liquid" modernity is characterized by the "nomadic" power games of explosive communities which trouble the security of national identification. As Declan Kiberd has argued, the text of the Belfast Agreement of 1998 promises a creative solution to the apparent intransigence of national identification by mobilizing concepts of hybridity and polymorphy within constitutional law (Kiberd 1999). That solution has broader implications than have so far been contemplated in Northern Irish politics, too, for the provision for political institutions which are based not just on territorial sovereignty but also on cross-territorial relationships, such as the North–South Ministerial Council and, more significantly, the British–Irish Council (or Council of the Isles, as it has been dubbed), contains within it the possibility of a devolved England (Agreement 1999). It is arguable, in this context, that the exemplary "bad" modernity of Northern Ireland's sectarian conflict may yet be instrumental in ushering in a new age of plural and hybrid identifications which have ramifications far beyond its own painted curbstones and mural-decorated walls. The question mark placed over the future of the agreement, however (and for the DUP the intercultural affiliations which Kiberd finds so promising have been somewhat problematic), registers the anxieties of hybridity, and the perceived danger that to leap into a future of heterogeneity is to lose one's identity altogether, is to be annihilated.

John Brannigan

The Peace Process as Fictional Space

Fiction in Northern Ireland has responded in various ways to the cultural politics of the interregnum, to the history of the region as one of recurrent trauma, and to the possibilities of imaginative trans-formation. My particular focus in this essay is the fiction produced in Northern Ireland during the current peace process, that is, since the British and Irish governments announced the Downing Street Decla-ration in December 1993, and paramilitary organizations announced the cessation of hostilities in late 1994. The peace process partly entails an imperative to avoid the repetition of historical trauma, but as the Belfast agreement document suggests in its too cursory treatment of culture, it is also an invitation to imagine new cultural narratives of Northern Irish society. It is, in other words, itself a fictional space, a space open to imaginative transformation, and yet continually haunted by the narratives of loss, trauma, and elegiac desires which are recur-rent features of the region's political rhetoric. The tension between these two poles has arguably existed for some time in Northern Irish fiction, as is evident in recent critical discussions.

As Elmer Kennedy-Andrews argues, literature in Northern Ireland during the conflict was compelled to make sense of the social problems and divisions inherent in the region, but this coexisted with a sense of "resistance to, and liberation from, orthodoxy and ideology, its commit-ment to the 'world elsewhere' made possible by language" (Kennedy-Andrews 2003: 7). This leads Kennedy-Andrews to deconstruct "the politics of difference encoded in texts," specifically in what he calls "Troubles fiction," and to argue that contemporary fiction in North-ern Ireland is engaged in a postmodern demythologizing of the monologic claims of identity politics. Kennedy-Andrews takes his cue specifically from Eve Patten's groundbreaking critique of the limita-tions of Troubles fiction. Patten argues that fiction in Northern Ire-land has adhered too closely to conservative forms of literary realism, and too often attempts to resolve the irreconcilable differences of the conflict through the consoling perspectives of liberal humanism (Patten 1995). She identifies three writers, however, who countered the "strait-ened territory" of traditional Northern Irish fiction in the 1980s – Frances Molloy, Glenn Patterson, and Robert McLiam Wilson – whose strategies of irony and dislocation Patten credits as subversive of the "established readings of their situation" (p. 146).

Joe Cleary similarly identifies the limitations of the "romance narrative," a dominant genre within Troubles fiction in which the symbolic union of lovers from across the political and social divisions of Northern Ireland attempts (unsuccessfully in most cases) to transcend those divisions. Cleary reads this genre as "an anxious and contradictory literary mode," which dramatizes the conflict as one involving state and paramilitary forces, and marginalizes the ways in which other social agents are involved. "Plot endings remain stalled in an unredeemed now: visions of collective social transformation are entirely absent," Cleary argues (Cleary 2002: 140), although like Patten, he commends writers such as Glenn Patterson, Robert McLiam Wilson, Seamus Deane, and Maurice Leitch for widening the social frame of Northern Irish fiction. Gerry Smyth, in his chapter on Northern Irish fiction in *The Novel and the Nation*, also looks forward to the imaginative reworking of traditional fictional forms, particularly to postmodern ironic and parodic forms (Smyth 1997), while Christine St Peter, in her chapter on women's fiction in Northern Ireland, offers a bleaker assessment that "the narrative voices and inscribed values of the northern women's fiction still carry a much more doubtful sense of an 'after'" (St Peter 2000: 121).

For other critics, it is the shift of emphasis in recent fiction toward urban settings as spaces of transformation, rather than ghettoes or criminal havens, which marks the potentially affirmative spirit of the interregnum. Laura Pelaschiar argues that the demythologizing of the rural as the traditional escape from the violence and chaos of the city has led to the rediscovery of the city in Northern Irish writing as "a laboratory for opportunities," a model of universal value not because of its terror, but "because of its enormous richness in terms of human histories, because of its being a global encyclopaedia of humanity in all its varieties" (Pelaschiar 1998: 134–5). Wilson's *Eureka Street* is particularly relevant to this argument. Linden Peach, in his traversal of both Irish and Northern Irish fiction, makes much the same case for seeing Wilson's and Patterson's treatments of the city as exemplary of postmodern concerns with free-floating signifiers and simulacra, part of a universalizing of Belfast as any postindustrial, financially prosperous city. But Peach argues that such novels are also engaged in a critique of the postmodern, marked as they are by "uncertainty" about "the way positive narratives of the brash, new consumer-oriented aspect of many late twentieth-century cities hide, as increasingly does their spatial organization, what challenges or undermines postmodern

society's celebration of itself" (Peach 2004: 37). One reason for the
mobilization of the city as a counter-hegemonic space, capable of resisting the political ideologies which fuel social and cultural divisions in
Northern Ireland, is offered in a recent collection of essays on Belfast
as a representational space, *The Cities of Belfast*. The editors argue that
"urban space threatens the social cartographies and restrictive spatial
visions of Irish nationalism and unionism, both rooted in a rural idealism that limits representations of place and society in Irish culture,"
that the city as a social arrangement opposes the filiative bonds central to nationalism and unionism, with the affiliative, volitional bonds
which the Belfast agreement strives to make central to the future of
the region (Allen & Kelly 2003: 8). While this risks dichotomizing the
country and city as entirely incommensurable to each other, and
places enormous strain upon the city as a civic ideal, it recognizes the
symbolic potential of lived space, and the constitutive capacity of
cities to incorporate the historical and the imaginary, the multiple and
the contradictory.

In recent critical discussions of Northern Irish fiction and culture,
then, it is evident that the tentative maneuvers toward peaceful co-
existence present potentially new avenues for fictional exploration,
even if such avenues are as yet unmapped and only dimly lit. This is
clear not just from the critiques of the limiting generic and political
province of "Troubles fiction," but also from the recognition that a new
generation of novelists, having grown up for the most part during
and through the Troubles, are themselves testing these limitations
and have proved willing to challenge the traditions of Northern Irish
fiction. In the critical analysis which follows, I trace some of the key
directions in which recent Northern Irish novels are rewriting the
figurative landscape and historiographical awareness of the region
through some exemplary texts. The argument is that the paradoxical
state of suspension which characterizes the interregnum is refracted
critically and imaginatively in Northern Irish fiction as a whole,
although obviously in variegated and contested forms in the novels
individually. As seems appropriate, I begin with questions of trauma
and haunting.

History as trauma

Even a cursory scan of the historical settings of contemporary fiction
in Northern Ireland might alert us to the significance of ruptured

time, of history as interrupted by the experience of trauma. Seamus Deane's *Reading in the Dark* (1997) ends on the eve of the outbreak of the Troubles, as do Patterson's *Burning Your Own* (1988) and *The International* (1999). Deirdre Madden's *One by One in the Darkness* shifts tellingly between 1968 and 1994, the beginning and the end of the conflict, as it were, as if wary of the space and time between. The moment before the Troubles begin, of course, is invested with the tragic poignancy of hindsight. It is already a haunted time, haunted by the past, of course, but also the dreadful future which it is about to release. Deane's *Reading in the Dark* is a self-consciously haunted narrative, not just in its treatment of haunting as a theme, but in that it is, in so many ways, a ghosted text itself, haunted by its many intertexts and precursors. The novel opens with a haunting, a scene which establishes the seething presence of the past making itself apparent to the present:

> On the stairs, there was a clear, plain silence.
> It was a short staircase, fourteen steps in all, covered in lino from which the original pattern had been polished away to the point where it had the look of a faint memory. . . .
> "Don't move," my mother said from the landing. "Don't cross that window."
> I was on the tenth step, she was on the landing. I could have touched her.
> "There's something there between us. A shadow. Don't move."
> I had no intention. I was enthralled. But I could see no shadow.
> "There's somebody there. Somebody unhappy. Go back down the stairs, son." (Deane 1997: 5)

The signs of the ghostly apparition for the unnamed narrator are silence and invisibility. He guesses that the smell of damp clothes indicates the presence of the ghost, but his mother dismisses this suggestion and admonishes that he shouldn't "talk himself into believing it." The narrator learns from this experience the paradoxical signification of the ghostly presence of the past, that presence is announced by absence, and that the seemingly incontestable "thereness" of the ghost is at the same time a mere construction, a matter of belief or disbelief. The ghost is no mere fancy of his mother's imagination, as she subsequently protests, however, but instead the figurative projection of a troubled past, which is slowly revealed in the course of the novel. The continuous echoes of the turbulent history of his republican family provide the boy-narrator with the sense that the present is overshadowed by the burden of the whispered mysteries of the past. This makes for something of a hybrid novel, as noted in Edna Longley's review (Longley 1996: 34). *Reading in the Dark* not only combines autobiography with history, national narrative with family saga, political mystery with childhood memoir, but it also combines the *bildung* narrative of formation and enlightenment with the narratives of loss, nostalgia, and exile. In the *bildungsroman* the narrative traces the awakening of the character or narrator into present consciousness, but in the case of Deane's novel, the narrator awakens into the consciousness of the belatedness and hauntedness of his own time. The past is constructed as a time of loss, from which the narrator is permanently exiled or banished. This exile from the past is suggested in the opening page, in which the ghost is a figure for the secret which the narrator's mother refuses to impart to him. The secret, along with the various shadows, ghosts, silences, and darknesses of the narrative, forms the absent center around which the abyssal structure of the novel is constructed. The landscape of the novel itself is abyssal, with domestic interiors represented by fading patterns and hidden secrets, the city streets depicted as dismembered and ruined, the graveyard labyrinthine, the distillery (which plays a central role in the misremembered scenes of history) collapsed and hollow, and, of course, the mythical "field of the disappeared," which resonates so powerfully with the boy-narrator whose uncle Eddie has himself "disappeared." "Disappeared" indeed is a word that recurs and echoes throughout the novel. People and places disappear, the past disappears, and, perhaps more strangely, the present disappears under the weight of the absent past. This is notable even in the pace of the novel, which begins in the slow, lingering time of nostalgia, wallowing in the sepia images of the vanished past, but races through the narrator's adult years in the sixties and seventies, as if the present is of little consequence when compared to the obsessively sifted and imagined past.

Reading in the Dark charts the narrator's attempt to read the secret of his family's past, and also to read himself into that past. "Reading," or perhaps more properly, the imaginative engagement with otherness which reading is made to signify, is thus constructed as the means of reconnecting with the past, and healing the turmoil of history. This is most evident in the chapter entitled "Reading in the Dark," where reading is associated with love (an aptly Proustian conceit in a novel which is a work of memory). The narrator reads a novel called *The Shan Van Vocht*, meaning The Poor Old Woman, a nationalist metaphor for an embattled Ireland:

The heroine was called Ann, and the hero was Robert. She was too good for him. When they whispered, she did all the interesting talking. He just kept on about dying and remembering her always, even when she was there in front of him with her dark hair and her deep golden-brown eyes and her olive skin. So I talked to her instead and told her how beautiful she was and how I wouldn't go out on the rebellion at all but just sit there and whisper in her ear and let her know that now was forever and not some time in the future when the shooting and the hacking would be over, when what was left of life would be spent listening to the night wind wailing on graveyards and empty hillsides. (Deane 1997: 19–20)

The novel is inscribed with his mother's maiden name, in faded ink, which signifies its strangeness as a memory object, and in his reading of it, the narrator identifies not with the implied masculine values of sacrifice and posterity, but with the apparent feminine values of love, talk, and commitment to life. Reading enables the narrator to live imaginatively among these shadows of history, not as a heroic participant, but as a recalcitrant. The imagined dialogue with the heroine of *The Shan Van Vocht* pits love, and reading, as antithetical to the "graveyards and empty hillsides" of history. The narrator here seems to desire the immediacy of living and loving rather than the posterity sought by the rebel, Robert. It is a desire for "thereness," for presence, and is constructed self-consciously in opposition to the phantasmal images of history recurrent in Deane's novel. As Liam Harte argues, the historical theme of *Reading in the Dark* is explored through the story of the boy-narrator's struggle with an unresolved subjectivity, through the impossibility of defining self-identity against the "suppressed trauma of his family's occluded history" (Harte 2000: 157). The narratives of nationalist history which surround the narrator through songs, novels, school lessons, history books, and the half-whispers of family history jostle constantly with his own shifting desires, identifications, and doubts. Even the trope of "darkness" shifts within the novel from the grimly oppressive darkness of the hidden, sinister past to the "endless possibilities in the dark," which the imaginative engagements of the narrator's reading seem to conjure into play.

"Reading in the dark" implies both of these meanings, of course, both the forbidden childhood pleasures of reading after bedtime, and the sullen, awkward attempts to read oneself in the darkness of a bleak and muted past. They represent the contrary impulses of the narrative toward openness and closure. The novel concludes with an openness to the possibilities which may emerge in the wake of the

149

narrator's father's death. The narrator remains unnamed, and no more certain of how to determine or delineate his place in the world, and this might signify a positive ending in the sense that he remains open to the future. The concluding paragraph returns to the stairwell with which the novel began, and finds that "there was no shadow there." The haunting has ostensibly ceased, and thus the narrative signals a new beginning. But there is also closure here, not least in the narrator's mother's stroke-induced silence, and in the literal eruption of the past into the present in the shape of political violence. History, it seems, has the last word. As the narrator's father lies in his coffin, the army is heard moving down his street:

> I lay awake until dawn, when the noise of horse-hooves roused me to the window again. As though in a dream, I watched a young gypsy boy jog sedately through the scurf of debris astride a grey-mottled horse. Bareback, he held lightly to the horse's mane and turned out of sight in the direction the army had taken hours before, although it was still curfew. The clip-clop of the hooves echoed in the still streets after he had disappeared. (Deane 1997: 232–3)

As Eamonn Hughes observes in his review of the novel, there is something of Elizabeth Bowen echoing through Deane's novel (Hughes 1997: 151–7). There is also something of Synge and Yeats. The hoof-beats of this passage echo the portentous hoof-beats of Synge's *Riders to the Sea* and Yeats's late, haunted play, *Purgatory*. In Synge's play, a mother's sighting of her dead fisherman son riding on his grey horse is an omen of the doom which hangs over her family. She lists the men of her family who have been drowned or lost in the sea, a litany which casts a shadow over all left alive. In Yeats's *Purgatory*, the old man returns to the house of his birth, there to hear the hoof-beats of his father's ghost approaching the house. The hoof-beats signal the eternal recurrence of the violent past of a cursed family, his mother condemned to live out the past in its exact detail, and the play concludes with the old man praying to God "Release my mother's soul from its dream! Mankind can do no more. Appease the misery of the living and the remorse of the dead." Both plays figure the echoing hoof-beats as the grim circularity of history, and the use of the trope in Deane's novel suggests that the narrator is to relive the history of political violence which has haunted his own family. The "misery of the living and the remorse of the dead" are to inhabit the same ruined landscape again. This is history as trauma, as the continual repetition of traumatic experience through time, each event in history re-enacting the trauma of the past. There is hope at the end of Deane's novel; the shadow has gone from the stairs. But the echoes and hauntings are interrupted, it seems, only by the sounds of soldiers on the streets outside.

Like Deane's novel, Deirdre Madden's *One by One in the Darkness* (1996) is structured around the wounds of the past. Madden's novel follows a week in the lives of the three Quinn sisters, who have grown up in a small rural homestead on the shores of Lough Neagh. The story gravitates toward Cate, in particular, who returns from her cosmopolitan, glamorous life as a fashion magazine editor in London with a secret to tell her family. The "secret," that she is pregnant by a man she has no intention of maintaining a relationship with, is balanced against the dark shadow cast over the sisters and their mother by the mistaken murder of their father, Charlie. Implicit in the story is the possibility that the impending birth of Cate's child, gradually accepted by her mother and sisters, may somehow compensate for the traumatic memories of their father's murder. But such an easy resolution of trauma is ultimately refused. The novel concludes with the same "uncanny silence" with which it began, with a home that is a "solid stone house," in which "one by one in the darkness, the sisters slept" (Madden 1996: 181). The "darkness" of Madden's novel is not so equivocal as Deane's: it closes back in on Madden's characters as a sign of the trauma that lies unresolved.

Trauma is marked throughout the novel, of course, by secrets and silences, by what is not said, by the failure of representation. For much of the novel, Charlie's death is a muted but pervasive subtext, alluded to fleetingly and sparingly. It is only in the concluding scene of the novel that Helen recounts in detail the scene of her father's murder, "repeated constantly, like a loop of film," with "the heavy feel of a nightmare" (p. 180). Her traumatic memory of her father's murder, moreover, is contrasted explicitly with the gently descending, beautiful, and compassionate visions of her childhood. From the intimate details of her father's smells and familiar habits, and the equally intimate, because all-too-familiar, scene of his murderers bursting in with guns and masks to shoot him point blank, "Helen's vision swung violently away":

> and now she was aware of the cold light of dead stars; the graceless immensity of a dark universe. Now her image of her father's death was infinitely small, infinitely tender: the searing grief came from the

tension between that smallness and the enormity of infinite time and space. No pity, no forgiveness, no justification: maybe if she could have conceived of a consciousness where every unique horror in the history of humanity was known and grieved for, it would have given her some comfort. Sometimes she felt that all she had was her grief, a grief she could scarcely bear. (p. 181)

As children, the sisters were invited to contemplate the "heavens" as the scene of ultimate redemption and reconciliation, but this religious narrative is thoroughly demythologized here by the secular vision of a sky offering only the enormity of suffering. Helen works as a solicitor dealing particularly in terrorist cases, and has to represent the kinds of men who might have murdered her father. She recognizes that the fate of both victim and perpetrator are "dreadful," but even this brings scant comfort (p. 52). For much of the novel, an uneasy tension exists between Helen and Cate, largely around Cate's pregnancy, and the full meaning of that tension is brought to light in this final scene. If Cate has her baby to look forward to, Helen has only her grief, "a grief she could scarcely bear" (p. 181). The choice of the verb "bear" in this phrase, implying comparison with Cate's pregnancy, makes clear the grim and barren legacy of the "troubles" for Helen and her family, and perhaps more widely for Northern Irish society.

Kennedy-Andrews utilizes Cathy Caruth's notion of trauma as "unclaimed experience" to analyse Madden's novel as "shaped by the psychological processes of repression, displacement, condensation and transference" (Kennedy-Andrews 2003: 153). The novel, according to this analysis, suggests in ways similar to Deane's novel that the Troubles cannot be understood at the time of their occurrence, but only through a belated engagement, often in dreams, flashbacks, and visions, which pervade the text. Madden sharpens this realization through a parallel theme of the media exposure of Northern Irish society. Through the constant media representations of the Troubles, the ever-present cameras, and ever-ready headlines, the region is over-exposed, excessively available as a trope, infinitely analogous with other conflicts in other times and other places. But paradoxically, despite or perhaps because of such over-exposure, the Troubles remain constitutively incapable of being "understood" or ingested, least of all by the victims and perpetrators. On the cusp of the IRA ceasefire in 1994, Madden's characters struggle to confront, let alone understand, the experiences which have marred their childhoods and which continue to haunt their adult lives.

The resistance to media narratives of Northern Ireland as what Joe Cleary calls "an atlas of atrocity" (Cleary 2002: 141) is evident throughout the novel. Helen's friend, David, for example, takes his English lover Steve on two very different tours of Belfast. The first tour is designed to show the beauties of the city, its lough and mountains, and how like an English city it is when you avoid the paraphernalia of militarization, images designed to counter the iconography of explosions, riots, and guns. The second tour, however, is designed to curb Steve's new-found passion for Belfast, by immersing him in the murals, fortifications, checkpoints, and terror landmarks of the city. The horrors of the TV version of Northern Ireland are real, not imagined, but they are also shown to be highly selective and repetitive. Lurking behind the imagery of Belfast as the dominant cinescape of the conflict, however, is the novel's more obvious fascination with the rural scene, particularly the pastoral idyll so abruptly punctured by violence. "Home" is understood in psychological terms to denote security, comfort, identity, but more than that, as an elemental force of nature: "The scope of their lives was tiny but it was profound, and to them, it was immense. The physical bounds of their world were confined to little more than a few fields and houses, but they knew these places with the deep, unconscious knowledge that a bird or a fox might have for its habitat" (Madden 1996: 75). The explosion of violence in such a seemingly idyllic place leads Madden's characters to question the meanings of home, and the wider notion of community. Helen and Cate's mother, Emily, for example, dreams that perhaps a retrospective and far-sighted vision will allow her to alter how she perceives the broken world around her: "She couldn't change the fact of things but she could change how she saw them, and in that way she could determine the effect they had on her" (p. 125). There is the glimmer of hope and reconciliation here. But Madden consistently counterpoints every possibility of hope with a qualification or deflation. Emily is also repeatedly haunted by dreams of a cowering young man begging for her forgiveness, which she cannot find it in herself to give: "To be a woman in her late sixties, to have prayed to God every day of her life, and to be left so that she could feel no compassion, no mercy, only bitterness and hate, was a kind of horror she had never imagined" (p. 125). The pressures upon this community are understood to have been there in the faded, half-perceived memories of life before the Troubles, but the ramifications of the dissolution of community, of the corpses lying lonely along quiet country roads, or buried somewhere unknown in fields or on beaches, are shown to be more problematic to comprehend.

Soft city

In Madden's novel, Belfast is the cold, unyielding, hard city, the antithesis of the warmth Helen associates with her rural home. She lives in the city as a transient, anonymous and antisocial, preferring to live in a characterless urban townhouse, "confident that it was, psychically, a blank" (p. 44). The advantage of her Belfast house for Helen is that it has no history and no ghosts, and consequently it serves as a contrast both to the comforting fullness of her family home, and to the traumatic history of her uncle's house, in which her father was murdered. Madden's depiction of Belfast contrasts starkly with the fictional exploration of the city in the novels of Glenn Patterson and Robert McLiam Wilson. For both novelists, Belfast is magnetic because of its rich history, crowded geography, and complicated, interwoven subcultures. For both, of course, Belfast is a hard city of fact, of murders and bombs, of territorial divisions policed and barricaded. But it is also the city of imagination, the soft city which sometimes yields to dreams and love.

Patterson's *The International* returns to an originary moment of softness in the recent troubled history of the city, the occasion of the foundation of the Civil Rights Movement in January 1967 in the International Hotel, Belfast. The hotel bar is the scene of multiple stories of humanity, warmth, community, and hope throughout the novel, the very name of the hotel suggesting a cosmopolitan transcendence of the petty sectarian passions fuelling the lurch toward murder and mayhem. It functions as a microcosm of the larger situation of Northern Ireland on the cusp of the 1970s, with some wealth, some dreams of stardom, its own success stories such as George Best on the international celebrity scene, and plans for motorways to bring the region into the twenty-first century. Northern Irish society is shown to be increasingly modern, reflecting the social changes and aspirations of people in Dublin and London, buying television sets and cars, listening to The Beatles and Elvis. The narrator, Danny, is himself a model of the sexual liberation and social mobility associated with the modernity of England and the USA, although he reflects more critically on that notion of himself toward the end of the novel. All of these stories and dreams pass through the bar of the hotel, where Danny works. The novel teases the reader with the impression of a pre-lapsarian world, of a city unaware of its impending fate, "another place entirely, the mere passage of years cannot account for the sense of rupture" (Patterson 1999: 307). The fire in Brand's Arcade which opens the novel is an "ordinary" fire, a source of some amusement to the barmen and customers of the International, but Patterson is also reflecting ironically on the prescience of the imagery of the fire, the ashes which several customers attempt to brush from their clothes, which are already haunting signs of the impending tragedy.

The hotel is also, of course, a reflection of the increasingly pressing signs of that tragedy. The conflictual lines of loyalist and nationalist politics intersect at the hotel, and both intertwine with the stories of the city councilors who patronize the hotel bar. We learn that the Civil Rights Movement was used as a vehicle to justify the emergence of the IRA in 1969. Loyalist violence against Catholics is also shown to have an intimate association with the hotel, since four of its barmen were murdered by loyalists in 1966. And the fictional stories which proliferate through the novel, many of them humanely comic and romantic, give way to the epitaphic conclusion, in which Danny tells of the loyalist ceasefire in 1994, and pays tribute to one of the young barmen murdered in 1966, Peter Ward: "He is, I realise, an absence in this story. I wish it were not so, but guns do that, create holes which no amount of words can fill" (p. 318). Trauma thus marks Patterson's depiction of Belfast as much as it registers in Madden's countryside, or Deane's Derry, but *The International* ultimately constitutes a work of mourning rather than a site of trauma. Among its concluding scenes, appropriately, is a funeral for one of the former hotel employees, at which Danny commemorates the people of the hotel. The novel, arguably, is involved in a commemorative, as much as a celebrative, act throughout. The "ordinariness" of Danny's life, and the possibilities of a return to such ordinariness in the future, is grasped thinly against the demand to mourn what Northern Ireland lost at this historic moment of rupture in the late 1960s.

Patterson's novel reads Belfast as a rich, plural, constantly changing city, tragically hijacked by narratives of war and hatred. Robert McLiam Wilson's *Eureka Street* revels even more wholeheartedly in this juxtaposition, while also constantly seeking to destabilize the narratives of terror with satire and irony. In *Eureka Street*, the city is imagined as a text, constantly being rewritten and overinscribed. "The city is a novel," it announces. "Cities are the meeting places of stories. The men and women there are narratives, endlessly complex and intriguing. The most humdrum of them constitutes a narrative that would defeat Tolstoy at his best and most voluminous" (McLiam Wilson 1998: 215).

When the novel describes an explosion in the city thereafter, the metaphor of the city as a repository of stories becomes sardonic: "Some stories had been shortened. Some stories had been ended. . . . The pages that follow are light with their loss. The text is less dense, the city is smaller" (p. 231). One implication of Patterson's structure of weaving from the "before" to the "after" (although the novel problematizes 1969 and 1994 as definitive points of beginning and ending) is that the "troubles" in between those years seem monolithic and unspeakable. Wilson pursues an alternative strategy to seeing the conflict as unspeakably traumatic, describing with caustic irony the effects of an explosion on people's lives, and the wrong-headed "political" justifications for violence. As a result, there is a sense throughout *Eureka Street* that the city is continually available for rewriting. This is particularly the implication of the elusive graffiti that appears on the city's walls, the letters OTG sending the inhabitants into a scurry of speculation about a new paramilitary movement. Later, the narrator explains that OTG means "almost everything":

> That was the point. All the other letters written on our walls were dark minority stuff. The world's grand, lazy majority will never be arsed writing anything anywhere and, anyway, they wouldn't know what to write. They would change their permissive, clement, heterogeneous minds half-way through. That's why OTG was written for them. It could mean anything they wanted. (p. 395)

The purpose of both Patterson's and Wilson's representation of Belfast as a complex, humane place, always open to be reinterpreted and rewritten, is that they clear a space for the "majority" to write the new narratives of Northern Irish identity, and demand that the same tired and bloody historical narratives of the region are not permitted to fill the silence. Joe Cleary rightly cautions against the limitations of some of the redemptive narratives offered up as alternatives, which uncritically endorse "the energies and excitements of global capital," or the liberatory properties of romance (Cleary 2002: 141). Arguably, the rags-to-riches narrative of arch-capitalist Chuckie Lurgan and the love story which ends *Eureka Street* are versions of what Cleary wishes to question. But it is more likely, given the novel's extensive critique of social deprivation and romantic idealism, that these redemptive narratives are themselves to be read as parodic, or critical fictions, within the genre which Kennedy-Andrews labels "postmodern humanism" (Kennedy-Andrews 2003: 92–195).

The pataphysical process

There is one further model of how fiction writing in Northern Ireland has responded to the cultural politics of suspension, which I believe merits attention here. If Wilson experiments with the historiographic and metafictional narrative turns associated with postmodernism, Ciaran Carson's *Shamrock Tea* (2002) takes this a stage further in working within the ludic sublime, in which the counter-realist conventions he deploys are never free from comic treatment themselves. Carson shifts to and from Belfast in his novel, but, in contrast with the other works I have discussed, this novel appears to have freed itself of the heavy burden of representing the Troubles. *Shamrock Tea* is about identity, art, time, and imagination. "Image begets image," writes Carson, "We float through the cloisters of memory, looking for our waking selves" (Carson 2002: 27). *Shamrock Tea* destabilizes the subject, and represents subjectivity through tropes of flotation, flight, transportation, and disappearance. The first-person narrator, the pseudo-autobiographical figure of Carson, gives the illusion of control, of a master narrative, but this is subverted throughout the novel, and particularly when Carson reads the secret colored books in which his life has already been written out for him. The narrator is thus the product of a text, and also appears in the Van Eyck painting "The Arnolfini Portrait," which is the central focus of the novel. This is a novel about an image, indeed a series of images begetting images, and not the *bildungs* narrative or autobiographical representation it appears to be from the beginning. "Perhaps I will return one day to the world I first entered," reads the opening line. "For now, I wish to record something of it, if only to remind myself of what I am" (p. 1).

Shamrock Tea opens with the promise of an autobiographical narrative, the recollection of "what I am," but it also suggests an altered notion of space and time, since the narrator hopes to return to the world "I first entered." This is a novel that plays with the fiction of alternative worlds, both in space and time. The narrator inhabits a landscape that is marked with holes and gaps through which it is possible to disappear, and "riddled with interconnecting subterranean channels" (p. 41). These subterranean channels suggest a labyrinthine landscape, endlessly connected, and impossible to know. Time is also labyrinthine in Carson's novel, as the narrator discovers that it is possible to travel through the image of Van Eyck's painting to other times, with the aid, of course, of the psychotropic properties of

"Shamrock Tea." Time travel, and the possibility that time folds in upon itself, is not just the effect of hallucinations, however, but is narrated as a condition of the real in Carson's world. This, in many ways, is the marvelous realism of this novel, that individuals travel in time, merge into other individuals, experience events which have strange correspondences and coincidences with the events of the past. The Troubles are not entirely absent from this novel, but they are ludically displaced by the centrality of tropes of transformation and deterritorialization.

Shamrock Tea proceeds not principally by a sequential plot structure, but according to the model which the novel itself discusses as "serendipity." "It would seem that we three are fated to be a part of a story whose purpose is as yet inscrutable," the character Maeterlinck announces:

> Indeed it puts me in mind of a story told to me by my uncle Maurice. It concerns the origin of the word "serendipity." One day he happened to send me on an errand to buy some turpentine, for which he gave me a one-franc piece. Alas! When I reached the artists' supplier and put my hand into my pocket, the money was missing. But when I retraced my steps, searching the pavement and the gutter for the lost coin, I found instead a five-franc note wedged in the bars of a storm-grating. When I related this to my uncle, he told me it was an instance of serendipity, an English word which had long intrigued him.
>
> After some research, he discovered that it had been coined by Horace Walpole, the author of the gothic novel, *The Castle of Otranto*. Walpole applied this notion of serendipity to curious or happy chains of events, on the model of a tale called *The Three Princes of Serendip*, in which the said princes, as they traveled, were always making discoveries, by accident or sagacity, of things they were not in quest of. (pp. 136–7)

The progress of Carson's narrative depends entirely upon such accidental discoveries, such curious coincidences and improbable juxtapositions, by which a pattern emerges out of a seemingly random set of events and experiences. Against the oppressive determinism of political ideologies, Carson's novel sets up narratives of chance and accidence. The model for Carson's novel here seems to be the unnamably hybrid texts of Iain Sinclair, in which dense mythic and symbolic patterns are discovered as if by accident in the apparently chaotic metropolitan spaces of London. In Sinclair, the impression is always of an obsessive magnification of detail and inscription, so that "we can only touch on a fraction of the possible relations" implied by the narrator's discoveries (Sinclair 1995: 16). Patterns emerge from seemingly disparate incidents, until they suggest no accidental design, but some mystical, predetermined form to which, unwittingly, the artists and dreamers are constantly drawn. In Carson's novel, as hybrid in its generic form as Sinclair's, the obsessive catalog of oil colors, herbs, saints, dates, historical events, objects, commercial brands, psychotropic substances, and mythic figures, as well as geometric details and artistic and literary references, reveals itself into a powerful, invisibly drawn design. Like Sinclair's texts, Carson's novel is a quest narrative, then, in which the narrator is dragged blindly through the labyrinths of space and time into the presence of "other historical rhythms."

Sinclair traces his visionary map of labyrinthine London through the mythologies of Blake, Yeats, and Stevenson. Carson charts the historical and imaginative webs of his fiction through the obsession with image and object in the works of Van Eyck, Wilde, and Conan Doyle, as well as the philosophies of language of Ludwig Wittgenstein. Wittgenstein in particular is the touchstone of the novel's understanding of the association between word and world. "The limits of my language mean the limits of my world," wrote Wittgenstein in his *Tractatus Logico-philosophicus*. Carson's novel pursues the implications of this understanding of the world as linguistically or textually constructed through its extensive use of quotation, paraphrase, allusion, derivation, and parody.

Shamrock Tea is a mad, obsessional work, which is encyclopedic in its reference to botany, which is structured according to a mosaic of one hundred colors, and which magnifies the real, the objective world, into unreal proportions. "One sausage alone is a very deep subject," observes Wittgenstein, who of course appears as a character in the novel (Carson 2001: 95). A sausage might yield an entire philosophical treatise, just as the narrator observes on the very first page that every color contains stories, each story unlocking another in a chain of stories and digressions which resembles the same associative flood of interlinking narratives we find in Rushdie, Sterne, or Joyce. Text begets text, stories beget stories. Carson weaves his readers within an infinite web of intertextuality, in which world is entirely and densely materialized in the word, in which the narrative embarks upon digression after digression, passing from one narrative voice to another, and in which the end of the novel repeats the beginning, thus figuring the circulatory movement of postmodern narrative.

"The whole universe is perfused with signs," the character Arthur Conan Doyle learns from his mind-bending experience of taking

"Shamrock Tea" (p. 230). They are signs which are not reflective of meaning, but which are performative, like the painting in *The Picture of Dorian Gray*, or the silhouetted bust of Sherlock Holmes in *The Empty House*, both texts which figure prominently in the novel. These signs or representations cause things to happen, and thus language itself in this magic realist text is always magical, always active in making things happen. Carson again here takes his cue from Wittgenstein, as Father Brown narrates a famous argument between Wittgenstein and Bertrand Russell:

> Wittgenstein, as I have remarked, had an acute visual imagination. It would have been no problem for him to see a rhinoceros – or a unicorn, for that matter – in his mind's eye; or, indeed, under Russell's table. When Russell, as he reports himself, made a great play of looking under tables and chairs in an effort to convince Wittgenstein that there was no rhinoceros present, this was a failure of Russell's imagination. It was also a refusal to acknowledge that a verbal rhinoceros had as much presence as a verbal unicorn. For both can be imagined, and described through language, which has the power of creating worlds beyond that of empirical observation. (p. 155)

This is the familiar premise of the linguistic turn in philosophy, the basis for poststructuralist thinking about the primacy of language over what it is assumed to represent. "Everything takes place in the brain," is another formulation of the same idea uttered elsewhere in the novel (p. 235). If this is the case, what wonderful journeys across time and space we can make, entirely through the magical power of language; what worlds of beauty and harmony can be conjured into existence through the imagination. Carson's novel is ultimately then about art, about the sublime experience of being moved or transported imaginatively by the power of art, or fiction, or stories of all kinds. It goes beyond Wilson's more tentative proposition that we can rewrite the existing narratives of our situations, and instead endorses, although not without comic irony, the potential of art or imagination to transform our existence. And Carson offers theories of art, which reflect this shift from the oppressive bonds of realism to the emancipatory potential of an art for which the rules have not yet been invented. Uncle Celestine tells Carson:

> Painting, he said, is the art of making things real, because you have looked at how things are. In order to paint a twig you must look at a

twig, and to paint a tree you must look &c. Only then do you bring the two things together. But you must also remember the injunction of Cennino, that the occupation known as painting requires you to discover things not seen, and present them to the eye as if they actually exist. (p. 50)

These are the "unknown arts" of representation pursued by Dedalus in Joyce's *A Portrait of the Artist as a Young Man*, the arts of presenting the "invisible in the visible," or, as Luis Leal wrote of magic realism, "to seize the mystery that breathes behind things" (Leal 1995: 123). But they are also close to the definition Jean-François Lyotard offers of the postmodern sublime. Lyotard argues that the task of art, of avant-garde painting in particular, is to present the unpresentable, to make visible in art what is not visible in the real. He calls, then, for a counter-realist art: "it must be clear that it is our business not to supply reality but to invent allusions to the conceivable which cannot be presented" (Lyotard 1984: 81). The universe presented by Carson is not the real, but the conceivable, and it is formulated within an art that is self-consciously in the making, which advertises itself as a hybrid art that is inventing its own rules as it unfolds. This makes Carson's fiction exemplary of the postmodern avant-garde, exemplary of the self-reflexive, intertextual, playful, and metafictional strategies of postmodern art, which conceives of art as the pataphysical laboratory in which history and the real might be remade.

Such pataphysical leaps as the ones Carson entertains in *Shamrock Tea* may take us on strange journeys. Indeed, in his introduction to his translation of Dante's *Inferno*, Carson finds himself mapping the "cramped and medieval" feel of North Belfast on to the hell of Dante's imagination. But ultimately, there is something more comically subversive about Carson's strategy in *Shamrock Tea*. He creates worlds of wonder out of an old joke about weak tea, known as "Shamrock Tea," "because they say there's only three leaves in it" (Carson 2001: 56). And when Carson discovers what might be the purpose of securing the consciousness-shifting properties of "Shamrock Tea," it turns out that Uncle Celestine has a plot to drug Belfast into an epiphanic hallucination of the wonders of a united Ireland. Even the serious, cosmopolitan play of postmodern aesthetics in the novel, then, may turn out to have more local and ludic functions. The labyrinthine interweaving of imaginative plots in *Shamrock Tea* may be another, yet more inventive, means of deploying literary fiction to desacralize the entrenched politics of Northern Ireland.

References and Further Reading

NONFICTION

Agreement (Belfast, or Good Friday), 10 April 1998 (endorsed electorally 22 May 1998). Available at: www.niassembly.gov.uk/io/agreement.htm.

Allen, Nicholas & Kelly, Aaron (eds.) (2003). *The Cities of Belfast*. Dublin: Four Courts.

Baudrillard, Jean (1994). *The Illusion of the End* (trans. Chris Turner). Cambridge: Polity Press (first published 1992).

Bauman, Zygmunt (2000). *Liquid Modernity*. Cambridge: Polity Press.

Cleary, Joe (2002). *Literature, Partition and the Nation State: Culture and conflict in Ireland, Israel and Palestine*. Cambridge: Cambridge University Press.

Derrida, Jacques (1995). Passages – from traumatism to promise. In: *Points: Interviews, 1974–1994* (ed. Elisabeth Weber, trans. Peggy Kamuf et al.). Stanford, CA: Stanford University Press (first published 1992).

Gramsci, A. (1971). State and civil society. In: *Selections from the Prison Notebooks* (ed. and trans. Quintin Hoare & Geoffrey Nowell Smith). London: Lawrence & Wishart.

Harte, Liam (2000). History lessons: postcolonialism and Seamus Deane's *Reading in the Dark*. *Irish University Review*, 30(1), 149–62.

Hughes, Eamonn (1997). Belfastards and Derriers. *The Irish Review*, 20, 151–7.

Kennedy-Andrews, Elmer (2003). *Fiction and the Northern Ireland Troubles Since 1969: (De-) constructing the North*. Dublin: Four Courts.

Kiberd, Declan (1999). Turning point: Wilde and the Belfast Agreement. *Textual Practice*, 13(3), 441–5.

Kirkland, Richard (1996). *Literature and Culture in Northern Ireland since 1965: Moments of danger*. London: Longman.

Leal, Luis (1995). Magical realism in Spanish American literature. In: Lois Parkinson Zamora & Wendy B. Faris (eds.), *Magical Realism: Theory, history, community* (pp. 119–24). Durham, NC: Duke University Press.

Longley, Edna (1996). Autobiography as history. *Fortnight*, 355, 34.

Lyotard, Jean-François F. (1984). *The Postmodern Condition: A report on knowledge* (trans. Geoff Bennington & Brian Massumi). Manchester: Manchester University Press.

Patten, Eve (1995). Fiction in conflict: Northern Ireland's prodigal novelists. In: I. A. Bell (ed.), *Peripheral Visions: Images of nationhood in contemporary British fiction* (pp. 128–48). Cardiff: University of Wales Press.

Peach, Linden (2004). *The Contemporary Irish Novel: Critical readings*. Basingstoke: Palgrave.

Pelaschiar, Laura (1998). *Writing the North: The contemporary novel in Northern Ireland*. Trieste: Edizioni Parnaso.

Smyth, Gerry (1997). *The Novel and the Nation: Studies in the new Irish fiction*. London: Pluto Press.

St Peter, Christine (2000). *Changing Ireland: Strategies in contemporary women's fiction*. Basingsroke: Macmillan.

FICTION

Carson, Ciaran (2001). *Shamrock Tea*. London: Granta.
Deane, Seamus (1997). *Reading in the Dark*. London: Vintage.
Madden, Deirdre (1996). *One by One in the Darkness*. London: Faber.
Patterson, Glenn (1988). *Burning Your Own*. London: Chatto & Windus.
Patterson, Glenn (1999). *The International*. London: Anchor/Transworld.
Sinclair, Iain (1995). *Lud Heat and Suicide Bridge*. London: Vintage.
Wilson, Robert McLiam (1998). *Eureka Street: A novel of Ireland like no other*. London: Vintage.

Part III

Mutations of Form

Chapter 8

The Historical Turn in British Fiction

Suzanne Keen

That recent British and anglophone fiction has taken a historical turn has become an axiom of critical commentary on the contemporary British literary scene. The historical novel, a subgenre of the English novel with a continuous presence since the eighteenth century, has in the past two decades flourished, enjoying popular success with a devoted readership, undergoing energetic feminist and postcolonial revisions, garnering significant prizes, inspiring film and television adaptations, and commanding significant critical attention (Byatt 2001; Connor 1996; Cowart 1989; Higdon 1984; McEwan 1987; Scanlan 1990). Historical fiction includes a wide range of works with a basis in biographical details and historical events, set in periods other than the writer's and contemporary readers' times, and representing characters in interaction with settings, cultures, events, and people of the past. Some writers, such as Patrick O'Brian and J. G. Farrell, built careers on historical fiction. Many more novelists (Penelope Fitzgerald, Hilary Mantel, Timothy Mo, Iris Murdoch, Jeanette Winterson) have written one or two critically acclaimed historical novels, while not dedicating themselves exclusively to this genre. A few writers (Peter Ackroyd and Stevie Davies) have written both nonfictional historical works or biographies and also fictional narratives set in the past. Their experiences in the archives and accomplishments in real history do not necessarily produce reverent attitudes toward the past handled fictionally: Ackroyd's *Last Testament of Oscar Wilde* (1983) bridges the two areas of his work in a tour-de-force performance of pastiche, full of invented

Wildean discourse, while his *Dickens* biography (1990) notoriously includes fictional episodes in which the author strolls with his subject and mixes with Dickens's creations. The generic boundaries are by no means tightly policed, and if historical fiction is taken to include works in other subgenres, such as Ellis Peters's Brother Cadfael mysteries and counterfactual alternate-timeline fantasies, then the saturation of the contemporary with versions of the past becomes even more striking.

What is the appropriate attitude of the novel critic to popular sub-genres of the novel? Though cultural studies encourages a wider range of enquiry than the heirs of the great tradition might approve, as broad-minded a critic as Malcolm Bradbury distinguishes "the novel" from its "soft rivals (film, television, popular or genre fiction)" (Bradbury 2000: x). This distinction places the subgenres firmly outside the zone of the serious novel. Even now, very few literary critics include the subgenres in literary historical narratives of the twentieth century, after the well-documented split of serious from popular fictional forms in the 1890s. Subgenres, including historical fiction, come back in as objects of study in and of themselves – as in the work of Jerry Palmer on potboilers or thrillers, or Martin Green on adventure tales (Palmer 1991; Green 1991) – or in accounts of individual writers' careers. Sometimes working under a pseudonym, a writer of serious literary fiction may float a career by turning out better-selling detective fiction, thrillers, or fantasy on the side. A few writers in the subgenres have transcended their status as authors of subliterary airport reading, at the rate of approximately one per subgenre per generation: the acceptance of John Le Carré, P. D. James, Ruth Rendell, and J. K. Rowling represents this largess on the part of academics and critical watchdogs, or perhaps indicates the cultural guardians' incapacity to keep all the subgenres out of the contemporary canon of seriousness in the face of real readers' enthusiasm. Most of the writers and works in the subgenres do not as a rule rate according to literary criticism, however: thrillers, westerns, and romances, or any subgenre that can be denigrated by the term formula fiction, must make do with sales, circulation, and no respect.

Historical fiction has in the past several decades defied this rule of thumb. It has, as Lindsay Duguid observes in a survey of reviewers' practices, "become respectable, even intellectual" (Duguid, 2002: 284). It has the advantage of a distinguished pedigree (going back to Walter Scott, with major Victorians trying the form at least once). Historical fiction has a leg up on popular forms of adventure and romance because it can allude to eminent figures, significant episodes, or other materials that command respect as matters of cultural literacy or a felt heritage. As I have argued elsewhere (Keen 2001: 105–9), the rise in popularity of historical fiction in a British context has exactly matched a de-emphasis on school history (no longer mandatory at Key Stage Four, for 14–16-year-old students, under the revised National Curriculum). Just because students may find history less emphasized in school does not mean that they are indifferent to it, however. The prominence of historical fiction has also accompanied, and arguably stimulated, a booming heritage industry's focus on a positive, marketable past capable of inspiring patriotism and attracting tourists (Hewison 1987; Lowenthal 1985, 1996; Samuel 1994). Historical fiction for children has been an area of distinctive achievement since the late 1960s and early 1970s, and may be partly responsible for the continued appetite for narratives based in the past despite history's de-emphasis in the schools.

A cohort growing up during a golden age of children's fiction may turn more readily to historical fiction. Rosemary Sutcliff's fictional accounts of the disintegration of Roman rule present a strong analogy with the British postimperial condition. Joan Aiken's feminist Dido Twite novels depict an alternative timeline in which things have turned out quite differently for the Stuarts and Hanoverians. Barbara Willard's superb Mantlemass Chronicles convey a sense of place (Sussex) through generations of women who witness and participate in historical changes from the Plantagenets through the English Civil War. Alan Garner's stoneworkers, Henry Treece's Vikings, Gillian Avery's (and later Philip Pullman's) Victorians, K. M. Peyton's early twentieth-century aviators, and Jill Paton Walsh's Dunkirk rescuers all contributed to the cultivation of the historical imaginations of a generation of writers – and readers – now come of age. It is not a huge leap from *Castors Away!* (Burton 1962) to *Master and Commander* (1970).

"How popular is historical fiction among adults?" the curious reader may ask. According to library circulation data, it lags well behind both mysteries and romances. The diffusion of historical fiction into an array of other subgenres may account for the slight decline in historical fiction's readership between 1988 and 1998, a period in which one might expect historical fiction to have risen in popularity. British library circulation data from 1988–89 and 1997–98 record a slight drop in total fiction loans, from 53.9% to 52%, despite a rise in borrowing of "general fiction" from 17.8% to 22.1%. Some of the decline derives from the drop of historical checkouts from 3.5% of the total books borrowed to 2.9%. In contrast, mysteries and detective stories held steady at 12.8%; at the end of the millennium, light romances still accounted for 10% of library borrowing (Bloom 2002: 247; for statistics on the 1970s and early 1980s, see Worpole 1984).

Though no match for the romance novel in this regard, historical fiction enjoys popularity and sales sufficient to inspire the publication of "How to Write and Sell" handbooks by Writer's Digest Books (Woolley 1997). A search for "historical fiction" on Amazon.com and Amazon UK produces 86,712 results, compared to 70,837 hits for "literary fiction," figures that do not account for overlap in the categories. While it may be argued that only a select group of texts attaining the middlebrow status of literary fiction need concern the student of historical fiction, factors of gender, genre, and popular readership alter the picture of the ostensible historical turn. Searching for "historical romance" by itself reveals a significant component of historical fiction not usually acknowledged by critical commentary on the "new historical fiction," but accounting for 46,218 editions of a kind of book avidly read by women readers. These readers matter to publishers because market research consistently reveals that women buy more fiction, read more novels, and read more books monthly than men (McLemee 2004; National Endowment for the Arts 2004; see also the National Literacy Trust website, www.literacytrust.or.uk). According to the survey conducted in 2000 on World Book Day (a UNESCO Literacy project), the top favorite author for adults in Britain was Catherine Cookson, a prolific writer of historical romances (Bloom 2002: 258).

The steady presence of women's "historicals" on library shelves and in paperback bookshops provides a backdrop for the consideration of the historical turn as a change in the status of a subgenre, a change that has been effected by regendering historical fiction as a respectable genre for male readers and writers. One may hypothesize that if a popular subgenre can rise from its subliterary zone into an arena of cultural respectability, it may do so by shedding its strong association with women readers, despite the fact that most actual readers are female. One consequence of this regendering of genre is that the presence of women writers among the authors of historical fiction can appear to be a notable new development rather than a constant feature of the kind, considered over time. Critic Lindsay Duguid, for instance, speculates that Beryl Bainbridge, Penelope Fitzgerald, Pat Barker, Hilary Mantel, Rose Tremain, and Jeanette Winterson turned to historical fiction in the 1980s "as a way of escaping the feminist straitjacket, or just getting out of the kitchen" (Duguid 2002: 296). This comment implies that either political correctness or dreary limitation to middle-class domestic realms drives female writers into a genre neither feminist nor traditionally female, a misunderstanding of historical fiction in the twentieth century.

"The New Historical Fiction"

Whether or not there has in fact been more or better historical fiction published recently, it has indisputably attracted significant attention since the 1970s, and has risen to prominence since the late 1980s. Critics have perceived changes in the fundamental attitude of some historical fiction, changes that appear to be related to a parallel narrative turn in historical writing, and to the impact of poststructuralism and postmodernism on literary fiction (Rozett 2003: 6–9). One version of this view receives powerful expression in Linda Hutcheon's (1988) identification of a theoretically aware *historiographic metafiction*, a quintessential postmodern genre and an important subset of historical fiction in the contemporary period. As aspects of postmodernist style permeate the mainstream, however, some fictional texts also take on the surface appearance of postmodernism without adopting all of its underlying philosophical positions.

An important conduit for both postmodern style and philosophy, Umberto Eco's *The Name of the Rose* (1980) appears to many observers to have stimulated a stylistic shift in historical fiction. The body of work appearing after the 1983 publication of Eco's novel in English translation has been treated by numerous commentators as "the new historical fiction" (Rozett 2003: 1–26). This innovative phase of an old genre emphasizes postmodern uncertainties in experimental styles, tells stories about the past that point to multiple truths or the overturning of an old received Truth, mixes genres, and adopts a parodic or irreverently playful attitude to history over an ostensibly normative mimesis. Some striking examples of contemporary British works in this category include Peter Ackroyd's *Hawksmoor* (1985) and *Chatterton* (1987), Martin Amis's *Time's Arrow* (1991), Julian Barnes's *The History of the World in 10¹/₂ Chapters* (1989), Louis de Bernières's *Captain Corelli's Mandolin* (1994), A. S. Byatt's *The Biographer's Tale* (2000), Kazuo Ishiguro's *The Remains of the Day* (1989), Ian McEwan's *Atonement* (2001), Lawrence Norfolk's *Lemprière's Dictionary* (1991), Graham Swift's *Waterland* (1983), Barry Unsworth's *Losing Nelson* (1999), Jill Paton Walsh's *Knowledge of Angels* (1994), and Jeanette Winterson's *The Passion* (1987).

When one expands the category of British fiction to include, as the Booker prize did from its inception in 1969, works published in English by writers from countries formerly colonized by the British, the ranks of writers of the new historical fiction swell: Margaret Atwood, Peter Carey, J. G. Farrell, Timothy Findlay, Amitav Ghosh, Thomas Keneally, Brian Moore, Michael Ondaatje, Caryl Phillips, and Salman Rushdie must be noted (among many others). Indeed, the success of Rushdie's magical realist chronicle of Indian independence, *Midnight's Children* (1981), coincides with the appearance of Eco's *The Name of the Rose*, and points to the huge influence not only on Rushdie, but also on world fiction generally, of Gabriel García Márquez's *One Hundred Years of Solitude* (1967; English translation 1970). The impress of García Márquez, Carlos Fuentes, Manuel Puig, and Isabel Allende on contemporary British historical fiction has been insufficiently emphasized, though Jorge Luis Borges, a significant exemplar of early postmodernism, receives tips of the hat. Eco's incorporation of references to Borges in his labyrinthine library and sinister librarian has ensured that one line of transmission from the New World to Old World remains in view. The worldwide popularity of Latin American magical realist texts in the 1970s and 1980s, including innovative historical chronicles that reinvent the generational saga, disseminated new techniques for representing traumatic histories with imaginative verve. Though *One Hundred Years of Solitude* is only one of Rushdie's intertexts, its impress on *Midnight's Children* was widely noted upon the novel's first publication and subsequent Booker Prize win (1981). The reselection of Rushdie's *Midnight's Children* as the Booker of Bookers in 1993 underscores the widespread perception that this fantastical historical fiction started something new in English language fiction.

The vogue for the new historical fiction, then, may be dated to Eco's *The Name of the Rose*, to Salman Rushdie's *Midnight's Children*, and to the continuing influence in the 1980s of the Latin American magical realism that everyone was reading in the 1970s. Homegrown British sources also deserve mention. Though he cuts a much smaller figure on the international stage today, John Fowles was a much-celebrated novelist in the 1970s, and his 1969 novel *The French Lieutenant's Woman* anticipates in many ways the traits of the new historical fiction. Winning both the Silver Pen Award and the W. H. Smith Literary Award, *The French Lieutenant's Woman* appeared in a film adaptation in 1981 (screenplay by Harold Pinter), just in time to add a historiographical look at the Victorians to the mix of influences. A. S. Byatt is quite right to decry the notion that Salman Rushdie started experimentation in the British novel (Byatt 2001: 3), and the point applies to innovative historical fiction as well (McEwan 1987). The explanations for the historical turn, and reactions to it, grow more complex as we consider historical fiction in all its forms, not only in the trendy category of the new historical fiction.

Emergent, Dominant, and Residual Forms of Historical Fiction

In Raymond Williams's terms, something new in historical fiction might be identified as an emergent form, representing "a new structure of feeling" that appears in a specific time period (Williams 1977: 132–4). The presence of an emergent form, as Williams describes it, coexists with prevailing (dominant) modes and even old-fashioned (residual) forms. Dominant and residual forms of historical fiction comprise the low and middlebrow historical novels already combining to make up most of literary production in the genre. The newer postmodern historical fiction represents an emergent form, one that has attracted a great deal of critical approbation, but which has not yet displaced its precursors. Women's historical romances remain the dominant form because of their sheer mass in the marketplace and the size of their dedicated readership. Despite the oft-repeated perception that historical fiction has left the tawdry bodice-rippers behind (White 2003: 12; Woodroof 2004), women's historical romances flourish, carrying on a tradition that includes George Eliot, Elizabeth Gaskell, Mary Butts, Mary Renault, Daphne DuMaurier, Margaret Mitchell, and Anya Seton. Traditional historical novels share with women's historical fiction dominance in the marketplace, but at this late date their authors still attempt to achieve verisimilar and historically accurate representation that might win the approval of historians. Thus they have more in common formally with nineteenth-century historical fiction after Walter Scott than women's historicals. The strong continuity with precursor texts in the tradition renders traditional historical novels examples of still vigorous residual forms. Dominant and residual historical fiction, despite the strong gender difference of their implied audiences, have a lot in common. Both women's historical romances and traditional historical fiction emphasize the marked difference of the past from the readers' era, and yet invite connection with characters, who may be either ordinary individuals caught up in historically significant moments, or famous people represented familiarly for fiction readers.

To return equipped with these terms to the early 1980s and the fiction scene at the time of the historical turn, then, we can see that Salman Rushdie's polyphonic, exuberant, and norm-defying Indian historical fiction could be called an emergent text representing a new postcolonial structure of feeling. What traces of the residual and dominant forms of historical fiction can be found? Rushdie and Umberto Eco, authors of the distinguished new historical novels, shared shelf-space with an enormously popular historical family chronicle of Australia's settling, Colleen McCullough's *The Thorn Birds* (1977). Also participating in postimperial recasting of a national story, McCullough's work belonged to the dominant form of the traditional generational saga. First reaching the public through an excerpt published in the women's magazine *Family Circle*, McCullough's novel earned an unprecedented $1.9 million for the American paperback rights (McCullough 1998). The publisher did not lose money on the deal, because *The Thorn Birds* became an international bestseller, ultimately rendered as a highly popular miniseries, aired in the early 1980s, starring Richard Chamberlain and Rachel Ward. Even taking the film of *The Name of the Rose* (1986) into account, McCullough's historical domestic epic certainly reached more readers in the 1980s than Rushdie and Eco combined. A variety of historical fiction in which passing time and changing mores matter most as they reflect on the developments of relationships, in which the challenges faced by characters arise from historical events and trends, but are always subordinated to the effects on character, remained the commercially dominant form of historical fiction in the 1980s.

What of the more traditional, residual form of historical fiction at this moment? Many examples testify to the health of the residual form. Patrick O'Brian's Aubrey/Maturin series had reached its eighth installment by 1981 with *The Ionian Mission*; seven books in this series appeared during the 1980s and had clearly built a loyal following. Less spectacularly popular than O'Brian's series, but a close runner-up for the 1980 Booker Prize, was Anthony Burgess's sweeping twentieth-century tome, *Earthly Powers* (1980). A rejoinder to the more insular twelve-book series by Anthony Powell, *A Dance to the Music of Time* (1951–75), Burgess presents the century in serio-comic splendor. Burgess did his research, taking care to ensure that even the details of women's clothing would ring true to a reader who had lived through the times he described. Though other works by Burgess can be counted among the postmodern new historical fictions, *Earthly Powers* represents the "ordinary people in extraordinary times" version of historical fiction, focused on the recent past, but otherwise true to the Walter Scott tradition.

It should be clear, but perhaps warrants mention, that historical fiction after Scott is still romance storytelling, with a strong relationship to another residual form of narrative, adventure fiction. Not coincidentally, all the novels discovered in dominant, residual, and emergent forms in the early 1980s are long books, either in series or in huge single volumes. Even in the pared-down publishing world of the twenty-first century, which favors quick reads and slim volumes, historical fiction can still be conceived by writers and pitched to publishers as big books, running to the hundreds of thousands of words. If extra-long novels are for the most part associated with *déclassé* subgenres (horror and thrillers), historical fiction preserves for voracious readers the pleasures of a long read, immersion, and repetition. This is true whether the reader favors the residual, dominant, or emergent varieties of historical fiction – emphasizing adventure, love story, or postmodern juggling of traces from the past.

If we were to take core samples of contemporary fiction at any time since the 1980s, the same contrasting bands of emergent, dominant, and residual forms of historical fiction would show. The method yields results when working by themes as well as by dates of publication. For instance, when Kazuo Ishiguro's *Remains of the Day*, a stylishly written novel looking back at the British flirtation with Fascism, came out in 1989, J. G. Ballard's 1984 *Empire of the Sun* was already on the shelves, and Isabel Colegate's more traditionally composed *Orlando Trilogy*, studying appeasement politics through three novels (*Orlando King* (1969), *Orlando at the Brazen Threshold* (1971), and *Agatha* (1973)), had been reissued in paperback in 1984. The fiftieth anniversary of World War II made that period especially attractive to historical novelists (and filmmakers) of all stripes. Those with a taste for the new historical fiction could turn to the oblique representation of war and empire depicted through a brewing dynasty in Graham Swift's brilliant 1983 novel *Waterland*.

Wartime broadly construed has inspired a great deal of traditional historical fiction since the late 1970s, not all of it focused on the European theatre. J. G. Farrell's *The Singapore Grip* (1978) treats the run-up to the Japanese occupation of Singapore in a popular novelistic style (the reader follows a family and set of friends through the events). Bapsi Sidhwa's *The Ice-Candy-Man* (1988) focuses on the 1947 Partition of India and Pakistan. Pat Barker's *Regeneration* (1991), *The Eye in the Door* (1993), and *The Ghost Road* (1995) retell the Great War experience from a set of perspectives including real people (famous war poets and their doctor) and invented characters, including women. Amitav Ghosh's *The Glass Palace* (2000) brings the history of Burma from its takeover by the British to the present day, and Helen Dunmore's *The Siege* (2001) relies on interviews with survivors and historical research to represent the tragic siege of Leningrad. Each of the books named in this brief catalog, in representing traumatic events, aspires to historical accuracy (as judged by historians and witness-participants) and attempts to invoke an empathetic response from readers situated far from the events and perhaps learning about them for the first time (Rigney 2001: 57). While these novels may participate in historiographical arguments by offering neglected perspectives or focusing on places whose history has been ignored, they employ traditional narrative strategies and they do not undermine their own truth claims as postmodern historical fiction often does. This commitment to historical accuracy sometimes coexists with an emphasis on a more positive heritage, as in Patrick O'Brian's Aubrey/Maturin novels and in books like Adam Thorpe's *Ulverton* (1992). In short, the residual form of historical fiction is going strong.

While some novelists strive to create fictional versions of past worlds "as they actually were," many others enthusiastically adopt historical settings and characters in order to address a wide range of present-day concerns, to redress perceived injustices, and to indulge in fancy-dress worldmaking. Among the lively reinventions of various pasts in fictional form are the group of texts I name romances of the archive. Like the most famous exemplar of the kind, A. S. Byatt's *Possession* (1989), these novels take place in libraries or collections, feature plots of research-questing, interpret the past through recovery of its material traces, and answer the postmodern critique of history with invented records full of hard facts. I have argued that the efflorescence of romances of the archive after the Falklands crisis reveals a form of literary nationalism that cuts across serious and popular genres to interrogate the uses of the past in a postimperial age (Keen 2001: 3–6). Residual in its romance adventure form, the English romance of the archive articulates a set of emergent responses to the cultural dominants of postmodernism and postcolonialism. The central fantasy of the romance of the archive lies in its recovery of the truth, making sense of confusion, resolving mystery, permitting satisfying closure, and redressing historic injustices (p. 14).

Several recent narratives break with the norm of prose fiction while otherwise participating in the revision of traditional historical fiction:

Craig Raine's *History: The home movie* (1994) blends epic poetry and filmic representational strategies in a narrative that sweeps from 1905 to 1984, telling the story of two families, one well-known and the other ordinary. Raine's first source is family history, a point he makes formally through the conceit of the home movie, rendered in triplets. Bernardine Evaristo's *The Emperor's Babe* (2001), by way of contrast, stems from research the author began when she was placed as a poet in residence at the Museum of London. Also in verse, Evaristo's text participates in the historical romance tradition of imagining the lives of the forgotten women who were attached to great men. Relating the life of Zulieka, a mistress of the Roman emperor Septimus Severus, Evaristo's novel of Roman Britain unfolds mainly in a sequence of poems written in couplets and blends Latin terms with an unabashedly contemporary idiom. A child of Sudanese immigrants to London and a would-be poet, Zulieka hosts a *recitatio*, immediately recognizable as a poetry slam. Evaristo's wry postimperial send-up of Roman Britain and the contemporary literary scene embraces presentism and anachronism, harvesting historical details from museums and popular sources to sketch a past of Britain that includes Blacks. Both texts emphasize heritage as much as history, and in this way these cutting edge narratives reach back at least as far as Walter Scott's poem *The Lay of the Last Minstrel* (1805), in which recovered materials of the heritage become the starting point for the development of the whole genre of historical fiction. Whether in one of these unusual books, which reclaim an area of narrative poetry much exploited in past centuries, or in one of Peter Ackroyd's celebrations of Albion, or in any number of popular historical treatments of great periods of the British past, heritage narratives invite a felt sense of connection with people, places, and events of the past.

Against the Historical Turn

It goes without saying that much of what writers present as the historical furniture in fiction is wildly inaccurate. The most common negative criticism of historical novels singles out bloopers – errors of chronology, geography, tone, cultural practices, turns of phrase, even (perhaps especially) dress and food. But this is not all that a contemporary historical novelist faces. A trend becomes most noticeable when it begins to attract negative criticism. The denouncers of historical fiction decry what they variously perceive as its misguided focus on the past, its deliberate misrepresentation of history, its manipulation of readers with an appetite for heritage sensations, and its neglect of the interesting present. Practically as soon as the recent historical turn is supposed to have begun, in the early 1980s, Salman Rushdie condemned its manifestations in films, television, and popular fiction, including the TV miniseries of Paul Scott's *Raj Quartet* (1966–75). Rushdie deplored the Orientalist stereotyping of their representations of India, their suggestion that the part of the story that mattered was "the doings of the officer class," with Indians relegated to bit parts "in their own history" (Rushdie 1991: 90). He saw pernicious nostalgia for the days of the Raj, writing:

> There can be little doubt that in Britain today the refurbishment of the Empire's tarnished image is under way. The continuing decline, the growing poverty and the meanness of spirit of much of Thatcherite Britain encourages many Britons to turn their eyes nostalgically to the lost hour of their precedence. The recrudescence of imperialist ideology and the popularity of Raj fictions put one in mind of the phantom twitchings of an amputated limb. Britain is in danger of entering a condition of cultural psychosis, in which it begins once again to strut and to posture like a great power while, in fact, its power diminishes every year. The jewel in the crown is made, these days, of paste. (pp. 91–2)

Rushdie's insight that nostalgia for a glorious Imperial past connected with the condition of Thatcher's Britain is borne out by jingoistic public rhetoric that accompanied the Falklands War (1982) and the subsequent revision of the secondary school history curriculum to reflect a more upbeat, nationalist, traditional version of English history.

The public emphasis in the 1980s and 1990s on a feel-good English heritage sets the recovery of history from below or examination of embarrassing parts of the national story in a productively oppositional stance. A variety of responses were forthcoming from historical novelists. Some, like Robert Goddard and Robert Harris, were frankly patriotic and, at least on Goddard's part, Little Englander in spirit. Others, like Rose Tremain's *Restoration* (1989), Jeanette Winterson's *Sexing the Cherry* (1989), and Ackroyd's dark time-shift novel *Hawksmoor* (1985), presented less pious views of English heritage. Gothic-inflected historical fiction joined detective fiction to suggest a sense of the past as containing criminal secrets. A grounding in postmodern skepticism or poststructuralist theory was not required to join the heritage debate. The proper uses of the past for the formation of citizens in a postimperial nation were matters of discussion in the weeklies and monthly magazines, with contributions from Prime Ministers and Members of Parliament, as well as teachers, historians, and opinion makers (Keen 2001: 97–131). Would that past be celebrated as the heritage, with its National Trust backdrop and strong relation to a healthy tourist industry, or would it be open to versions of historians' accounts, including the painful and unpleasant discoveries of social history and the mortifying reminders of racism, dispossession, exploitation, slavery, and even genocide that a full story of empire would include?

Looking back to expose the crimes of the past, to engage in revisionist story-telling, or to bring up-to-date historical insights to readers of fiction have proven strong motivations for contemporary historical fiction: Barry Unsworth's *Sacred Hunger* (1992), the Booker Prize-winning epic novel about the eighteenth-century slave trade, exemplifies this use of the novel. Other historical novels that embark on projects at least partly didactic include Timothy Mo's *An Insular Possession* (1986), about Hong Kong; Brian Moore's *Black Robe* (1985), about Jesuit encounters with the Native American Hurons; and Roddy Doyle's *A Star Called Henry* (1999), about the Easter Rising. These often subversive texts nonetheless aim for a high degree of verisimilitude, cultivate empathy, and make truth claims that gesture toward historical accuracy rather than toward the undermining playfulness of postmodern historical fiction. As Edmund White writes in defense of his recent novel *Fanny* (2003b), he intends to "unearth the past, not as we would have it be but as it was. After all it is a past – shameful, all too human, hopeful – that we all share" (2003a: 13). The post-Auschwitz view that some experiences have simply been rendered unrepresentable has not deterred novelists and filmmakers from tackling even the most horrifying of historical topics (Vice 2000; Wagner 2003).

The history you thought you already knew receives vigorous challenge from novels such as these, but the techniques employed have more to do with the insights produced by writing history from below or from alternative perspectives, than with the frontal assault on the nature of facts, evidence, and the very possibility of a knowable past often found in postmodern fiction. These historical novels bear a strong relationship in their revisionist spirit to the feminist and postcolonial tradition stemming from Jean Rhys's *Wide Sargasso Sea* (1966). As A. S. Byatt observes, "One very powerful impulse towards the writing of historical novels has been the political desire to write the

179

histories of the marginalized, the forgotten, the unrecorded. In Britain this has included the histories of blacks and women, and the whole flourishing and brilliant culture of the post-colonial novel." Byatt suggests a ripple effect from women and minority writers' works: their "often polemical revisionist tales [have] given other British writers the impulse to range further historically and geographically than the immediately postwar social realists" (Byatt 2001: 12).

That concern with this historical trend should be expressed by one of the century's most distinguished writers of social realism, South African Nobel laureate Nadine Gordimer, suggests that a preoccupation with redressing injuries of the past has its limitations. Gordimer has recently worried in an interview about young South African writers' obsession with history:

> Of course there is a tendency, especially among young writers, to write about the past rather than the present. This worries me a little bit because the present is so interesting. It is a new way in which we are all living. And so far it is not even a decade. There are not many works, whether poetry, stories or novels that deal with the present. I suppose it is a repression of the past where you couldn't say this, or didn't think you could get away with it, but people tend to write more and more about what happened in the apartheid past than in the post-apartheid present. (Lee 2003: 5)

Gordimer's comments may simply come too soon for a generation of writers who came of age during the end of Apartheid or the period of the Truth Commissions. Her critique avoids noticing that a great deal of historical fiction represents the past to approach contemporary issues. This frank presentism is less about judging the past by present-day standards and more about creating fictive worlds in which to explore current social problems or conditions.

For instance, since the *fatwa* condemning Salman Rushdie to death for blaspheming in *The Satanic Verses* (1988) (itself a hybrid historical novel divided between events of the seventh century and events of the late twentieth century), and perhaps even more after the terrorist attacks on September 11, 2001, the seventeenth century and the English Civil War period have been frequently represented in historical fiction (Victorian times, Shakespearean England, the eighteenth century and the Regency, the medieval period – especially for mysteries – and Greek and Roman times have been perennial favorites). Peter Ackroyd's *Milton in America* (1996), Iain Pears's *An Instance of the Fingerpost* (1997),

Stevie Davies's *Impassioned Clay* (1999), Maria McCann's *As Meat Loves Salt* (2001), and James Robertson's *The Fanatic* (2000) all turn to a period characterized by religious fervor, persecution, and fanaticism. Contemporary concerns about censorship, blasphemy, death sentences, and migration all receive attention, and the remote period allows writers of a mainly secular nation to ponder intense religious conviction expressed in community life, politics, and in private.

The emphasis in several of these novels (*Impassioned Clay* and *As Meat Loves Salt*) on both the spirituality and sexuality of characters who would be labeled lesbian or gay in our time permits not only a rewriting of the history of sexual identities, but also an escape from contemporary sexual politics. For a writer like Stevie Davies, a connected past accommodates feminist revisionist aims, allowing assumptions about traditional gender roles and women's relationships to be challenged. Indeed, a notable cluster of novels representing characters that alter hetero-normative expectations about sexuality include Philip Hensher's *Mulberry Empire* (2002), Sarah Waters's *Affinity* (1999) Sarah Dunant's *The Birth of Venus* (2003), and Edmund White's *Fanny* (2003b). Edmund White, defending his novel in *TLS*, opines:

> If as historical novelists we do not show these ever-changing practices and definitions of love then we are guilty of replacing history with nature. We mislead our readers into believing that nothing has ever been different from the way it is now . . . The job of the enlightened historical novelist is to show that the sun never rises twice on the same human sentiments. Each period has its own character, and no sentiment is natural, uninflected by the prevailing social forces. (2003a: 11)

Some younger writers decry the imaginative license that paradoxically appears to be required in order to achieve the goals White sets out. In *All Hail the New Puritans* (2000), a group of young English writers presents a manifesto rejecting the past and embracing the contemporary as a proper subject: "As faithful representations of the present, our texts will avoid all improbable or unknowable speculation about the past or the future" (Blincoe & Thorne 2000: i). Matt Thorne and Nicolas Blincoe lament the dominance of the historical mode, which they see as sopping up prizes and wasting the energies of the young. Others have seen the turn to the past more neutrally, as a typically contemporary preoccupation; the archaeologist, the historian, and the researcher embody the spirit of a backward-looking postwar period

(Higdon 1984: 11–12), but it may be time for twenty-first century novelists to define themselves by reversing that direction.

The future of historical fiction is not a matter of consensus, even among those who write it. Hilary Mantel, whose first written novel, *A Place of Greater Safety* (not published until 1992), is about the French Revolution, defends the historical author against the charge of ignoring the here-and-now. Indeed, writing historical fiction may prove a liberating choice: "For the constant and passionate imagination, no documents or passes are needed. It did not seem to me that I was writing of dead people or events that were distant and frozen. I was working at a transformative moment in the history of Europe. . . . By writing a novel one performs a revolutionary act. A novel is an act of hope. It allows us to imagine that things may be other than they are" (Mantel 2002: 97). While judging the historical novel quite impossible, P. N. Furbank suggests that all it can ever hope to do properly is represent the concerns of the present: "The historical novelist can hardly hope to illuminate the past. What he or she can do, on the other hand, is use the past to cast light on the present – to highlight those parts of our way of thinking that were not known to a past period – and this is the secret of historical novels that succeed" (p. 112). While Furbank reminds us that there are no neutral representations of obviously true history, his deeper point is that all (good) historical fiction is fundamentally historiographical.

If we can conceive of the historical fiction of a period as a conversation about past and present in emergent, dominant, and residual forms, with a variety of attitudes toward truth, accuracy, evidence, events, causation, human beings, and fictional characters, then we need not choose sides. More complicated understandings of the continuing taste for historical fiction in an ever-changing market will arise if we can practice a little bit of what Franco Moretti calls "distant reading," a more rational literary history based on large numbers of texts (Moretti 2003). The literary historical narratives that we tell about the rise and fall of subgenres also deserve our skeptical scrutiny, and we should wonder why the celebrated historical turn in contemporary fiction must situate itself against the historical romances and traditional historical novels that still dominate the marketplace. Distant readings, such as I have only begun to suggest in this essay, can open up to historically specific arguments about changes in the publishing industry, swings in fashions for the "nouveau" and the "retro," hierarchies of taste, and the influence of lived context itself on narrative forms.

References and Further Reading

NONFICTION

Barth, John (1967). The Literature of exhaustion. In: David H. Richter (ed.), *Narrative/Theory* (pp. 77–86). London: Longman.

Blincoe, Nicholas & Thorne, Matt (eds.) (2000). *All Hail the New Puritans*. London: Fourth Estate.

Bloom, Clive (2002). *Bestsellers: Popular fiction since 1900*. Houndmills: Palgrave Macmillan.

Bradbury, Malcolm (2002). Introduction. In: Iris Murduch, *The Philosopher's Pupil* (pp. ix–xx). Harmondsworth: Penguin.

Byatt, A. S. (2001). *On Histories and Stories*. Cambridge, MA: Harvard University Press.

Connor, Steven (1996). *The English Novel in History 1950–1995*. London: Routledge.

Cowart, David (1989). *History and the Contemporary Novel*. Carbondale, IL: Southern Illinois University Press.

Duguid, Lindsay (2002). Before it becomes literature: how fiction reviewers have dealt with the English novel. In: Zachary Leader (ed.), *On Modern British Fiction* (pp. 284–303). Oxford: Oxford University Press.

Elias, Amy J. (2001). *Sublime Desire: History and post-1960s fiction*. Baltimore, MD: Johns Hopkins University Press.

Fleishman, Avrom (1971). *The English Historical Novel*. Baltimore, MD: Johns Hopkins University Press.

Furbank, P. N. (2004). On the historical novel. *Raritan*, Winter, 94–114.

Green, Martin (1991). *Seven Types of Adventure Tale: An etiology of a major genre*. University Park, PA: Pennsylvania State University Press.

Hewison, Robert (1987). *The Heritage Industry: Britain in a climate of decline*. London: Methuen.

Higdon, David L. 1984. *Shadows of the Past in Contemporary British Fiction*. London: Macmillan.

Hutcheon, Linda (1988). *A Poetics of Postmodernism: History, theory, fiction*. London: Routledge.

Hutcheon, Linda (1989). *The Politics of Postmodernism*. London: Routledge.

Karlin, Daniel (2003) Wanting in on history: Edmund White's way with first-person historical fiction. *Times Literary Supplement*, August 15, 19–20.

Keen, Suzanne (2001). *Romances of the Archive in Contemporary British Fiction*. Toronto: University of Toronto Press.

Lee, Hermione (2003). In conversation with Nadine Gordimer. *Wasafiri*, 39, Summer, 3–7.

Lowenthal, David (1985). *The Past is a Foreign Country*. Cambridge: Cambridge University Press.

Lowenthal, David (1996). *Possessed by the Past: The heritage crusade and the spoils of history*. New York: Free Press.

Mantel, Hilary (2002). No passes or documents are needed: the writer at home in Europe. In: Zachary Leader (ed.), *On Modern British Fiction* (pp. 93–106). Oxford: Oxford University Press.

McCullough, Colleen (1998). Colleen McCullough on . . . Colleen McCullough. A *Current Affair* Online. Available at: http://acurrentaffair.ninemsn.com.au/stories/397.asp (accessed February 20, 2005).

McEwan, Neil (1987). *Perspective in British Historical Fiction Today*. London: Macmillan.

McLemee, Scott (2004). Literary reading is declining faster than before, Arts Endowment's New Report Says. *Chronicle of Higher Education*, 9 July, A1, A16.

Moretti, Franco (2003). Graphs, maps, trees: abstract models for literary history – 1. *New Left Review*, 24, 67–93.

National Endowment for the Arts (2004). *Reading at Risk: A survey of literary reading in America*, Research Division Report no. 46. Washington, DC: National Endowment for the Arts.

Palmer, Jerry (1978). *Thrillers: Genesis and structure of a popular genre*. London: Edward Arnold.

Palmer, Jerry (1991). *Potboilers: Methods, concepts, and case studies in popular fiction*. London: Routledge.

Rigney, Ann (2001). *Imperfect Histories: The elusive past and the legacy of romantic historicism*. Ithaca, NY: Cornell University Press.

Rozett, Martha T. (2003). *Constructing a World: Shakespeare's England and the New Historical Fiction*. Albany, NY: State University of New York Press.

Rushdie, Salman (1991). Outside the whale. In: *Imaginary Homelands: Essays and criticism 1981–1991* (pp. 87–101). London: Granta (first published 1984).

Samuel, Raphael (1994). *Theatres of Memory*, vol. 1: *Past and Present in Contemporary Culture*. London: Verso.

Scanlan, Margaret (1990). *Traces of Another Time: History and politics in postwar British fiction*. Princeton, NJ: Princeton University Press.

Vice, Sue (2000). *Holocaust Fiction*. London: Routledge.

Wagner, Tamara S. (2003). "After another round of tissues": "bad time" fiction and the Amy Tan-syndrome in recent Singaporean novels. *Journal of Commonwealth Literature*, 38(2), 19–39.

White, Edmund (2003a). More history, less nature: the new historical novel must not sanitize the past for contemporary tastes. *Times Literary Supplement*, July 25, 11–13.

Williams, Raymond (1977). *Marxism and Literature*. New York: Oxford University Press.

Woodroof, M., reporting, with Hansen, L. hosting (2004). Well researched historical fiction makes a comeback. *Weekend Edition Sunday*, May 30.

Woolley, Persia (1997). *How to Write and Sell Historical Fiction*. Cincinnati, OH: Writers' Digest Books.

Worpole, Ken (1984). *Reading by Numbers: Contemporary publishing and popular fiction*. London: Comedia.

FICTION

Ackroyd, Peter (1983). *The Last Testament of Oscar Wilde*. London: Hamish Hamilton.

Ackroyd, Peter (1985). *Hawksmoor*. London: Hamish Hamilton.

Ackroyd, Peter (1987). *Chatterton*. London: Hamish Hamilton.

Ackroyd, Peter (1990). *Dickens*. London: Sinclair Stevenson.

Ackroyd, Peter (1996). *Milton in America*. London: Sinclair Stevenson

Aiken, Joan (1964). *Black Hearts in Battersea*. NY: Doubleday.

Amis, Martin (1991). *Time's Arrow*. London: Jonathan Cape.

Atwood, Margaret (1996). *Alias Grace*. London: Bloomsbury.

Avery, Gillian (1960). *The Elephant War*. London: Collins.

Bainbridge, Beryl (1996). *Every Man for Himself*. London: Duckworth.

Ballard, J. G. (1984). *Empire of the Sun*. London: Victor Gollancz.

Barker, Pat (1991). *Regeneration*. London: Viking.

Barker, Pat (1993). *The Eye in the Door*. London: Viking.

Barker, Pat (1995). *The Ghost Road*. London: Viking.

Barnes, Julian (1989). *A History of the World in 10^1/$_2$ Chapters*. London: Jonathan Cape.

Barth, John (1960). *The Sot Weed Factor*. New York: Doubleday.

de Bernières, Louis (1994). *Captain Corelli's Mandolin*. London: Secker & Warburg.

Borges, Jorge Luis (1964). *Labyrinths* (Donald A. Yates & James E. Irby, eds.). New York: New Directions (first published 1962).

Burgess, Anthony (1980). *Earthly Powers*. London: Hutchinson.

Burton, Hester (1962). *Castors Away!* Oxford: Oxford University Press.

Byatt, A. S. (1989). *Possession: A romance*. London: Chatto & Windus.

Byatt, A. S. (2000). *The Biographer's Tale*. London: Chatto & Windus.

Carey, Peter (1997). *Jack Maggs*. London: Faber.

Carey, Peter (2000). *The True History of the Kelly Gang*. St Lucia: University of Queensland Press.

Colegate, Isabel (1984). *The Orlando Trilogy*. London: Penguin (first published 1969–73).

Davies, Stevie (1999). *Impassioned Clay*. London: Women's Press.

DeLillo, Don (1988) *Libra*. New York: Viking.

Donoghue, Emma (2000). *Slammerkin*. London: Virago.

Doyle, Roddy (1999). *A Star Called Henry*. London: Jonathan Cape.

Dunant, Sarah (2003). *The Birth of Venus*. London: Little, Brown.

Dunmore, Helen (2001). *The Siege*. London: Viking.

Eco, Umberto (1983). *The Name of the Rose* (trans. William Weaver). London: Secker & Warburg (first published 1980).

Evaristo, Bernardine (2001). *The Emperor's Babe*. London: Viking.

Farrell, J. G. (1978). *The Singapore Grip*. London: Weidenfeld & Nicolson.

Fowles, John (1969). *The French Lieutenant's Woman*. London: Jonathan Cape.

Fraser, George Macdonald (1969). *Flashman: From the Flashman Papers, 1839–1842*. London: Herbert Jenkins.

García Màrquez, Gabriel (1970). *One Hundred Years of Solitude* (trans. Gregory Rabassa). London: Jonathan Cape (first published 1967).

Garner, Alan (1976). *The Stone Book.* London: Collins.

Ghosh, Amitav (2000). *The Glass Palace.* London: HarperCollins.

Goddard, Robert (1986). *Past Caring.* London: Robert Hale.

Goddard, Robert (1998). *Caught in the Light.* London: Bantam.

Harris, Robert (1992). *Fatherland.* London: Hutchinson.

Hensher, Philip (2002). *The Mulberry Empire.* London: Flamingo.

Ishiguro, Kazuo (1989). *The Remains of the Day.* London: Faber.

Keneally, Thomas (1982). *Schindler's Ark.* London: Serpentine.

Mantel, Hilary (1992). *A Place of Greater Safety.* London: Viking.

McCann, Maria (2001). *As Meat Loves Salt.* London: Flamingo.

McCullough, Colleen (1977). *The Thorn Birds.* London: Macdonald & Jane.

McEwan, Ian (2001). *Atonement.* London: Jonathan Cape.

Mo, Timothy (1986). *An Insular Possession.* London: Chatto & Windus.

Moore, Brian (1985). *Black Robe.* London: Jonathan Cape.

Mosley, Nicholas (1990). *Hopeful Monsters.* London: Secker & Warburg.

Norfolk, Lawrence (1991). *Lemprière's Dictionary.* London: Sinclair Stevenson.

O'Brian, Patrick (1970). *Master and Commander.* London: Collins.

O'Brian, Patrick (1980). *The Surgeon's Mate.* London: Collins.

O'Brian, Patrick (1981). *The Ionian Mission.* London: Collins.

O'Brian, Patrick (1983). *Treason's Harbour.* London: Collins.

O'Brian, Patrick (1984). *The Far Side of the World.* London: Collins.

O'Brian, Patrick (1986). *The Reverse of the Medal.* London: Collins.

O'Brian, Patrick (1988). *The Letter of Marque.* London: Collins.

O'Brian, Patrick (1989). *The Thirteen-gun Salute.* London: Collins.

Ondaatje, Michael (1976). *Coming Through Slaughter.* Toronto: Anansi Press.

Ondaatje, Michael (1987). *In the Skin of a Lion.* Toronto: McClelland & Stewart.

Pears, Ian (1997). *An Instance of the Fingerpost.* London: Jonathan Cape.

Peters, Ellis (1977). *A Morbid Taste for Bones.* London: Macmillan.

Peyton, K. M. (1969). *Flambards in Summer.* Oxford: Oxford University Press.

Phillips, Caryl (1993). *Crossing the River.* London: Bloomsbury.

Powell, Anthony (1951–75). *A Dance to the Music of Time,* 12 vols. London: Heinemann.

Raine, Craig (1994). *History: The home movie.* London: Penguin.

Rhys, Jean (1966). *Wide Sargasso Sea.* London: Andre Deutsch.

Robertson, James (2000). *The Fanatic.* London: Fourth Estate.

Rushdie, Salman (1981). *Midnight's Children.* London: Jonathan Cape.

Rushdie, Salman (1988). *The Satanic Verses.* London: Viking.

Scott, Paul (1966–75). *The Raj Quartet,* 4 vols. London: Heinemann.

Sidhwa, Bapsi (1988). *Ice-Candy-Man.* London: Heinemann.

Sutcliff, Rosemary (1954). *The Eagle of the Ninth.* Oxford: Oxford University Press.

Swift, Graham (1983). *Waterland.* London: Heinemann.

Thorpe, Adam (1992). *Ulverton*. London: Secker & Warburg.

Treece, Henry (1963). *Horned Helmet*. Leicester: Brockhamton.

Tremain, Rose (1989). *Restoration*. London: Hamish Hamilton.

Turtledove, Harry (2002). *Ruled Britannia*. London: Penguin.

Unsworth, Barry (1992). *Sacred Hunger*. London: Hamish Hamilton.

Unsworth, Barry (1999). *Losing Nelson*. London: Hamish Hamilton.

Walsh, Jill Paton (1967). *Dolphin Crossing*. London: Macmillan.

Walsh, Jill Paton (1994). *Knowledge of Angels*. Cambridge: Green Bay.

Waters, Sarah (1999). *Affinity*. London: Virago.

White, Edmund (2003b). *Fanny*. London: Chatto & Windus.

Willard, Barbara (1970). *The Lark and the Laurel. The Mantlemass Chronicles.*
    London: Penguin

Winterson, Jeanette (1987). *The Passion*. London: Bloomsbury.

Winterson, Jeanette (1989). *Sexing the Cherry*. London: Bloomsbury.

Chapter 9

The Woman Writer and the Continuities of Feminism

Patricia Waugh

In *The Whole Woman* (2000), her rallying call for a new, third-wave feminism, Germaine Greer lambastes the apostasy of feminists of her own generation who think the battles have all been won. Her real ire, however, is reserved for those contemporary "lifestyle" feminists who assume the movement was only ever about having it all: the success-ful career, the perfect relationship, the modelesque body. In her view, the womanpower of the seventies has given way to girl power; the rounded contours of the adult female form to the body-fascistic linea-ments of a Barbie doll. The feminine mystique has passed from the magic of the perfectly hygienic home to the mirage of unblemished but entirely cosmeticized feminine beauty. A female obsession with routing the final mote of dust is now transferred to the eradication of that last pucker of cellulite. Postfeminism has embraced artifice, endless performance, self-fashioning, and empowered sexuality. According to Greer, its perspective on seventies' feminists is to regard them as literal-minded, naive, flat-chested, puritanical, and politically correct team-players for whom the achievement of equality required the erasure of individual pleasure and freedom. But for Greer, the new "girl power" of postfeminism is entirely a betrayal of that political feminism which sought to liberate women from a patriarchally controlled and socially constructed femininity. Once again, women have become "illusionists. They fake light-heartedness, girlishness and orgasm; they also fake the roses in their cheeks, the thickness, colour and curliness of their hair, the tininess of their waists, the longness of their legs and the size and shape of their breasts" (Greer 2000: 33). Women have become female impersonators of themselves. Dungarees and dreams of utopia have been abandoned for big hair and business suits and then again for bad-girl sluttishness and ladette-style japes. Distinctions between self-mutilation and self-fashioning dissolve and, like Ruth, the heroine of Fay Weldon's *Life and Loves of a She-Devil* (1983), woman has become Dr Frankenstein to her own monstrous body, asserting herself in gestures of resistance which entirely collude with and acknowledge the hegemony of the oppressive system, the Iron Maiden of feminine attractiveness. Self-fashioning is self-assertion and self-esteem and self-control. Performance is power. The answer to the question of "what is a woman" seems as remote in 2005 as it did in 1968: the difference is that the very unanswerability of the question is now regarded as a source of empowerment rather than oppression. Neither custom nor politics seems to have staled the infinite variety of the feminine. De Beauvoir's words resonate, but with irony: one is not born, but becomes a woman.

So it would seem that feminism has run aground on the groundlessness of feminine identity. To talk of women's writing might seem as much of a tautology as to speak of "men's writing" (but imagine an essay in a volume such as this on the construction and deconstruction of "the male writer" of the period). Much is made therefore of the need to distinguish between prefeminist, feminist, and postfeminist phases in women's writing, with the period covered by the present volume marked by the turn of the "post-." For critics like Greer, the specifically postmodern obsession with gender-performance has now killed off feminism, and young women have fallen for the performatives of Judith Butler and the Beauty Myth without seeing any contradiction between them. Feminist polemicists such as Greer, Naomi Wolf, and Natasha Walters have therefore called for a New Wave where feminism renounces its complicity with the postmodern, reclaims nature for women, and abandons the obsession with identity for more traditional political questions of rights, equality, and justice. All bemoan the postmodern dissipation of female writerly energies previously directed toward political commitment into an obsession, not so much with sexual politics, as with *sex*, plain and simple. Greer cites the market success of Helen Fielding's 1996 novel *Bridget Jones's Diary* as evidence of the extent to which the contemporary woman writer has renounced her commitment to feminist politics: "Bridget, whose head has room for little other than beauty routines, sexual fantasies, envious thoughts and narcissistic panic about her looks, is thin enough to get her man. She will soon be baring her empty little soul in cinemas and on video" (Greer 2000: 314). For Greer, just as women had begun to digest and somehow believe in that ubiquitous line of feminist graffiti that had announced that "a woman needs a man like a fish needs a bicycle," along comes Bridget, thirty-something successful career woman, well-versed in seventies' feminism, but still thoroughly reveling in and parading her emotional neediness, her fears about cellulite, her continuous romantic fantasies, and her various sexual hang-ups.

Bridget Jones began life as a successful column in the *Independent* newspaper, written in the form of a diary addressed to a close friend, but transferred to novel format, it immediately rose to bestseller status. Rather than seeing its popularity as evidence of a now dominant postfeminist mindset, one might point to similarities between it and the so-called "novel of liberation" by writers such as Erica Jong, Lisa Alter, Marilyn French, and Kate Millett, in the seventies. Like Erica Jong's *Fear of Flying* (1973), for example, *Bridget Jones* seemed to capture the *zeitgeist*. Both novels are responses to the pressure of feminism as a utopian politics in that they depict heroines who come to recognize that happiness lies precisely in not striving for perfection. But to so-called "third wave" theorists and other critics of the supposedly postmodern, postfeminist phase in contemporary British fiction, *Bridget* is a symptom of feminism's current midlife crisis: her daughters are ungrateful and leaving home; the "sacred cows" of her life's mission are in question; and she is under pressure to submit to a complete makeover, or risk stagnation as retro without the *chic*.

Such concerns are perfectly understandable, but the apocalypticism is unnecessary. Turning from feminist polemic to women's literary writing, it is apparent that there have always been plenty of women writers who have not only reveled in their "illusionism," but have seen it as perfectly compatible with an entirely serious commitment to fight for the political liberation of their sex. Virginia Woolf has been such an iconic figure for women writers in the contemporary period because she combined a serious, rational, and clear-eyed sense of the gender injustices of modernity with a writerly, playful, and self-consciously "feminine" attitude to the gendering of rationality itself. This is evident not only in the more hortatory texts such as *Three Guineas* (1938), but throughout much of the fiction and in the lectures which were written up as *A Room of One's Own* (1929), or the parodic biography *Orlando* (1928), dedicated to Vita Sackville-West, with its dizzying constructions and deconstructions of gender positions. Woolf recognized early on that to write as a woman within the rationalistic terms of post-Cartesian modernity is to risk abandonment of the sexed body and the embodied voice as constitutive of difference. But she realized, as well, that to turn the "feminine" simply into writing, or semiotic practice, clothing, and performance, is equally to risk dissolving her into a convenient cipher of marginality for a male avant-garde willing its own exclusion from bourgeois mores and constraining rationalities. So she recommends in *Three Guineas* that women form a "society of outsiders" who resist assimilation into patriarchal structures by rewriting the plots and stories, who are self-conscious mimics and ventriloquists, but who can speak in tropes *and* walk in sensible shoes (to use Nancy Miller's arresting phrase; Miller 1982: 53). Despite her qualms and concerns, Woolf killed the Angel in the House not with the weapons of war or anger, but through writing, aesthetic play, and performance.

This essay will therefore diverge not only from the generational partisanship of critics like Greer, but also to some extent from the emphases of the Companion as a whole. Rather than stressing the unique concerns or qualities of post-1978 – i.e. "postmodern" or ostensibly "postfeminist" – women's writing, I will be arguing a case for underlying continuities in British women's fiction since even before the emergence of the women's liberation movement in the late 1960s. To be sure, the political and discursive valences of feminism have shifted since 1978, becoming, depending on one's point of view, either more complex and sophisticated or more frivolous and irrelevant. And these changes have been effected by, as well as reflected in, contemporary women's fiction. But this does not mean that earlier fiction writers were somehow naive about gender politics, nor that women writers of the contemporary period have written about nothing else, nor that by now the entire issue of gender and authorship has been consigned to history. If there are shifts and phases in women's writing and feminist theory from the so-called "personal" to the so-called "postmodern," we should not be too rigid in our attempts at periodization, nor assume that there is only one way to be personal, one way to be postmodern. A preferable option might be to see various phases characterized by a rhetorical "dominant," but each drawing on aesthetic strategies and thematic preoccupations which predate and outlast that particular historical moment.

191

Theory, Politics, and the Tradition of "Cautious Feminism"

How might these phases be characterized? First, a pre-theorized and ambivalent phase beginning in the sixties and involving writers such as Iris Murdoch, Doris Lessing, Sylvia Plath, Simone de Beauvoir, and Muriel Spark. Second, a phase of explicitly "writing as a woman," and involving, above all, a quest to reconcile the collective with the personal voice, to explore the reverberations of "the personal is political" as in the continuing work of Lessing, Greer, Millett, Rich; the "midd-leground" or in the metafictionalized realism of writers such as Margaret Drabble, Anita Brookner, Pat Barker, A. S. Byatt, and early Margaret Atwood; as well as the Gothic and carnivalesque fiction of the early Fay Weldon and Angela Carter. Finally, emerging in the 1980s, a third phase of explicit engagement with the challenges of postmodernism and postcolonialism, the moment when feminism enters fully the "wilderness": the moment of high (poststructuralist) theory and the proliferation of difference, as women writers turn self-consciously and deliberately to the parodic and the fantastic, to masquerade and monstrosity, as, for example, in the later work of Weldon and Carter, and in the writing of Jeanette Winterson, Zadie Smith, and Monica Ali.

Feminism itself seems at present to have embarked upon a moment of Hegelian synthesis, working over the expressive realist thesis of the early years and the antithetical deconstructions of the eighties and early nineties, to return to a reconsideration of experience, rights, and subjectivities, in the context of a new era of globalization and multiculturalism and in response to new threats from biotechnologies and the recently rejuvenated discourses of sociobiology. Whereas for some this might seem to constitute a falling off from the utopianism of the seventies, it may represent an attempt to integrate feminist perspectives into the Realpolitik of broader social and political concerns. One could read both *Bridget Jones* and *White Teeth* (2000) from either perspective, of course. But both interpretations could equally be made of the fiction of Iris Murdoch, Doris Lessing, and Simone de Beauvoir, all of them born just as World War I came to an end and who began writing in the decade before feminist activism. Indeed, women novelists throughout the past four decades have refused to confine themselves to a narrow feminist agenda and have often taken up positions antithetical to those of the dominant feminist politics of their time. Doris Lessing's *Memoirs of a Survivor*, for example, published in 1974, was criticized by feminist theorists for biological essentialism. In her vision of a post-nuclear future, she dared to engage seriously with revived evolutionary theories and with sociobiological ideas about gender roles, leadership, group survival, and sexual selection at a time when any departure from culturalist assumptions tended to be regarded by academic theorists as potentially fascistic.

In fact, social constructionisms and postmodern textualisms have been cautiously assimilated into an indigenous fictional tradition where ethical commitment has often allied itself with a broad empiricism skeptical of the claims and preoccupations of academic high theory. In A. S. Byatt's 1990 Booker Prize-winning novel, *Possession*, for example, her literary academics Maud and Roland begin by conducting their historical research into a Victorian passionate romance entirely within the sterile discourses of late twentieth-century theory, with its talk of decentering, dissolution, and desire. Byatt enjoys herself enormously parodying the excesses of theory. The plot is ostentatiously manipulated so that their initially unacknowledged feelings for each other are only recognized and their researches completed when theory is abandoned for the sensual pleasures of the text and (ironically of course) the authorial voice of Byatt herself. This skeptical orientation reflects a mainstream intellectual temper broadly left liberal in ethos; concerned with moral considerations and the ongoing need for contracts protecting human rights; and requiring the belief that being reasonable requires assertions to be supported by evidence that is not simply the property of one group or "language game" but is, as far as possible, universalizable and applicable to all human beings. So most fiction writers in the period have been as wary of political correctness as they have of academic "theory," and women writers have been no exception, despite the mounting pressures as feminism has become, since the late 1970s, both a major subfield of academic theory and an arena in which political agendas are fiercely scrutinized and critiqued.

In 1980, for example, in an interview with Diana Cooper-Clark in *Atlantic Monthly*, the novelist Margaret Drabble complained of her sense of the pressure on the contemporary woman writer to produce politically correct role models that might contribute to the emancipation of women: "If I end with marriage, it's going to be seen as a mistake; if I end with a woman alone, it's going to be regarded as a triumph. All you can do is to write about how it seems to you to happen at the time" (Cooper-Clark 1980). The interview was entitled "Margaret Drabble: cautious feminist." Indeed, Drabble's stance of measured

193

political engagement tempered by a commitment to artistic integrity was not unusual for a woman writer speaking just 12 years after the inauguration of the Women's Liberation Movement and the headiest decade of second-wave feminism. Also not unusual for the time is her assumption that the two sets of demands, for political activism and an aesthetic honesty in holding the mirror up to culture, rarely if ever entirely coalesce: commitment, to either art or politics, is likely to be hindered rather than helped by correctness.

Drabble has resisted the artifice of the ideal political role model, demonstrating a preference for the broadly realist sense of the novelist as a recorder of "the way things are." But even those writers such as Angela Carter, for example, who are more explicitly committed to feminist politics and more formally adventurous in their engagements with the postmodern, are equally resistant to the indiscriminate aestheticization, or idealization of female experience and identities. For Carter, Byatt, and Drabble began writing in the shadow of that earlier generation of women writers, Lessing, Spark, and Murdoch, who had come of age during World War II. After Nazism, it had seemed evident to them that the projection of Promethean desire beyond the controlled realm of art had, as often as not, realized a hell of violence rather then an aestheticized utopia. The countercultural and situationist slogans which fed into the liberation movements of the sixties, of taking one's desires for reality, even more than the technocratic state, could be seen to invest in a potentially destructive aestheticization of experience. Women writers of this generation therefore were often both cautious about utopian politics and also anxious to explore the issue of female authorship in the context of broader ethical and political commitments. Given their concern with differentiating between the intentional fictions of the artistic imagination and those epistemologically distinct orders in the world beyond art, these writers deployed metafictional textualism as an ethical tool rather than one of indiscriminate ontological pluralization – and in this respect they have exerted an enduring influence. We can trace forward from the 1970s an unbroken line of women writers whose "cautious," rationalist engagement with metafictionality and formal experimentalism stands as a useful corrective in an era which has increasingly revealed the complicity of the postmodern with the commercial, and of self-fashioning with late capitalist consumption.

Iris Murdoch's *The Black Prince* (1973), *A Fairly Honourable Defeat* (1970), or *The Flight from the Enchanter* (1955), for example, or Spark's

The Prime of Miss Jean Brodie (1961), or *Not to Disturb* (1971), or *The Abbess of Crewe* (1974) are ostensibly comically metafictional stories about the gendered illusions of romantic love or of comedic institutionalized role play, but they also explore the myth-making imperatives of power politics and totalitarianism and the dangerous uses of fictionality and self-fashioning. This deployment of the formal properties of fantasy and postmodern experimentalism in the service of a skeptical rationalism is equally evident in the more explicitly feminist writers of the next generation. Angela Carter's fiction from the beginning deployed postmodern performativity and fantasy in the service of a realistic and broadly rational but never "correct" feminist politics. In her novel *The Infernal Desire Machines of Doctor Hoffman* (1972), for example, she paints a darkly negative picture of a world liberated (Situationist-style) into the materialization of desire. The militaristic rationalism of the Minister is equally condemned, however, as a similarly fantastical scholasticism, and the novel suggests the need to work toward a representation of human subjectivity where reason and desire are neither opposed nor split along gender lines, and where utopian rationalisms and irrationalisms finally bow to an empirical skepticism which keeps political feet securely on the ground of an Orwellian two plus two equals four. In the worlds of both Dr Hoffman and the Minister, women are abused and subjugated eunuchs. The narrator, Desiderio (a kind of latter-day Winston Smith), learns that the disconnection of reason from affect has produced only superficially opposed political regimes: a politics grounded in the indiscriminate liberation of desire is as likely to produce a totalitarian regime as one grounded in the rational formalisms of pure logic.

Carter's resistance to a fully postmodern semiosis was always based in her recognition that without an identity grounded in "experiences of the body," even one fractured by differences of race, class, sexuality, and ethnicity, feminism could hardly survive as a political movement of solidarity among women. What would it mean otherwise to talk about "the woman writer"? For if gender is a "free-floating artifice, with the consequence that man and masculinity might just as easily signify a female body as a male one, and women and feminine a male body as easily as a feminine one" (Butler 1993), then the body, paradoxically, and as in Descartes' *Discourse on Method*, ceases to matter and, as matter, becomes expendable in the very construction of subjectivity and authorship. Judith Butler's theoretical project of the 1980s and 1990s, for example, began with the familiar insistence that it is "wrong to assume that there is a category of 'women' that simply needs to be filled in with various components of race, class, age, ethnicity and sexuality in order to become complete," reiterating the idea that the meaning of woman and of the feminine must always be indeterminate (Butler 1990: 209). But she goes much further than this in claiming that the sexed body is itself always ever an imitation that actually produces what it claims to imitate. For Butler's performative body is entirely *disembodied*: within speech-act theory, a performative is a discursive practice that produces what it names, so that, "the norm of sex takes hold to the extent that it is 'cited' as such a norm, but it also derives its power from the citations that it compels" (Butler 1993: 15). In the end, "body matters" in poststructuralist feminism seems to mean that the body as matter does not matter: a Cartesian claim if ever there was one. But the body does matter, at least to what has been the dominant perspective within British women's fiction for more than 30 years. Even as seemingly frivolous a novelistic treatment of the woman's body as *Bridget Jones*, in which the diarist begins every entry with a calorie count and thigh measurement, can be seen as a skeptical antidote not only to the puritanical associations of political correctness but to the excesses of textualist theory.

Greer herself has declared in *The Whole Woman* that "a woman's body is the battlefield where she fights for liberation. It is through her body that oppression works, reifying her, sexualizing her, victimizing her, disabling her" (Greer 2000: 135). Most women novelists of recent decades have thoroughly engaged with this perception, and in a variety of literary modes. Monstrous bodies, anorectic bodies, hybrid bodies, cyborg bodies, fantastic bodies, zombies (bodies without souls) fill the pages of women writers from the sixties to the nineties: Muriel Spark's *The Public Image* (1968) and *The Hothouse by the East River* (1973), Fay Weldon's *Puffball* (1980) and *The Life and Loves of a She-Devil* (1983), Lessing's *Memoirs of a Survivor* (1974) and *The Fifth Child* (1988), Carter's *The Passion of New Eve* (1977) and *Nights at the Circus* (1984), Winterson's *Sexing the Cherry* (1989) and *Written on the Body* (1992). In all of these fictions, the monstrous body functions not only as a means to voice and overcome anxieties concerning dominant constructions of femininity as uncontrollability and irrationality, but also as a way of asserting the contingency of matter over and against the crystalline perfections of rationalistic philosophy. The body, in this indigenous novelistic tradition, is both the topos of a "cautious" feminist politics and a firewall against the more extravagant claims of academic feminist theory.

Identity, Experience, and Female Authorship

Perhaps because the women's liberation movement as such lasted for only a decade, from 1968 to 1978, after which it seemed to splinter into a bewildering diversity of identity politics and abstruse theoretical disputes, commentators often argue for sharp distinctions between a pre-1968 and a post-1978 generation of women writers, with the latter far more alert to the instabilities of the very category of woman. But here again, I would insist on strong lines of continuity; there has in fact been an anxious dialogue on the nature of feminine identity and female authorship throughout the entire period. The Movement for Women's Liberation emerged out of the upsurge of countercultural political activism of the sixties and alongside radical movements such as Gay Liberation, Black Power, and the Civil Rights Movement. In 1968, the grassroots women's movement set out to analyze the sources of oppression within patriarchal societies and began its task of liberating women by campaigning for equal pay and opportunities, equal human rights, the eradication of sexist assumptions, and the deconstruction of woman as "the second sex." Almost immediately, however, feminists recognized that issues about rights and freedoms are not easily dissociated from representations of human needs, and that the procedural discourses of the legal system are woefully inadequate tools for the articulation of such human requirements as respect, affection, dignity, and recognition. Consequently, the energies of the movement came to be absorbed more and more with questions concerning identity – "who am I," as much as "what is to be done?"

Such questions are traditionally the concern of literature and culture rather than activist or campaigning politics. Early on, therefore, feminists turned to art and literature as a means of working through contradictions that seemed intractable when addressed through traditional political and philosophical discourses. The power of symbolic representation and cultural embodiment in constructing and containing identities and subjectivities was recognized from the first as a definitive aspect of a new kind of political movement. Given these expectations, it has long been necessary for women writers to grapple with their status and function as "women writers," and to conceive their work as bearing some relation with the new feminist politics.

Though Drabble suggests otherwise, it was precisely the capacity of the literary text to explore and represent contradiction, ambivalence, and paradox that recommended literary forms to feminist writers in

197

the early seventies. As a political movement seeking equality and the recognition of gendered identities, feminism had very quickly come up against the contradiction which would preoccupy theorists throughout the seventies and eighties: how might women affirm a feminine identity historically constructed through the very cultural and ideological formations which feminism as a movement was also seeking to challenge and deconstruct? So that, despite the early commitment to the uncovering of a unified and collective women's "voice," the idea of the "feminine" seemed only sustainable, even then, as an ambiguously double-voiced affirmation and negation of identity. As Elaine Showalter argued in her important essay of 1981, "Feminist criticism in the wilderness," any feminist re-visioning (to use Adrienne Rich's term) will require both an impulse toward, and a resistance to, the concept of the feminine, to identity as Woman (Showalter: 1985: 247–8). Like the Derridean "trace," women's voice and identity seemed from the start both available and under erasure. The idea that women might liberate themselves from false consciousness to uncover a buried but authentic female self was quickly recognized as having the potential simply to facilitate the reproduction of that patriarchal construction of femininity which feminists had set out to contest. For what could such a self be except a construction of patriarchy? And if one asserted the radical feminist belief in a female essence marginalized and undervalued and residing somehow in "the body" then the danger here was of collapsing gender back into sex and biological essentialism. Not only must feminism engage with profound differences in women's cultural situations, but also with the problem that, even allowing for such difference, the entry into the symbolic order of culture entails that one's voice, unlike one's room, may never be one's own.

This problematic of the "woman writer" took particularly vexing shape because the rise of the women's movement coincided with the impact of postmodern critiques of authorship as such. Foremost among these critiques was Roland Barthes' seminal essay "The death of the author," published in French in 1968 and translated into English in the mid-1970s. Just as popular and academic feminism had begun to take up the metaphor of authorship as a means of describing the need to rewrite patriarchal scripts, Barthes' essay became the center-plank of a new literary theory which proposed to unravel the very concept of authorship together with all its liberal humanist underpinnings: the unified subject, "voice," "expression," "intentionality," and intellectual property. The essay was an assault generally on humanist and essentialist notions of authorship and, in particular, on the idea that an author "expresses" (him)self by translating inner feelings, moods, and ideas into words on the page: the suggestion is of something anterior to or buried being forced from inside to an outside and of some abstract condition as yet unspoken finding concrete formulation in words. Barthes argued that it was time to dispense altogether with the idea of an author as an antecedent intentionality and to reconceive the literary enterprise as a play of intertextualities, a writing that writes, a figure that insistently becomes its own ground. For it is language that speaks and not the author. Words would no longer express a personality but simply translate an already-formed diction-ary of endless deferral and intertextuality.

This is not Virginia Woolf's conscious formulation of a tradition, the thinking back through one's mothers, the patient task of constructing a literary lineage: Barthes' writing is liberation from filiation altogether, from the author conceived as the "past of his own book ... in the same relation of antecedence to his work as a father to his child" (Barthes 1977: 145). Not surprisingly, therefore, muting the vocal optimism of early confessional women's writing is a strain of ambiva-lence and self-reflexive doubt. From the late sixties onwards, writers such as Drabble, Lessing, Murdoch, and Spark would begin to use their fictions specifically to raise formal and existential questions about voice and authorship. Such formalist self-reflexivity exists well before the splintering of the women's movement into the identity politics of the eighties. Such fictions often depict alter-ego writer-protagonists, so that Doris Lessing's *The Golden Notebook* (1962) could be regarded almost as the prototype of a new genre of *Kunstlerroman* concerned specifically with the plight of the female author. By 1978, feminism had established itself as a broad cultural politics working on a plural-ity of fronts. Major academic journals flourished in the eighties and nineties: *Signs* (launched in 1976), *m/f* in (1978), and *Feminist Review* (1979). Independent feminist and women's presses, negotiating the terrain between the academic and the broader literary culture, were established at the same time: Virago in 1973, Onlywomen (1974), The Women's Press (1977), Sheba (1980), and Pandora (1981), and the seventies and eighties saw a "woman-centered" publishing boom of unprecedented scale. Certainly this discursive plurality, wherein lay its capacity to avoid definitive capture, ultimately threw up difficulties for feminism as an activist movement and led by the nineties to both the idea of a postfeminism and a new third-wave feminism. Factions and splinterings occurred not only across differences of class, race, and sexuality, but at the interfaces of the popular and the academic and between earlier and later phases. Any account of such inter-relationships within feminism, however, cannot afford to ignore the significance of shifting cultural contexts outside of feminism. There was a marked tendency in the eighties and nineties, for example, for postmodern feminists to regard women's writing of the seventies as naïve and undertheorized, concerned to articulate a non-problematic feminine identity through expressive realist and confessional modes of writing. But this is to read that work purely within the frame of our own cultural preoccupations. As feminism strengthened itself within the academy, taking on the professionalized apparatus of scholarship and theory, personal and confessional discourses began to seem unsophisticated and lacking in rigor. Moreover, the personal and the confessional were appropriated in the nineties as powerful and effective media tools in the patriarchal hands of Western national governments and global superpowers seeking to control the political agenda through strategies of domestication and sentimentalization. The Jerry Springer-style confession and the newsworthy eyewitness account have become ways of distracting attention from more fundamental issues concerning those relations of economics and power which finally underpin lifestyles and intimate relationships. It is not surprising that feminism in the eighties began to take flight from "experience" and to develop a romance with those high theorists of deconstruction for whom the "subject" was only ever a position in discourse. But the situation was very different in the seventies. Consciousness-raising, confessional writing, and the quest to find new forms in which to explore women's experience, were practiced in conjunction with a Marxist-feminist analysis of economic oppression and an existential critique of liberal exclusion and separation of the public and the private. Confession was part of an attempt to forge, for the very first time, the political solidarity of a woman-centered culture organized to subvert the patriarchal structures (political and economic) of the liberal state. I am suggesting there are more continuities between writers of the earlier and the later period than is sometimes thought, and that even those writers who appear more conservative or traditionalist or reactionary often turn out, on closer inspection, to be more experimental and more sympathetic to the concerns of contemporary feminism than either a narrowly politically correct or explicitly postmodern agenda might suggest.

Most of the important women writers of the sixties and early seventies drew quite self-consciously on the resources of the aesthetic to resist what Lessing explicitly identified in *The Golden Notebook* (1962) as that intellectual form of ideological "bullying" (whether patriarchal or matriarchal) that favors the abstract and systematic over the fluid, the material, and the contingent. Drabble's sense too of the difficulty of finding a comfortable mode of authorship as a woman is about the need to avoid stepping out of patriarchal straightjackets into those of political or any kind of correctness. Viewed in this light, novels that predate the women's liberation movement and that seem indifferent to feminist politics can be seen to engage with such issues. Muriel Spark's Jean Brodie, for example, in *The Prime of Miss Jean Brodie* (1961) is eventually betrayed by one of her set, the soon-to-be-converted Sandy Stranger, and condemned for her romantic and (politically) dangerous confusion of art and life; but in the context of the morally puritanical and "correct" culture of her own time (middle class, "respectable" Edinburgh in the thirties), she is also curiously sympathetic and genuinely charismatic. Spark's novel, though ostensibly about an egotistical and romantic schoolteacher who flirts with Fascism, is also an early self-reflection on the problem of female authorship. Jean Brodie is a brilliant creation because she is genuinely monstrous and yet her monstrosity is largely the consequence of the restricted possibility for revolt against the patriarchs of a narrow Presbyterianism. Her author, like Sandy Stranger, rightly condemns her ethical blindness, yet also presents her stubborn waywardness in a proto-feminist, as well as an austerely Augustinian light. Viewed from this perspective, one of the most fascinating aspects of the writing of radical women who begin their careers before but continued writing into the sixties and seventies (de Beauvoir, Murdoch, Lessing, Spark) and beyond, is their attempt to sustain universalist or transcendent modes of representation while reconciling them with a sense of identity as perspectival and radically situated in specific bodies. The strategy is often to interrogate a grand narrative and to reveal it as wanting *from the woman's point of view*: communism for Lessing, liberalism for Murdoch, existentialism for De Beauvoir, and Christian doctrine for Spark. Each of them longs to write a "book powered with an intellectual or moral passion strong enough to create order, to create a new way of looking at life" (Lessing 1973: 61). Of these three, Iris Murdoch might seem the least interested in a feminist perspective on cultural politics, reflecting her preference for writing "about things on the whole where it doesn't matter whether you're male or female, in which case you'd better be male, because a man represents ordinary human beings, unfortunately as things stand at the moment, whereas a woman is always a woman! . . . It's a freer world that you are in as

201

a man than a woman" (Murdoch 1978: 82). But De Beauvoir too announced in the preface to *The Second Sex* (published in France in 1949) that "enough ink has been spilled in quarrelling over feminism, now practically over, and perhaps we should say no more about it" (de Beauvoir 1972: xix). And Lessing herself never revised her opinion that we should "stop talking about men and women writers. Our whole language, the way we think, is set up for putting things into departments. We've got far more in common with each other than what separates us" (Lessing 1996: 61).

But as humanists who profoundly challenge the assumptions of humanism from within, these three writers are still relevant to a feminism now trying to negotiate its way out of the impasses of the postmodern. What unites them as writers is their search for a model of self-reflexive consciousness as an opening out into the world which proceeds from a radical embeddedness in which the "body" is not simply a text overwritten by culture, but a situation through which we experience our very subjectivity: for "the body is not a thing, it is a situation . . . it is the instrument of our grasp on the world" (de Beauvoir 1972: 34). Despite Murdoch's shared ambivalence about writing as a woman and her famous preference for male narrators, she too uses her fiction to demonstrate the negative consequences for human flourishing of scientific liberalism's acceptance of the so-called "naturalistic fallacy," the assumption that human values must be radically, that is to say logically, divorced from the facts of human biology. She was often regarded as (embarrassingly) essentialist by feminist theorists of the eighties. Yet her insistence on recognizing our bodily condition offered an alternative vision of the human where each of us is situated as an embodied but self-reflexive consciousness engaging a world that never presents itself simply as neutral "facts." Again, though, the more "universalist" position engages gender issues. In this world, goodness ever escapes the frantic egomaniacal fantasies and desires of her loquacious male artist-narrators and enchanters, and is more often to be discovered in the muted and tacit responses of those women characters or "feminized" males who, accepting the contingent, the brute materiality of the world, serve (often self-sacrificially) as the means to expose the seductive egotism of masculine desire in its will to absorb the world and the other into self-projected and crystalline schemes. Accordingly, good art is that which tempers a will to transcendence with an acceptance of immanence and, as "the most educational thing we have," art is valuable because of its "pierced nature . . . its limitless connection with ordinary life, even its defencelessness against its client" (Murdoch 1977: 86). Art is a means of countering what Lessing has also described as the thinning of language against the density of experience.

De Beauvoir too insisted on our radical embodiment. Biological facts are woefully insufficient as a justification for the "hierarchy of the sexes," but nevertheless, if our situated bodies are still, fundamentally, the "instrument of our grasp on the world" then "the world is bound to seem a very different thing when apprehended in one manner or another" (de Beauvoir 1972: 33). But for women, held merely as bodies within the defining gaze of the male, experience has been forcefully limited to an immanence precluding that projection forth into the full existence of participation in the universal. Like Murdoch, and unlike Sartre, she rejects the Hegelian concept of a subjectivity ever premised on the objectification of the other, and calls for an "ethics of ambiguity" which would recognize that "equivalent centre of self" (George Eliot's term) and allow for one's own ambiguous positioning as both subject and object. Though de Beauvoir retained a horror of the female body and a fear of being regarded as "just a woman," and though she refrains from the kind of critique of liberal universalism central to Murdoch's writing, she too offers a thoroughgoing critique of those Cartesian assumptions which have been instrumental in separating a feminized body from a masculinized model of rationality and mind.

Just as *The Second Sex* has been easily the most influential work of political philosophy on women writers in the period, Doris Lessing's *The Golden Notebook* was the earliest and most influential work of fiction to analyze the construction of femininity in the second half of the twentieth century. Both texts were often the chosen butts of feminist theory in the eighties. In the preface to the novel, Lessing justified her commitment to the Lukàcsian ideal of humanist character and to the writing of fiction as a means of exploring contingent experience, the "raw feel" of being a woman or a man living in the late twentieth century: "The way to deal with the problem of 'subjectivity', that shocking business of being preoccupied with the tiny individual who is at the same time caught up in such an explosion of terrible and marvellous possibilities, is to see him as a microcosm and in this way to break through the personal, the subjective, making the personal general, as indeed life always does, transforming a private experience . . . into something larger." But she also voiced her unease with the capacity of expressive realism to articulate the complex fragmentariness of late modernity in terms that neither reduce social experience to particularized flashes of insular personal emotion, nor subsume the particular into the generalized impersonality of the rationalized discourses of social science and political theory. Initially, Anna Wulf, the writer, tries to work her way through the problem and overcome her writer's block by separating herself out into distinct voices, one for each of her four notebooks, convinced that if the essence of neurosis is conflict, then dividing up, separating out the voices, is the way to stay sane. But in the final, golden notebook, she begins to break down and to experience a complete dissolution of the voices into each other and into those of other characters. For Lessing, only *immersion* in the cacophonous vocal chorus which is the "small personal voice" of the late twentieth century, offers a way of breaking through to new political identities for, as Martha Quest observes in *The Four-Gated City*, "when people open up a new area in themselves, start doing something new, then it must be clumsy and raw, like a baby trying to walk" (Lessing 1969). Lessing insisted that after the writing of *The Golden Notebook*, she had ceased to believe in the personal: but this is not some mode of poststructuralism *avant la lettre*; it is simply one of the ways in which, throughout the century, and particularly in the contemporary period, women writers have tried to expand and explore a semiotic feminine subjectivity without abandoning the category of "women's experience" and the concept of an authorial voice.

Since Woolf's time at least, then, women writers have explored the contradictoriness of female identity and recognized that the formulation of a unified "woman's voice" is as risky a strategy as its dissolution into a fluid and free-floating semiosis. Women writers have certainly plotted their escape from the common sitting room of domestic realism whose identification with femininity has produced a history of patriarchal constructions of the woman writer as variously silly, scribbling, confessional, irrationalist, miniaturist, imitative, baggy, or strident. But equally, they have sought to think back through their mothers and to valorize those aspects of women's experience that have been associated with the domestic activities of nurturance, care, and attendance. Often they have used fiction to explore the contradictions inherent in these various imperatives and in feminist theory. While affirming the concept of the feminine, for example, Angela Carter's *The Passion of New Eve* (1977) is also an exuberant critique of the fascistic tendencies in some versions of radical feminism. Fay Weldon's *The Cloning of Joanna May* (1989) comically upholds the gender liberationist potential of new biotechnologies while also providing a

riposte to Donna Haraway's utopian and postmodern feminist reading
of the cyborg in its insistence on the intimate relationship between
the new genetic intellectual property and the patriarchal long arm of
global capitalism. Many novels of the late sixties and seventies were
explicitly about the difficulties of female authorship. Muriel Spark's
The Driver's Seat (1970) explored the effects of the cultural hystericiza-
tion of the female body through her character Lise, who sets out to
take over the "driver's seat," to give authorship to her life by plotting
her own (clean) murder. But in her author's vocal control over the
verbal tense of the novel, and in its unnerving proleptic descriptions
of her actual demise (raped and then murdered), is reflected a measure of all the agency we have, as ruthless narrative projection brings
the future into the present and reminds us of those larger plots which
frustrate our authorial desires and impulses to scriptoral autonomy.
Each of Margaret Drabble's novels of the sixties is narrated by a writer
figure. *The Waterfall* (1969) used an unstable narrative voice to present
a critical view of a love affair through a first-person voice which
alternates with a third-person romance narrative. Her protagonist Jane
Grey comes to recognize how "I split myself. I went underground" in
order to avoid the direct vocalization of an anger which she fears
might "annihilate everything, any word of mine . . . might shatter them
all into fragments" (Drabble 1981: 114). Even Anita Brookner, who
repeatedly repudiated any association with feminist politics, produced
ambivalent romances such as *Hotel du Lac* (1984) and *Altered States*
(1996), which explored the split consciousnesses of literary women
who can neither comfortably masquerade in the public world of am-
bition, efficiency, and autonomy nor accept their feminine condition
of self-effacement, dependency, and silence.

Given the problematic relationship between women and voice, it is
hardly surprising that most of the great innovators in the use of free
indirect discourse (the quintessential mode of double-voicing, and the
perfect vehicle for mimicry, masquerade, subversion, satire, contested
authority, intimacy, dialogism, and irony) have been women writers.
Such experimentation with voice connects contemporary women
novelists like Weldon and Winterson not only to their immediate
predecessors in the generation of Lessing, Spark, and Murdoch, but
back to Woolf and even Austen. But it connects them, as well, to
contemporary feminist criticism and theory, in which we find an
equal fascination with varieties of simulation: with "strategy," for
example, as in the self-consciously adopted positionality of Spivak's
"strategic essentialism"; or with duplicitous masquerade as in Butler's

"drag performances"; or with "mimicry" as a form of reverse discourse in the writing of Luce Irigaray. Again, these are not utterly new and unprecedented discursive moves; to some degree, they might be viewed as variations on what Susan Sontag in the sixties referred to as a discourse of "camp," a subversive politics waged through the erotic pleasures of the (aesthetic) text.

Whether we are looking at women's fiction of the last quarter century or at the feminist theory of that period, then, we find a postmodernism which is more an elaboration and exaggeration of already available codes than an apocalyptic break with aesthetic tradition. Feminist writers such as Greer herself have been using vocal play since the very dawn of the women's liberation movement in the service of a cultural polemic arguably as slippery and polyphonic as any poststructuralist performance. Greer defied academic convention in producing confessional and polemical texts that repudiated the usual scholarly procedures of genuflection to authority, even-handed distribution of argument and counterargument, and extensive citations and referencing. In *The Female Eunuch* (1970), she claimed authorship as an independent voice whose authority to speak for others arose from a boldness in contesting distinctions between the academic and the popular, the scholarly and the journalistic, and the literary and the critical. This work combined the devices of popular oratory (denunciation, exhortation, *reductio ad absurdam*, mimicry, and ridicule) with those more restrained and impersonal conventions of academic "research" (factual citation, sociological analysis) and with the direct appeal of personal testimonial (intimate anecdotes and narrative reconstructions of experiences as a woman, elision of the split between the narrating and the narrated I) to induce a sense of shared intimacy with her readers, a rallying call to a "we," a collective first person who must speak out and denounce the "they" of oppression. There is no single voice of the "real" Germaine Greer in *The Female Eunuch* but a playful orchestration of multiple voices creating a polyphonic re-vision of the political treatise. For all her concerns about the "new," "postmodern" culture of performativity, Greer, like so many women writers before as well as after her, knows that authorial selves are always constructions and that in the end the "whole woman" herself is only ever an idealized projection of desire from within the degenerate myth of the "female eunuch."

References and Further Reading

NONFICTION

Barthes, Roland (1977). The death of the author. In: *Image–Music–Text* (trans. Stephen Heath). London: Fontana.

Butler, Judith (1990). *Gender Trouble: Feminism and the subversion of identity*. London: Routledge.

Butler, Judith (1993). *Bodies that Matter: On the discursive limits of "sex"*. London: Routledge.

Cooper-Clark, Diana (1980). Margaret Drabble: cautious feminist. *Atlantic Monthly*, November, 69–75.

de Beauvoir, Simone (1972). *The Second Sex* (trans. H. M. Parshley). Harmondsworth: Penguin (first published 1949).

Firestone, Shulamith (1971). *The Dialectic of Sex: The case for feminist revolution*. London: Paladin.

Greer, Germaine (1970). *The Female Eunuch*. London: MacGibbon & Kee.

Greer, Germaine (2000). *The Whole Woman*. London: Anchor.

Haraway, Donna J. (1991). A cyborg manifesto: science, technology and socialist-feminism in the late twentieth century. In: *Simians, Cyborgs and Women: The reinvention of nature*. New York: Routledge.

Lessing, Doris (1996). *Putting the Questions Differently: Interviews with Doris Lessing 1964–94* (ed. Earl G. Ingersoll). London: Flamingo.

Miller, Nancy (1982). The text's heroine: a feminist critic and her fiction. *Diacritics*, 12(2), 48–53.

Murdoch, Iris (1977). *The Fire and the Sun: Why Plato banished the artists*. Oxford: Oxford University Press.

Murdoch, Iris (1978). *Recontres avec Iris Murdoch*. Caen, France: Centre de Recherches de Litterature et Linguistique des Pays de Langue Anglaise.

Raskin, Jonah (1972). Doris Lessing at Stony Brook: an interview. In: Paul Schleuter (ed.), *A Small Personal Voice*. New York: Vintage.

Showalter, Elaine (1981). Feminist criticism in the wilderness. *Critical Inquiry*, 8(2). Reprinted in Showalter, Elaine (1985), *The New Feminist Criticism: Essays on women, literature and theory*, New York: Pantheon.

Walter, Natasha (1998). *The New Feminism*. London: Little, Brown and Company.

Wolf, Naomi (1998). *Promiscuities: A secret history of female desire*. London: Vintage.

Woolf, Virginia (1929). *A Room of One's Own*. London: Hogarth Press.

Woolf, Virginia (1938). *Three Guineas*. London: Hogarth Press.

Woolf, Virginia (1979). Professions for women. In: *Virginia Woolf: Women and Writing*, ed. Michèle Barrett. London: Women's Press.

FICTION

Brookner, Anita (1984). *Hotel du Lac*. London: Jonathan Cape.
Brookner, Anita (1996). *Altered States*. London: Jonathan Cape.
Byatt, A. S. (1990). *Possession: A romance*. London: Chatto & Windus.
Carter, Angela (1972). *The Infernal Desire Machines of Doctor Hoffman*. London: Rupert Hart-Davis.
Carter, Angela (1977). *The Passion of New Eve*. London: Victor Gollancz.
Carter, Angela (1984). *Nights at the Circus*. London: Chatto & Windus.
Drabble, Margaret (1981). *The Waterfall*. Harmondsworth: Penguin (first published 1969).
Fielding, Helen (1996). *Bridget Jones's Diary*. London: Picador.
Jong, Erica (1973). *Fear of Flying: A novel*. New York: Henry Holt & Co.
Lessing, Doris (1969) *The Four-Gated City*. London: MacGibbon & Kee.
Lessing, Doris (1973). *The Golden Notebook*. St Albans: Panther.
Lessing, Doris (1974). *Memoirs of a Survivor*. London: Octagon.
Lessing, Doris (1988). *The Fifth Child*. London: Jonathan Cape.
Murdoch, Iris (1956). *The Flight from the Enchanter*. London: Chatto & Windus.
Murdoch, Iris (1970). *A Fairly Honourable Defeat*. London: Chatto & Windus.
Murdoch, Iris (1973). *The Black Prince*. London: Chatto & Windus.
Smith, Zadie (2000). *White Teeth*. Harmondsworth: Penguin.
Spark, Muriel (1961). *The Prime of Miss Jean Brodie*. London: Macmillan.
Spark, Muriel (1968). *The Public Image*. London: Macmillan.
Spark, Muriel (1970). *The Driver's Seat*. London: Macmillan.
Spark, Muriel (1971). *Not to Disturb*. London: Macmillan.
Spark, Muriel (1973). *The Hothouse by the East River*. London: Macmillan.
Spark, Muriel (1974). *The Abbess of Crewe*. London: Macmillan.
Weldon, Fay (1980). *Puffball: A novel*. London: Hodder & Stoughton.
Weldon, Fay (1983). *The Life and Loves of a She-Devil*. London: Hodder & Stoughton.
Weldon, Fay (1989). *The Cloning of Joanna May*. London: HarperCollins.
Winterson, Jeanette (1989). *Sexing the Cherry*. London: Bloomsbury.
Winterson, Jeanette (1992). *Written on the Body*. London: Jonathan Cape.
Woolf, Virginia (1928). *Orlando: A biography*. London: Hogarth Press.

Chapter 10

Queer Fiction: The Ambiguous Emergence of a Genre

Robert L. Caserio

Fiction about gays and lesbians, by writers who themselves avowed same-sex or bisexual desire, rapidly emerged as an identifiable and important literary category in Britain during the 1970s and 1980s. Building on post-1945 representations of homosexuality by homosexual and heterosexual authors alike, encouraged by decriminalization of homosexuality between consenting adults in 1967, and inspired by post-1968 political movements in favor of dissident minorities, gay and lesbian fiction stimulated a growth of publishers (Gay Men's Press, Onlywomen Press) and bookstores devoted to gay and lesbian markets, and had an impact on publishers' lists in general. By 1993, the *Writers and Artists' Yearbook* was including separate listings of publishers of gay and lesbian books, and the general booksellers had begun to dedicate specially designated shelves to gay and lesbian texts. Such successful courting of public attention to representations of homosexual life was unprecedented.

That public success, however, has been pervaded by contradictions. Gay writing's new prominence in the 1970s was part of a concerted movement toward full-scale public acceptance of homosexuality. Gay and lesbian storytelling, especially "coming out" narratives, "helped shape a new public language" about homosexual lives (Plummer 1996: 45). Brigid Brophy's monumental reclamation of Ronald Firbank's life and work in *Prancing Novelist* (1973) pointed a way to join the new public language to art. The influence of the American Stonewall rebellion of 1969 led to the formation of new British gay rights groups.

Christopher Isherwood's *Christopher and His Kind* (1976), an example of shared Anglo-American desire for public acknowledgment, imagines an international queer brotherhood. But at the very moment of this gay and lesbian bid for a public world, the public world itself began to disappear: The advent of Thatcherism in 1979 signaled an end of collective-minded progressive values that might have offered homosexual men and women full standing as citizens. Privatization – of everything from state industry to personal "choice" of sexual orientation – became the order of the day. Accordingly, by 1987, despite the decriminalization of private consensual homosexuality 20 years earlier, Clause 28 of a Conservative Local Government bill prohibited public "promotion" of homosexuality in education and affirmed the "superior" status of heterosexual family life.

Such prejudicial legislation made clear that, despite its increased representation in fiction and its wider social recognition, homosexuality faces ongoing resistance. Although the age of consent for homosexual relations was lowered in 1994 from 21 to 18 (and in 2001 to 17 in Northern Ireland and to 16 elsewhere); although protest against Clause 28 led to the formation of Stonewall, a strong advocacy lobby; and although a return of the Labour Party to power in 1997 brought openly gay persons into government positions, nevertheless, an era that began in hopes of continuing progress has turned out to be liberated yet still not free. The chance advent of the HIV-AIDS pandemic in 1982 among gay male populations renewed prejudicial associations of homosexuality with disease, cruelly undermining the aspirations of the previous decade. Extension of the 1967 decriminalization law to Scotland and Northern Ireland was variously resisted until the 1990s. Police raids on gay bookshops in London and Scotland in 1984 were a portent of the Conservative government's abolition of the gay-friendly Greater London Council in 1985 (the same year a gay couple was arrested and fined £100 for kissing on Oxford Street). Homosexuality in the military was prohibited until 1999, when the European Court of Human Rights forced Britain to allow gays to serve openly in the armed forces. Repeal of Clause 28 was resisted until late 2003.

Obstacles to liberation have emerged from within homosexual populations as well as from outside. As gays and lesbians sought political power and simultaneously became objects of marketing, some realized that visibility and commodification would newly misrepresent homosexual life, and would suture gay experience to conventional norms that it had suffered from, and fought against, since at least the 1890s. Politically motivated struggles and antagonisms among gay

constituencies became at least as common as protests against heterosexual norms, which could no longer be regarded as the sole basis of
derogatory stereotypes and misrepresentations. As the new academic
field of gay and lesbian studies began to take shape in the 1980s and
1990s (and to exert an increasing influence over gay and lesbian
fiction), scholars in the field argued compellingly that gay or lesbian
claims to a common eros or group identity across the lines of gender,
class, ethnicity, nationality, and history were simply untenable. Accordingly, it was not only a meaningful public world that had eroded at
the moment gay and lesbians thought they might enter it. Their
assumed identity had also begun to dissolve, even as booksellers and
readers – and scholars too – were busily constructing it as a market
niche. To be sure, the disappearance was said to be an advantage:
homosexuality would henceforth call itself "queer" as a sign of its
having many identities, ranging from "traditional" gays and lesbians,
to bisexual and transgendered persons, to heterosexuals who repudi-
ate normative or superior status in heterosexual orientation. That
new regard for queer identities promised shared libertarian coalitions
with groups whose aims had no basis in a uniform sexual desire. But
realization of such promise remains uncertain, and suspect as well.
Having long considered themselves as a minority more sinned against
than sinning, gays and lesbians have had to face their complicity in
exploiting others. Queer (or gay or lesbian) desire for enduring institutionalized public power is also suspect, because the desire might
mimic oppressive heterosexual regimes of self-perpetuation. As Lee
Edelman, among others, has argued, heterosexuality's constitutive
investment in biological reproduction tends to support the demand
that all heterosexual cultural institutions and values reproduce themselves infinitely, as a guarantee of heterosexual victory over disrup-
tion, loss, mortality itself. Homosexual desire, in contrast, stands at a
distance from oppressive compulsions to reproduce, and is more at-
tuned to loss and limitation. Whenever gay eros pursues heterosexually
conditioned political and cultural forms of self-perpetuation, it might
weaken the countercultural potential of homosexuality's inwardness
with finitude and mortality (Edelman 2004).

These various and uneven developments are the context in which
queer fiction as a genre has made its impact; they have furnished the
content of the genre as well. Two novels of the early 1980s by lesbian
authors, Maureen Duffy's *Londoners: An elegy* (1983) and Kay Dick's
The Shelf (1984), chronicling life just before the advent of HIV and AIDS,
exhibit gay desires for a recognized place in a progressive society and

state – and gay awareness that, with the rise of Thatcherism, there perhaps are no creditable political or state institutions left to share. Although Dick's book has a despairing lesbian's suicide at its center, nevertheless, sad to say, it is the more hopeful of the two. A suicidal fate for homosexuality is stock matter in earlier twentieth-century writing. But Dick uses the stock matter to emphasize remarkable changes: by the 1960s, the time of the novel's retrospective narrative, the story's women accept all varieties of sexual experience. Cass the narrator estimates her bisexuality as "in no way unusual" (p. 15). Anne, the suicide in love with Cass, also takes her own bisexuality for granted, and lives in a world "where normal sexual and social taboos did not exist" (p. 15). Dick's point is that Anne's sorrows are not a simple result of social repression of homosexuality, or of any single class of antagonists.

What happens after the suicide, occurring at the novel's mid-point, is most significant. Dick introduces a new character, who reviews – and, so to speak, reads – Anne's death along with Cass, who must come to terms with her own failures in loving Anne. The new character is a coroner at the suicide inquest. A married man in a provincial town, he is fascinated by the dead woman and by Cass, having had access to love letters from the latter that Anne placed under her pillow when she took a fatal overdose. Dick presents the coroner's fascination as a mixture of eroticism and respectful intelligence, interested and disinterested – Cass is a novelist, and he is something of a novelist himself. It is his interest that makes it possible for Cass to do the dead woman justice with self-critical exactitude. The police have put Cass's letters to Anne "on the shelf," a place for unclaimed papers; and the coroner returns them to their writer. In their chance circulation, and on their way back to their origin, the letters have an effect on the imagination, and the eros, of an unintended audience. The result figures an unexpected alliance of gay author and straight reader. The coroner's place in the story also exhibits an institution – the state's police apparatus, of all things – feeling its way forward into sympathy with a taboo desire. Like the coroner, the narrator, who writes her story to a tolerant male friend, circulates what she has on her shelf, hoping others, whatever their sexuality, will read her with disinterestedness. Meanwhile, Dick never discloses the actual text of her narrative's love letters. Her motive for secrecy appears to be a desire that readers not subject sexual desire to any exact, hence confining or limiting, transcription. Cass's sin against Anne was a frantic need to define her. The truth about love, whether gay or straight, Dick's novel acknowledges, is too queer for classification. Just that queerness suggests an alliance among multiple erotic orientations.

A similar suggestion of alliance underpins Duffy's *Londoners*. Assuming a transgendered role by making her narrator male, Duffy keeps her reader's identity-fixated curiosity about Al's sexual orientation in suspense. Al, a translator-poet-scholar who lives a marginal existence, is a regular at two pubs, one straight, one gay. His close relations with habitués at those establishments argue past attachments at both. If Duffy does not want to make Al's desire or object-choices definite, it is because she wants to emphasize hybrid identities and attachments that newly constitute London's under-life. Everything about London as it once was identified has become indefinite, thanks to 40 years of change that have brought foreigners and former colonials into its midst. Its latest population of strangers, "denizens of cosmopolis" (p. 23), does not feel at home in London, or expect to belong to it; and Al feels that he too is a stranger. As a writer who has trouble finding a publisher for his translations of Villon, he wryly notes that Hindu and Muslim immigrants "have colonized our imagination and our literature" (p. 32). Yet Al is intimate with such companions as Jemal, an Indian from Zimbabwe and Raffael, a gay hustler who hails from Khartoum. There are rootless white "others," as well: Wolfgang, a German businessman expecting a transfer to Pakistan; a suicidal young Irishman in rebellious flight from home; Frank, a gay Australian in danger of losing his visa and his London lover; a French businesswoman impregnated by Jemal. Even the native Londoners among Al's friends are rootless and afloat. And yet, in their very dislocation, Duffy's characters constitute a multicultural bohemia that promises to include straight and gay in a shared new "cosmopolite" life.

But no hybrid order can come to birth, Duffy's finale argues, under an erosion of socialist traditions by conservative reaction and renascent capitalism. A lockstep unity will absorb the new bohemians, or stamp them down: "capitalism is moving us all," Al laments, "yes ironically capitalism, towards a uniform society of identical consumer goods and shopping precincts." And, with Labour's power disappearing, politics brooks no variety or difference: "The new middle class . . . want a new party, a coalition. In the age of the computer the old two-party system won't do" (p. 53). When Al protests to a Parliamentary subcommittee that publishing consortiums' power over marketing amounts to censorship, he is rebuked: "sixties liberalism isn't possible in the economic climate of the eighties" (p. 93). A journalist who interviews Al about censorship also rebukes him, insisting that because taxpayers pay for freedom of expression, they have a consumers' right to curtail it. Mounting intimidation of the very minorities that might create an alternative political order demoralizes a gay friend of Al's when he is arrested for kissing another man in public. His arrest is counterpointed by commodification of dissident sexuality: a film producer wants Al to write a lurid biopic about Villon's bisexuality. Alternative eros sells at the box office, but it is a different matter on the street. To exemplify a hardening cultural opposition to the "strangers" Al fraternizes with, Duffy ends *Londoners* with a hate-crime or terrorist bombing of the novel's gay pub, and with Al's economically enforced removal from the city.

In the same year as *Londoners*, Adam Mars-Jones edited *Mae West Is Dead*, an important collection of short stories by gay authors, intended to remind readers that enemies of queer life are not only external. Combating gay writers' – and gay readers' – market-driven falsifica-tion of gay experience, Mars-Jones's introduction to the collection finds that 15 years of "a lavish fraction of civil rights" have produced "improvised moralities combining . . . reaction against, and imitation of heterosexual precedents" (p. 13). That combination has reduced gays and lesbians to a "subculture," dissolving their status as a "counterculture" (p. 42), and turning representations of them into mere "exonerations" (p. 21). The exonerating impulse does not leave out sex. But it removes sex "from the realm of the personal, the emotional, and the subjective" (p. 28), and garnishes that removal with commodity-friendly role models and pin-ups. "For a gay reader," Mars-Jones protests, "the hero of a novel can be a role-model or a pin-up . . . only if [the hero's] behavior remains studiedly vague" (p. 37). Mars-Jones concedes that "legitimate fears" of "isolation" and "dependence" in "a community which is constantly being reminded of its provisional status" (p. 40) disposes gay readers to celebrate unreal role models and pin-ups. But gay writing must express those fears of isolation and dependence if it is not to be overwhelmed by self-promoting misrepresentation and marketing.

Whether or not the 1983 *Mae West Is Dead* confronts gay and lesbian isolation and dependence in relation to other communities is debat-able. Most compellingly the collection represents gay and lesbian self-scrutiny. In Aileen LaTourette's terse stories, a lesbian narrator recounts how, having fallen for a man, she must recognize that "once again I was a person without integrity, a sexual double agent" (p. 179); another lesbian narrator faces her own culpability for bungling an affair: "I'm what's the matter" (p. 228). The intention of such stories is to move their readers beyond stock approval and disapproval. Such movement is obtained when writers invite readers to identify with characters and events, and simultaneously mix detachment or satiric aggression into those identifications. Simon Burt's stories especially enlist that admixture. One story, about what goes on behind the scenes of a fading dance club, examines repetitive experiences that are at once bemoaned and unbreakable: among them, sex that is never adequate. "If people go on and on behaving in the same way," asks a narrator who is trapped in repetition, "it must mean they like it, mustn't it?" (p. 59). A reader is asked to sympathize with the questioner – and simultaneously to distance himself from the character's immobilization. Burt's story "Floral Street," which contains a passage that gives the collection its title, has a shocking male protagonist. He is bisexual; his wife and teenage son know he is a gay porn star by night. During the day, he painstakingly counsels a friend, and, in his job as a teacher, he strongly resists sexual overtures from a hysterical male student. But at his night work, the pornography star is another being. When his son turns up at the porn studio as a new actor, expressly for the purpose of consummating incest, the father accommodates him. "Ultimately," the father insists, "one has only one loyalty, to honesty" (p. 163). The outcome of loyalty and honesty here argue Burt's desire to unsettle a reader's attitudes and judgments about everything Burt has represented. Such unsettling is in line with Mars-Jones's polemical intention for the collection.

As the advent of HIV disease heightened the gay male population's visibility and its dependence on a larger public world, and as the disease intensified the isolated and provisional character of the gay community by increasing homophobic aggression against it, gay fiction might have responded by continuing to pursue "studied vagueness." But Mars-Jones dedicated his own fiction to representing gay men with AIDS in terms of a realism that would not compromise the polemic of *Mae West Is Dead*. A new edition in 1987 (the same year a British Social Attitudes Survey reported 74 percent of the public disapproved of homosexual relationships (Jivani 1997: 195)) included Mars-Jones's "Slim," a story that focuses on its narrator's aggressive envy of his volunteer "buddy" helper. Rather than stressing the pathos of the disease, the story highlights its narrator's self-absorption prior to the disease, and his extreme competitiveness, which even illness does not abate. Hoping that "fiction might create a psychological space in which the epidemic could be contemplated, with detachment rather than denial or apocalyptic fear" (p. 2), Mars-Jones continued to write

215

about the disease in an unsparing series of stories, collected in *Monopolies of Loss* (1992).

Mars-Jones applies fiction's powers of detachment to the subject of gay pornography in his novel *The Waters of Thirst* (1994). The novel's posthumous narrator suffers when alive from congenital kidney disease, which provokes a thirst that never can be slaked – in part because the thirst always must be monitored. The thirst is a metaphor for gay desire, monitored by disapproving institutions. Pornography promises an escape from the monitor. For most gay males, for whom representations of their contemned eros are only available through pornographic fantasy, such fantasy is, as Mars-Jones knows, compelling. The narrator of *The Waters of Thirst* lives in the afterlife in the arms of his favorite porn star, Peter Hunter. In life the narrator had tracked every photo of the star; had discovered Hunter's entrepreneurship in the pornography industry; and had lovingly deduced signs of Hunter's HIV infection. Mars-Jones makes his narrator's absorption with pornography sympathetic. At the same time Mars-Jones, true to his aesthetics of detachment, makes his narrator's absorption appear a human failure. Peter and pornography are big business, representing an ersatz rebellion and escape – and subjecting the narrator further to unslaked thirst and monitoring. Moreover, the narrator while alive has an ordinary lover, Terry, to whom, on account of fantastical Peter, he invariably condescends. With life behind him, the narrator realizes the sorrow of his loss of Terry, his over-investment in fantasy at the expense of the partnered life he undervalued on earth: "the reliable elusiveness of another person in the same space, the same life, the predictability that never grows stale. I miss that" (p. 157). Underneath its satirical detachment, or by way of it, *The Waters of Thirst* celebrates gay monogamy. Such a celebration, given gay liberation's tradition of resistance to domestic values, is intended to provoke controversial response from gay readers.

Mars-Jones's refusal to shirk thorny aspects of homosexual life and desire, even in an age of AIDS and Conservative hostility, leads to what might be a period style for current gay fiction: a mode of expression that invests gay life with glamorous or daring eroticism yet finds such eroticism not self-justifying. Such a style comes to full flower in the work of Alan Hollinghurst. His writing's cool, flat tonality results from two counterpoised intentions: to protect gay sex and gay lives from external aggression; and to subject gay sex and gay lives to internal criticism, an alternative form of aggression.

Hollinghurst's *The Swimming-Pool Library* (1988, the year of the Clause 28 controversy) takes place just after the 1982 Tory conflict with Argentina over the Malvinas (the "Falklands War"). When the novelist's narrator, Will Beckwith, has a sexual encounter with an Argentinean leather man who exclaims, "I could whip you for what you did to my country in the war," Beckwith protests, "I think that might be to take the sex and politics metaphor a bit too seriously, old chap" (p. 322). But the joke is on Beckwith. With all seriousness Hollinghurst's narrative takes homosexuality and politics as metaphors for each other. The story of their identity is not pretty: it is a historical as well as a political tale, whereby late twentieth-century homosexuality in Britain remains anchored to the British imperial past. That is because, according to the novel, the imperial project stimulated an enlistment of homosexual men (even while outwardly forbidding their service) who saw foreign adventure as an erotic opportunity. Such opportunity inevitably was interracial, with a result that gay sex became repellently involved with political and social domination. The repulsiveness hits home when Beckwith realizes that a patrician elderly gay man whose biography he intends to write, a former colonial officer (in the 1920s) who prides himself on his love of blacks and his anti-racism ("I've always had to be among them, you know, Negroes, and I've always gone straight for them" (p. 283)), is unscrupulous. When self-interested opportunity serves, the aged imperialist self-contradictorily oppresses his own homosexual kind, whether they be "Negroes" or whites (especially if the latter are not of his class). The old man's incoherence is the more stunning because he went to prison in the 1950s as a result of a gay witchhunt initiated by Beckwith's grandfather. Beckwith expected his biography to avenge both his subject and his eros, but he realizes he must drop the project. He has discovered that the oppressor is internal. Beckwith himself – he also sexually pursues blacks and working class men – repeats in the 1980s psychosexual social patterns that are continuous with imperialist patterns of the 1920s. Outside of Hollinghurst's fiction, and corroborating it, those same patterns were to appear in gay self-help AIDS organizations, which initially overlooked the needs of black and other less privileged communities (Weeks et al. 1996).

Echoing Simon Burt, Hollinghurst's novel asks if gay men's historical repetition compulsion means that they must like what a century of history has shaped for them: modern homosexuality's infection – *pace* HIV – by domination, class snobbery, and racism. Because

Robert L. Caserio

Hollinghurst's Will is a rich 25-year-old whose personal glamour pervades everything he narrates, the harshness of historical vision he communicates is masked by the style I have described. But despite glamour and style, in *The Swimming-Pool Library* historical infection appears immedicable. Instead of being redeemers of historical or political malaise – as Duffy's Al hopes his new Londoners might be – Hollinghurst's figures deceive themselves into thinking they instance an alternative to a long-enduring status quo. And when in a later novel, *The Spell* (1998), Hollinghurst depicts three post-1950 genera-tions of gay men who have by century's end created a virtually altern-ative world, apart from the wider public realm (they have no political passions, and manage to bracket off their personal relation to AIDS deaths of the 1980s), their self-enclosed subculture appears, at best, to be ludicrously claustrophobic. The protagonists include a gay father and his gay son, whose relationship hews to cliché ("he didn't want his boy," the father worries, "turning into a slut" (p. 60)); but a fusion of "the spell of the family" (p. 70) with "sex magic" (p. 219) turns the lives of father and son and their lovers – all of them "troublingly perfect" in appearance (p. 116) – into a sexual round robin consum-ing in its intensity, yet simultaneously flat. When *The Spell*'s charac-ters occasionally feel driven to break out of their tightly woven private world their very impulse baffles them.

Repeatedly, British gay fiction of the last quarter century witnesses the defeat of homosexual life in any form beyond "privatization." A case in point is Colm Tóibín's *The Story of the Night* (from 1996, the year after Tony Blair's undoing of the Labour Party constitution's Clause IV, committing the Party to further privatization of industry). An account of a gay son of an English émigré family in Argentina (the English too are part of a diaspora), Tóibín's narrative shows its pro-tagonist's homosexuality helping him grow beyond his conservative Anglo-Argentine origins. As the protagonist's world expands, he comes in touch with "political dissidents," including a Chilean victim of political torture. And he hears about torture at home: one night, during love-making, a partner explains an unusual noise in a nearby building as a sound of generators that power cattle prods used by the police to torture political prisoners. Despite what he hears, however, the protagonist remains insulated from politics: "the famous disap-pearances we hear so much about now" (p. 6) are not stories to which he can feel attachment. Private relations rather than public ones retain an upper hand. Just after the protagonist allies himself with Argentine nationalist feelings, he accepts work with the International Monetary

Fund that involves him in the privatization of Argentine national industry. Nationalism, global internationalism, and intensifying privatization paradoxically go together. Bodily life repeats the paradox. In 1988, the protagonist and his closeted Argentine lover discover that they are suffering from AIDS, their HIV infection having predated identification of the virus and their own safe-sex practices. Their experience of disease will be "like . . . being tortured and punished" (p. 251). They too will enter the realm of the disappeared; and their private story will find no adequate public hearing.

Given persistent pessimism about homosexuality's achievement of public stature, forms or themes that divert the pessimism, or compensate for it, have helped shape contemporary gay genres. Departures from realism into modes of allegory and romance might be understood as a diverting compensation at the level of form. Efforts in fiction (and in queer theory) to reveal queerness in all sexual desire might be understood as compensation at the level of theme. Such compensatory thematics suggest that homosexuality appears not to have a public place because homosexuality is assigned a fixedly transgressive character, hence is regarded as altogether external to the social order. More rightly considered, sexual desires and identities are – at least in present historical circumstances – fluid; their queerness is already inside "normal" experience, and therefore already installed in a public realm. Such a thematic perspective is to be found in novels by gay and straight writers alike.

Allegory, romance quest, and pastoral idyll combine in Neil Bartlett's *Ready To Catch Him Should He Fall* (1990), as if Bartlett intends his novel to simulate a text from the Renaissance or the ancient world. Indeed, the novel is presented as a story of an antiquated, albeit legendary, past of homosexual experience. By the narrative's end, the bar that has fostered a gay marriage (an "open" one) between fabulous O (Older Man) and perfect Boy, has closed its doors; and the married couple have faced down a knife-wielding street gang, homophobes who now – in the idyllic narrative present – have become innocuous. As a long preface to such utopian resolution, Boy undergoes rituals that traverse a gamut of gay history's styles and transgressions. Those rituals pollute Boy and purify him. His exposure to disease and death in the AIDS era constitutes another polluting purification. Because of Bartlett's allegorical intentions, however, Boy's intimacy with mortality takes on multiple meanings: he nurses a dying man who might represent his former lover or a father or both, as well as the Closet, the Gay Past, AIDS, or Death. A single characterization does not matter. What matters, Bartlett suggests, is that his novel itself serve as a rite of passage for gay (and gay-friendly) readers into a polysemous queer future, and as a kind of prayer or talisman in support of such passage. Given that there are no institutional "arms" into which any O or Boy can fall, Bartlett's fiction seeks to act as a transitional public institution, leading to a more sexually tolerant body politic.

To believe that fiction can take on responsibility for such transition might sound like belief in magic (*The Spell* perhaps parodies Bartlett's talismanic tale). Nevertheless, gay fiction's flights of fancy, however hopeful of surmounting real prejudice, keep close touch with what everyday life cannot overcome. Jeanette Winterson's novel *Oranges Are Not the Only Fruit* (1985), widely read and celebrated for its picture of a young female evangelical's discovery and embrace of lesbian desire, interweaves realism, and facts of Winterson's own life, with fairy tales and romance narratives that parallel the main plot. Those parallel fables suggest that "coming out" is magical, endowing gay and lesbian subjects with liberty to soar above real life's constraints. But at the same time the fables are tinged with melancholy, as if coming out were also a new type of bafflement. Similar self-divided suggestions inform Winterson's *The Passion* (1987). The novel enlists magical elements to affirm political and erotic desires as world-conquering forces. A female protagonist, daughter of a Venetian gondolier in the Napoleonic era, is "queer" from birth, inasmuch as she is born with webbed feet, enabling her to walk on water. More magically and queerly yet, after she surprises herself by falling in love with a woman, she discovers that she can live after her beloved has taken her heart outside of her body. Webbed feet and lost sapphic heart make the heroine superhuman, more powerful rather than less. Eventually, however, historical reality and ordinary limitations subvert queer desire's heightening of human agency. Winterson's heroine gets her heart back, but remains, like the novel's other figures – including Napoleon – subject to desire, rather than in command of it. "Passion . . . commands us and very rarely in the way we would choose" (p. 144); certainly not in ways that correspond to hopes for a world-transforming order of desire. Meanwhile, despite having thematized dissident sexualities, Winterson herself, in her critical writing in *Art Objects* (1995), protests readings of her work – and her life – that emphasize "sex": "To continually ask someone about their homosexuality . . . is harassment . . . The Queer world has colluded in the misreading of art as sexuality. Art is difference, not necessarily sexual difference" (p. 104).

Historical realist fiction by Hanif Kureishi (who does not identify as gay but whose work "queers" eros) and Jackie Kay exhibits queer desire's permeation of everyday life more than Bartlett and Winterson's departures from realism. Kureishi's *The Buddha of Suburbia* (1990), re-enlisting Duffy's dissident multicultural Londoners but jettisoning her elegiac tone, demonstrates an upward mobility for such figures in the 1970s, indeed celebrates their emergence as cosmopolitan insiders with cultural capital. Acquisition of such capital depends on their exploitation of their multiple class and ethnic positions, and on their transgression of gender and sexual norms. Kureishi's eponymous hero, a suburban father, rejects the position he won as a London civil servant in the 1950s in order to reclaim his South Asian identity and become a Buddhist guru. The father's oldest friend, a Muslim émigré, believes that the father's Buddhism shows him to be merely "seduced by the West" (p. 211), more white-identified than ever. Yet the father has at least two identities, and his mobilization of them initiates for himself and other characters – above all for his bisexual son Karim – liberties and powers otherwise not available. Karim's polymorphous sexual identities are complemented by his talents as a mimic: he becomes an actor whose specialty is playing roles that represent his own mobile background. At the novel's end, in 1979, Karim has landed a role in a soap opera "which would tangle with the latest contemporary issues: . . . I'd play the rebellious student son of an Indian shopkeeper" (p. 259). Because Karim's eros remains an unsettled, indefinite energy, interwoven with his public celebrity, Kureishi's novel shows homosexuality threading the public world, reducing prohibitions against it to impotence.

It would be wrong, however, to assert an unqualified triumph of identity-dissolving, mobile sexual orientation in Kureishi's book. Its latter pages make a case for the value after all of fixed selves and desires, even though such fixity is to be reached through experiments in metamorphosis. Karim's oldest friend, Jamila, is forced by her Muslim father into marriage with a new immigrant, Changez. In response to Jamila's refusal to consummate the marriage, Changez divests himself of his Muslim identity and practices. By the novel's end he lives in a commune with Jamila, helping her raise a child that she conceived by another man, before she realized her sexual preference for women. Karim's ultimate respect for Changez and Jamila, focusing the narrative's especial admiration of them, responds to their fixed final commitments, limiting change. Karim also is shown to find limits for himself. Meanwhile, Kureishi's narrative implicitly criticizes all of Karim's success in the London theater, inasmuch as the plays in which he appears and the roles he performs are all tied to clichés about gender, race, and class – and to clichés about mobility of identity and eros. Karim lands his soap opera job, tangling "with the latest contemporary issues," on the eve of the 1979 victory over Labour. The coincidence suggests that contemporary social problems henceforth will occupy a sphere of entertainment, relegated there by the State's abandonment of progressive collective welfare in favor of conservative "values" and private gain. Given that *The Buddha of Suburbia* suggests queer eros succeeds in and as soap opera performance more than it succeeds as a vehicle of social or political transformation (*pace* Jamila's private achievement), one finds the novel's thematizing of liberation to be more pessimistic than commentary has assumed.

Whether realistic or fantastical, a desire to endow transgressive sexual and gender orientations (and art, too) with the power to induce progressive change persists in Jackie Kay's *Trumpet* (1998). *Trumpet*, in contrast to *The Swimming-Pool Library* and more than in Kureishi, envisions homosexual love as a reconciler of racial tensions. The novel is about a famous Afro-Scottish jazz trumpeter, whose death reveals to the public that he has always been a woman. The trumpeter's Scottish–Irish wife falls in love with him before discovering his secret; then marries him, living passionately with him, for decades. She and the trumpeter adopt a bi-racial son. The novel is about the son's response to the revelation that his adoptive father was female. At first, rage leads the son to reject his parents, and to team up with an opportunistic journalist who wants to write a biography of the trumpeter because "the nineties love the private life . . . that turns suddenly and horrifically public . . . [And] lesbian stories are in . . . Lesbians who adopted a son; one playing mommy, one playing daddy. The big butch frauds" (pp. 169–70). The son cedes his rage, however, and rejects collaboration with the sensational press, when he encounters the trumpeter's mother, who for decades received letters and money from her daughter, but was not visited by her. Kay presents the reunion of white grandmother and bi-racial son as a triumphant consummation of an African diaspora narrative, in which interracial and intergenerational unity is achieved through a transvestite lesbian eros and a kindred transgendering impulse. The utopian power of these queering tendencies to dissolve invidious group labels and identities is signaled by the music of Kay's trumpeter: "When [the trumpeter] gets down, he loses his sex, his race, his memory . . . All his self collapses . . . It doesn't matter a damn that he is somebody he is not . . . Only the music knows everything. The dark sweet heart of the music" (pp. 131–5). Likening her own fiction to such music, and dissociating it from more commercially opportunistic media, Kay suggests that the imperialist struggles that once issued in *Heart of Darkness* can issue in a heart of sweetness, especially when the matrix of union – as in her union of grandmother and grandson – is family feeling.

Kay's recourse to familial tenderness is perhaps incoherent, given that her narrative's sexual components promise to depart from conventional sentiment. *Trumpet*'s potential for incoherence is abetted by strains on its realism: the trumpeter's wife immediately adjusts to her husband's female body, free of conflict in regard to her previous inclinations; a minor character, a Bangladeshi Muslim registrar of deaths in a London office, faced with the trumpeter's gender-bending death certificate and enthralled by the wife, feels – within eight-pages – that "the intimacy between [himself and the wife] had been like love" (p. 81); another minor character, a funeral director, preparing the trumpeter for burial in male clothes, speaks to himself as if he has taken a course in queer theory. *Trumpet*'s near-indifference to plausibility in such instances suggests that by the end of the 1990s, with the AIDS crisis under medical supervision for nearly two decades, and with Clause 28 protests only a memory, gay and lesbian fiction had returned to "studied vagueness." Perhaps vagueness is an inevitable response to a public world that, despite the shift in governance from the Conservatives to New Labour, has kept gay culture under assault for a quarter century.

Two aspects of British gay and lesbian fiction in the last decade sum up homosexuality's uneven progress in relation to dominant culture. *The Shelf*'s interest in sharing stories has succeeded: fiction about homosexual lives, or fiction inspired by gay and lesbian texts, circulates beyond its originary sites, and has come to be written by novelists – like Kureishi – who loan themselves to their gay characters' orientations. Such sharing attests to, and probably is facilitated by, a compelling persuasiveness in queer theory's picture of an essential fluidity of identities – evading fixed determinations of eros, gender, ethnicity, or class. To have established the truth of such fluidity for a broad audience argues a queer capture of public imagination, whatever the status of homosexuality in actual public life. The capture is counterbalanced, nevertheless, by a recent trend in gay and lesbian fiction that argues doubts about public progress once again. The trend involves looking backwards rather than forwards – back to late Victorian and modernist periods, not as sites of unqualified repression, but as eras of homosexual and bisexual heroism. Given such retrospection, gay hopes for actual public influence – in contrast to status in the realm of fiction – appear to have more of a past than a future.

The avatar of gay fiction's return to a heroic queer past is the *Regeneration* trilogy of historical novels (1991–1995) by Pat Barker, who also does not identify herself as homosexual but who makes gay and bisexual characters central to *Regeneration* and its sequels. The trilogy, about a crisis in English sexual practices and public allegiances during World War I, recycles queer theory's multiple identities, in this version presenting them initially as traumatic products of global conflict. Curing such trauma, according to Barker, means living consciously and tolerantly with plural selves, rather than sealing them off from each other or aggressively subordinating one or more to a single ego. To be sure, Barker suggests a limit to multiple identities: a core of being that must not be violated. One of the trilogy's protagonists, bisexual Billy Prior, undergoes psychic splits when his work for a war ministry requires him to persecute childhood friends who have become conscientious objectors. Reconciliation or identification with nation or State violates Prior's wayward eros and his alliance with "socialists, sodomites, and shop stewards" (p. 304). Because his core of being stands with the latter, eventually Prior gives himself up to death at the front, not for the sake of the State, but to escape *its* refusal to permit multiple identities – including socialists and sodomites – to flourish. Prior's death reaches forward, albeit blindly, to some unformulated community. Perhaps through Prior Barker reminds gay readers of their countercultural calling, a thing of the past but awaiting regeneration. Meanwhile, Prior's psychiatrist in the novels, who also is an anthropologist, comes to identify with his patients' personalities, and also finds in his patients confirmation of his "cross-cultural" (p. 659) discovery in Melanesia that no one culture's values can act as a "measure" for another (p. 242). Cultural identities, no less than erotic ones, must not be made to conform to any coercive assumptions.

The *Regeneration* trilogy places Prior in the company of real-life modernists – anthropologist W. H. Rivers, bisexual poet Siegfried Sassoon, and gay poet Wilfred Owen – and portrays their struggles against convention as heroically intense. The modernist era was indeed a period of homosexual self-assertion: prior to 1914 gay liberationist Edward Carpenter insisted that homosexual love was to become a heroic agent in establishing universal democracy. Another version of modernist heroism, bathed in the light of Carpenter and of novelists James Joyce and Flann O'Brien, is offered by Jamie O'Neill in *At Swim, Two Boys* (2001). A yearning for a public world of gay men, indeed for "a nation of their own" (p. 286) (of the sort imagined by post-Stonewall Isherwood), undergirds the book. In fact, the yearning organizes O'Neill's representation of the 1916 Easter Uprising so thoroughly that it makes historical fiction, and Joycian inspiration, inseparable from political and sexual daydream. The novel's protagonists are a trio of Irish gay men, a pair of boys (16 and 17, they constitute an object lesson for opponents of lowering the age of homosexual consent to 16) and a man in his 30s. The older man has been imprisoned in England for sodomy; his consequently self-torturing sexual life is characterized by Prior-like multiple personality. But as he falls in love with the adolescents – who are in love with each other, but must overcome religious and class obstacles to consummation – his identity becomes single. The older man becomes aggressively, openly proud of his queerness, as do the boys. The three men, uninterested in multiple identities, and enacting their eros as inseparable from socialism and anti-imperialism, commit themselves equally to sexual love for each other and to Ireland's liberation. Epitomizing an intergenerational and inter-class alliance, the trio is intransigently oppositional. The novel demonstrates remarkable social effects of their intransigence: inter-class solidarity between the boys' fathers, and liberty for women whose lives touch the gay men. Antithetical to Mars-Jones's and Hollinghurst's pictures of gay present and past (and emotionally at odds with the Blair government's IRA disarmament commission), O'Neill's novel is something like a séance with modernist icons of sexual, political, and artistic rebellion: Carpenter, Wilde, gay Irish rebel Roger Casement, "queer" Joyce, and proto-postmodernist O'Brien. *At Swim, Two Boys* seeks to contact them for reassurance in the face of continuing setbacks for homosexuality's revolutionary place in the world.

The current era of homosexual writing in Britain began with American inspiration, with shared post-Stonewall public advocacy for Isherwood's queer "kind." In light of what has been called New Labour's "unthinking Americophilia" (Fishman 1998: 98), and Tony Blair's alliance with a presidency that has renewed public aggression against American gays and lesbians, a recent example of American inspiration for British fiction, and one that also reaches back to modernism, might best close this survey. Colm Tóibín's latest novel, *The Master* (2004), evokes the American modernist expatriate novelist Henry James to hear what James has to say to the queer present. Tóibín's James does not figure the injustice of closeted life, or the pathos of unmitigated repression. Although Toíbín's protagonist is reticent about his sexuality, he is aware of his longing for male love (the world around him also is aware of, and even supportive of, his longing), and is willing, if not able, to yield to it. What Toíbín's James is more aware of than eros, and thinks of continually, is mortality; indeed James is figured as speaking ceaselessly, in thought, with dead friends and relations, with whom he has more converse than with the living. Such inward conversation practices and expresses, oddly, a remarkable self-possession. Toíbín's James receives inspiration for that self-possession from the one man in the novel he sleeps with. The man, a Civil War veteran, "had stared evenly at death, had suffered painful injuries, and, more importantly . . . had learned a steely fear-lessness" – one that could make its way "completely into the private realm" (p. 94). On the model of such "steely fearlessness," resulting from sexual experience with another man, the "master" founds both his self-possession and his art. Because of steely aspects of both, Toíbín's James is never fully a social or familial or erotic being. All his worldly relations are backed by a private realm of self-possessed (rather than self-repressed) reserve.

Toíbín's treatment of privacy here differs from his treatment in *The Story of the Night* (1996). In the latter, the private realm meant depri-vation; in *The Master* it is a full potential for public effect – the public effect that is James's writing. One is tempted to understand Toíbín's characterization of the master's reserve as an epitome of gay fiction's relation to the present, or of what Toíbín thinks that relation should be in an age when Britain finds itself officially allied with a conservative-reactionary American government. Gay writing's relation to the pre-sent is, or should be, as reserved as James's, simultaneously sociable and fearlessly detached, conversing with both the contemporary moment and the modernist past as a form of *memento mori*, a way of staying mindful of mortality. To be sure, at first sight a *memento mori* scarcely seems to promise a political resource for gays and lesbians in search of new public status. But *The Master*'s emphasis on mortality perhaps consolingly reminds readers (queer readers, at least) that even the most oppressive powers and institutions, even heterosexual ones as they currently are ordered, will pass away, to become mere ghosts in the future.

References and Further Reading

NONFICTION

Bersani, Leo (1995). *Homos*. Cambridge, MA: Harvard University Press.

Brophy, Brigid (1973). *Prancing Novelist*. New York: Harper & Row.

Edelman, Lee (2004). *No Future*. Durham, NC: Duke University Press.

Fishman, Nina (1998). Towards a radical reformism. In: Anne Coddington & Mark Perryman (eds.), *The Moderniser's Dilemma* (pp. 91–110). London: Lawrence & Wishart.

Ilona, Anthony (2003). Hanif Kureishi's *The Buddha of Suburbia*. In: Richard J. Lane, Rod Mengham, & Philip Tew (eds.), *Contemporary British Fiction* (pp. 87–105). Cambridge: Polity Press.

Jeffery-Poulter, Stephen (1991). *Peers, Queers, and Commons*. London: Routledge.

Jivani, Alkarim (1997). *It's Not Unusual*. Bloomington, IN: Indiana University Press.

Plummer, Ken (1996). Intimate citizenship and the culture of sexual story telling. In: Jeffrey Weeks & Janet Holland (eds.), *Sexual Cultures* (pp. 34–52). New York: St Martin's Press.

Reitan, Earl A. *The Thatcher Revolution*. Lanham, MD: Rowman & Littlefield.

Sedgwick, Eve Kosofsky (1990). *Epistemology of the Closet*. Berkeley, CA: University of California Press.

Sinfield, Alan (2000). Culture, consensus and difference. In: Alistair Davies & Alan Sinfield (eds.), *British Culture of the Postwar* (pp. 83–102). London: Routledge.

Warner, Michael (1993). *Fear of a Queer Planet*. Minneapolis, MN: University of Minnesota Press.

Warner, Michael (1999). *The Trouble with Normal*. New York: Free Press.

Weeks, Jeffrey. (1977). *Coming Out*. London: Quartet Books.

Weeks, Jeffrey, Aggleton, Peter, McKevitt, Chris, Parkinson, Kay & Taylor-Laybourn, Austin (1996). "Community Responses to HIV and AIDS: the de-gaying and re-gaying of AIDS. In: Jeffrey Weeks & Janet Holland (eds.), *Sexual Cultures: Communities, values and intimacy* (pp. 161–79). New York: St Martin's Press.

Winterson, Jeanette (1995). *Art Objects*. London: Jonathan Cape.

Woodhouse, Reed (1998). *Unlimited Embrace*. Amherst, MA: University of Massachusetts Press.

FICTION

Barker, Pat (1991). *Regeneration*. London: Viking.

Barker, Pat (1993). *The Eye in the Door*. London: Viking.

Barker, Pat (1995). *The Ghost Road*. London: Viking.

Bartlett, Neil (1990). *Ready to Catch Him Should He Fall*. London: Serpent's Tail.

Dick, Kay (1984). *The Shelf*. London: Hamish Hamilton.

Duffy, Maureen (1983). *Londoners: An elegy*. London: Methuen.

Hollinghurst, Alan (1988). *The Swimming-Pool Library*. London: Chatto & Windus.

Hollinghurst, Alan (1998). *The Spell*. London: Viking Penguin.

Isherwood, Christopher (1977). *Christopher and His Kind*. New York: Farrar, Straus, & Giroux.

Kay, Jackie (1998). *Trumpet*. London: Macmillan.

Kureishi, Hanif (1990). *The Buddha of Suburbia*. London: Viking Penguin.

Mars-Jones, Adam (ed.) (1983). *Mae West Is Dead*. London: Faber & Faber.

Mars-Jones, Adam (1992). *Monopolies of Loss*. London: Faber & Faber.

Mars-Jones, Adam (1994). *The Waters of Thirst*. New York: Knopf.

O'Neill, Jamie (2001). *At Swim, Two Boys*. London: Simon & Schuster.

Toíbín, Colm (1996). *The Story of the Night*. London: Picador.

Toíbín, Colm (2004). *The Master*. London: Picador.

Winterson, Jeanette (1985). *Oranges Are Not the Only Fruit*. London: Pandora.

Winterson, Jeanette (1987). *The Passion*. London: Bloomsbury.

Chapter 11

The Demise of Class Fiction

Dominic Head

Class in Britain remains a topic fraught with contradictions and confusion. In a perceptive overview from 1998, David Cannadine shows how three mutually exclusive versions or models of the class system have recurred in British perceptions: "the hierarchical view of society as a seamless web; the triadic version with upper, middle and lower collective groups; and the dichotomous, adversarial picture, where society is sundered between 'us' and 'them.'" Of these three models, Cannadine writes: "all of them are ignorant over-simplifications of the complexity of society. Yet they have remained remarkably enduring, and they are still in existence today." For all the confusion, he is surely right to conclude that the very persistence of these competing explanatory models is itself evidence enough that "Britain cannot possibly be described as a 'classless society'" (Cannadine 1998: 19–21).

Attempts to specify distinctions or divisions between classes may therefore be more divisive than illuminating. With respect to the poorest social groups, discourses of class can have the perverse effect of generating false social identities, and colluding with broader economic and political effects that militate against collective understanding. In contemporary Britain, poverty is no longer the province of wage-laborers, whose toil is defended by an effective union, and ameliorated by factory clubs and socials. Changes that have taken place since the rise of Thatcherism – the curbing of union powers, the imposition of strict productivity regimes, and the disappearance of traditional working-class communities – have meant that there is no longer a collective working-class experience with which to identify (as there still was in the 1960s and 1970s).

Manual labor has declined in post-industrial Britain, and this has been another factor in the decreasing relevance of traditional class categories (even where these persist in the popular consciousness). But this has produced a new brand of inequality. The period since 1980 has witnessed the development of a growing salaried middle class, covering a wide range of occupations, and this is not something to be easily dismissed or condemned (at least not by academics, who are themselves integral members of the new professional salariat). However, what unites this group, rather than a shared social conscience, is the financial status of its members, who can be categorized as consumers, wielding economic power. On the other side of this equation, a new "underclass" has emerged to support the prosperity of the majority. Here one thinks first of that "servant class" which comprises "the army of cleaners and menial service workers, paid a pittance, often working only a few hours here and there, cash-in-hand, no questions asked, ministering to the world above in its homes, offices, hospitals and schools" (Adonis & Pollard 1997: 12). But beneath even this servant class is the truly disenfranchised sector of society, which includes not just those bypassed by technological change, and disadvantaged by the increasing rarity of unskilled manual labor, but the homeless, and those from the sink-estates whose lives are broken by prostitution and drug addiction, sometimes before they reach their teens (Davies 1997).

In trying to assess how the novel has fared in addressing the new questions of class and status – those questions that the rise of the underclass in the 1980s and 1990s leaves in its wake – an initial answer would have to be: not very well. Class is not an issue that has figured very centrally in British fiction over the last 25 years. However, before enlarging upon this, and raising the question of just how reasonable it is to expect novelists to attempt interventions in these social questions, it is worth recalling how fundamental the notion of class had been for novelists of the preceding generation.

The Working-Class Novel in Retrospect: Identity and Contradiction

Most readers conversant with British fiction since World War II would have a ready answer if asked about treatments of class in the novel:

they would point to those novels of the 1950s and 1960s noted for depicting northern working-class experience in a style of "gritty realism." *Room at the Top, A Kind of Loving, This Sporting Life, Saturday Night and Sunday Morning,* and *A Kestrel for a Knave* would all figure prominently in any such survey (a prominence augmented by the fact that all were adapted to the screen by major practitioners of British cinematic realism). A point to note at once is that the first two titles on the list are concerned with social mobility and the break up of a notional stable class hierarchy. *This Sporting Life* (1960) stages the conflict between economic mobility and ideological stasis, while the class solidarity of Arthur Seaton in Alan Sillitoe's *Saturday Night and Sunday Morning* (1958) seems contradictory, his anger finding outlet in merely hedonistic pleasures. From this list only Barry Hines's *A Kestrel for a Knave* (1968) implies the continuing oppressiveness of working-class experience in a constant social model: the ending clearly indicates that Billy Casper, emotionally numb and his kestrel now dead, will follow his brother down the pit. But even this bleak novel registers a changing culture, as when the headmaster Gryce remarks that young people now are "just fodder for the mass media" (Hines 1968: 56). This suspicion of popular mass culture is also a tacit recognition that there are forces abroad that will transform working-class identity.

Few readers would dispute that the novels I have mentioned seem dated after 40 or 50 years, that they are set in a now unrecognizable social milieu. What is not often acknowledged, however, is that the novels commonly associated with working-class identity since 1950 might also be about the actual, or impending break-up of that identity, clearly signaling the demise of the world they evoke so vividly – and thus anticipating, and connecting with, the novels of the 1980s and 1990s. John Braine's *Room at the Top* (1957), for example, is a cautionary tale of class mobility. The material successes of Joe Lampton see him overcoming a series of traditional class obstacles, in particular the advantages bestowed by family connections, inherited wealth, and an Oxbridge education. Although set in the year 1946–7, the action of the novel is connected to the consumer boom of the 1950s, with the "success" of Lampton providing a wry commentary on this social phenomenon: material acquisitiveness displaces emotional responsiveness. Vic Brown in Stan Barstow's *A Kind of Loving* (1960) is also emblematic of social change. He is a miner's son who becomes an entrepreneur and purveyor of those electrical goods – such as radiograms and televisions – that signify the new mass consumer culture.

In *This Sporting Life* (1960), David Storey, too, examines the problem of class mobility. Admittedly, in Arthur Machin he creates a protagonist whose sporting success and celebrity cannot expunge the working-class markers that others are apt to see in him, and his relationship with Mrs Hammond seems doomed by a wider net of exploitation that encompasses industrial relations and the world of rugby league. Yet the novel does not deny the availability of a wider horizon. It suggests that alienation is pervasive and systemic, even beyond the traditional class struggle.

Not all of the best-known novels of class from this period are written by men about the north: Nell Dunn's *Poor Cow* (1967), for example, is a sober corrective to the glamorized version of swinging sixties London. But, like the other novels mentioned, it offers a surprising slant on class relations: it is centrally about female self-assertion in the face of both gender and economic oppression, implying the emergence of a new consciousness, a new identity for a working-class woman. Indeed, nearly all of the novels I have mentioned register, to some degree, a growing sense of class mobility – or at least the pressing need for such mobility – in economic terms, and a weakening of the traditional British class system. There are other novels that one could mention in the same breath, such as *Lucky Jim* (1954) by Kingsley Amis, *Billy Liar* (1959) by Keith Waterhouse, and Raymond Williams's *Border Country* (1960): each one, in its own way, investigates a new kind of social mobility and the dramatic impact this has on settled class communities of different kinds. For 15 or 20 years, it seems, novels treating (usually) upward mobility and the consequent dismantling (and reimagining) of the social fabric – however problematically – caught the imagination of novelists and the reading public.

A problem already alluded to should color how we read these earlier treatments of class: conventional class distinctions (especially "middle class" and "working class") live on in the popular imagination – and in the active processes of class formation, it should be recognized – long after the economic basis for traditional class affiliation has changed beyond recognition. The important thing to understand is that World War II gave an impetus to the radical changes in the class structure that were soon to emerge. The postwar Labour government did enact policies that favored the working class, and which made possible a wider distribution of the new prosperity of the 1950s, after the austerity of the war years and the later 1940s. Despite the emergence of new, later forms of inequality, we can still see the expansion (and transformation) of the middle class, together with the dramatic success of middlebrow culture, as a very influential factor in British social and political life since 1950. But it took a generation for the inevitability of these changes to seem less heady, and so a generation of novelists – those quintessentially middlebrow cultural practitioners – could examine and re-examine the thrills and the pitfalls of social mobility, using a transparent form of realism to mediate a topic that did not immediately dull the enthusiasm of the reading public. Of course, these were writers who, in most cases, were experiencing the kinds of social transition that their works recorded, progressing toward the bourgeois condition that is the condition of possibility for novel production (and reception).

The career of Raymond Williams, as novelist, suggests why working-class experience, and the topic of class tension, both became less compelling in the later twentieth-century novel. Williams's first (auto-biographical) novel, *Border Country* (1960), presents a theme that is very familiar in the novel of this period: the dilemma of the working-class scholarship boy, and the fear of class betrayal. Williams's especial concern is changing class identity and the loss of traditional community values. Matthew Price, a university lecturer in economic history, is summoned from London to Glynmawr, his Welsh border village home, by news of his father's illness. Price thus begins a journey of self-evaluation, based on the troublesome negotiation between intellectual and working-class kinship.

Williams's narrative method in the novel gestures toward a broad historical treatment of working-class experience: for much of the novel, he juxtaposes scenes from the narrative present in the 1950s with episodes from the past, centered around the impact of the General Strike of 1926. But, as Williams indicated, this serves to underscore the rapidity of change, rather than continuity (Williams 1960: 106). The crucial figure in this phase of transition is Morgan Rosser, the impassioned NUR (National Union of Railwaymen) Branch Secretary during the strike, and the staunchest upholder of traditional values of collective support, within the tight-knit community. The strike, however, leads him in a new individualistic and entrepreneurial direction, selling produce for himself. Rosser establishes his own factory, selling jam from local fruit, but the factory is sold shortly after the war, and becomes in effect a depot, "labelling the pulp from abroad" (p. 330). Rosser's actions are representative of a kind of economics that signals class defeat: his personal profit motive allows external interests to disrupt the settled community's concerns.

Border Country and its sequel, *Second Generation* (1964), now read like works of traditional realism, distinctly of their time, certainly when compared with Williams's later, more innovative fiction. Yet Williams went to great lengths to achieve exactly the form he wanted, rewriting the novel six times between 1947 and 1960 (Williams 1979: 271). He was acutely conscious that the new social experience of class transition required a new form, and despite appearances his early works do actually engage closely with the problem of realism. His model was the working-class novel of the interwar years, which, for Williams, had become "a kind of regional form" – for example, in the works of Jack Jones and Gwyn Jones. Williams felt this was a type of novel deft at describing "the internally seen working-class community," and it was this crucial capacity that he sought to retain, and which lends his early novels their conventional air. However, he wished to combine that internal dynamic with a sense of "a movement of people" away from those communities to which they are still connected (Williams 1979: 272–3).

At this stage in his career, it is clear that Williams felt that an authentic form for working-class fiction required a subtle development of available models, rather than a dramatic overhaul of them. But, in a larger context, he was aware of the relative impoverishment of the twentieth-century novel: in comparison with the novels of the nineteenth-century realists, Williams found an absence of history in twentieth-century fiction, where a character's experiences may not appear to be determined "by any larger forces." The reason for this was the situation of the novelist, and the brute economic pressures that, certainly at that time, obliged speed and brevity in a publishable, profitable novel marketed as "serious" fiction. From the vantage point of literary history it is this economic reality that produces an ideological squeeze on the novel, necessitating the omission of the kind of detailed social history that a fully realized working-class novel would require. However, as Williams observes, "the nineteenth-century forms of the novel were shaped within a bourgeois world" (Williams 1979: 271, 275). One might also wonder whether or not the ideological squeeze on the novelist is impelled by the same economic factors that are life-altering for so many characters in the novels of the 1950s and 1960s – like Morgan Rosser – and which may signal a waning of class-consciousness for the novelist, too.

Of course, Williams was well aware that broader social changes have a direct bearing on the novelist's ability to identify community. Indeed, he felt that a crisis in the portrayal of a "knowable community" was the central problem for the English novel since the mid-nineteenth century, since the meaning of community becomes increasingly uncertain with the rapid social change that accompanies a "transforming urban and industrial civilization" (Williams 1987: 12, 14). Williams's aim in *Border Country*, in fact, was to stimulate a new understanding of community, to make it knowable once more, if only as a kind of provisional gesture. This is done, chiefly, through the experience of Matthew Price coming to terms with his working-class roots through the defining experience of grieving for his father. Yet one cannot help feeling that this accommodation is specific to one generation, and that the kind of community he comes to know again must become increasingly unknowable in the future.

The limitations inherent in Williams's hopes for a fictional form that might fruitfully play off older perceptions of class continuity with newer experiences of discontinuity are demonstrated by the direction his fiction was to take. Partly this has to do with his personal experience of the economic pressures of publishing, and the social history that is "written out" by any viable schedule of book making. But the role of the intellectual (a role filled by all serious novelists, I would venture, not just academic novelists like Williams) is also transformed in crucial ways. Thus, the dilemma of the working-class scholarship boy – the personal dilemma that Williams projects onto successive protagonists, in one form or another (most notably onto Matthew Price in *Border Country* and Peter Owen in *Second Generation*) – has no relevance to the plight of Lewis Redfern in *The Volunteers* (1978). This is not, I think, because of the economic exigencies that force Williams to give up working-class realism for genre work (in this case, a political thriller), but, rather, because a complex of social changes has, by the late 1970s, produced a new affiliation and a new dilemma for the intellectual.

An important aspect of the social restructuring that has occurred since 1950 is the repositioning of intellectual work as one aspect of new kinds of class formation. Toward the end of the twentieth century the transformative processes of globalization produced new hierarchies based on very different indices of power and wealth to those that determined class in Britain before World War II. For the intellectual – whether circumscribed by institutional life, or by the requirements of a publishing conglomerate – there are new affiliations and complicities to negotiate. The individual belonging to this class may find his or her convictions compromised, defined in a world of "professional" standards and expectations. In *Towards 2000*, Williams succinctly describes the new social model that generates the new dilemma, where he suggests that "a scheme of production for the market has . . . substituted itself for a society" (Williams 1983: 89).

The Volunteers (1978) represents one formal alternative for treating this new (global) context. The novel describes a future, ten years on from the date of publication, in which there is a National Government (and no Labour party), and where a form of terrorism represents the only source of political challenge. The narrator, Lewis Redfern, now a journalist for an international television satellite service, but once a political activist, has been recruited to infiltrate the political underground.

The novel is very much about political choice in an age where traditional class affiliations no longer pertain. The "volunteers" of the title are both the radical activists, and a group of Fabian-style intellectuals whose project is to advance the socialist cause through a slow process of infiltration of the state apparatus: through pursuing a career. This very long-term (and unannounced) revolution makes professionalism a kind of gradualist activism in itself, though it is constantly under threat of absorption and incorporation.

Hindsight makes aspects of the novel's political vision seem closer to realism than they really were. The portrayal of a dominant global media corporation, as well as Williams's anticipation of the complete disappearance of the Labour party's socialist principles, no longer register as facets of the book's deliberately futuristic orientation. Williams had consciously set out in this novel to move beyond realism, and this intention was reinforced by commercial pressures as the book moved toward publication. In explaining why his characters' motivations are often left curiously undeveloped, for example, Williams mentions enforced editorial cuts. But rather than resisting these interventions, he took them as an opportunity for formal development: he was pleased not to have "been driven back to more conventional or received forms, with their greater amplitude" (Williams 1979: 271).

Williams's rationale for pursuing a new style was clear. Now unable – and disinclined – to rely on the features of realist exposition, he sought to dramatize the blend of class discontinuity and continuity through a form of linguistic juxtaposition. In this way he hoped to have found a new formal solution to the problem of rendering the "disjuncture of consciousness" between old notions of industrial disputes, and the experience of the workers. It is not a perfect solution: the terse hard-boiled style of Redfern, for instance, can seem to be at odds with any development of his moral standing. The formal problems evident in *The Volunteers* highlight the difficulty that has come to color the treatment of class-based politics in the post-consensus era (Williams 1979: 298–300).

Williams's later novels represent not so much a failure of the traditional working-class novel as a tacit acknowledgement of its increasing irrelevance in the face of rapid social change. In 1976, pondering "why there is not yet socialism in Britain," Williams attributed this absence to the emergence of "mixed communities" which require that the "struggle for class consciousness" now "be waged on . . . more socially neutral ground" (Williams 1989: 109). But his turn toward this new ground of social neutrality also suggests that class-consciousness had already been diluted.

Sequels and Reworkings: The Problem of Class in Post-Thatcher Fiction

A crude (but revealing) index of this shifting and diminishment of political class loyalty in British society is voting tendency. A glance at voting habits in general elections from 1974 demonstrates how quickly the tribalism formerly associated with British politics – with the Conservative Party seen as the party of capitalism, the Labour Party perceived as the party of the workers – was to disappear. Though still strong, working-class support for Labour was already declining in the mid-1970s. By the time of the first Thatcher victory, in 1979, it was down to 50 percent, and by 1983, it had plummeted to 38 percent (Kavanagh 1990: 168–9). With the old adversarial model of British political and social life effectively at an end, what kind of response might one expect from novelists?

As I have suggested, even in the novels of the 1950s and 1960s, where that old adversarial view seems to motivate a working-class character, inconsistencies or contradictions in class-consciousness are exposed. Alan Sillitoe's Arthur Seaton, in *Saturday Night and Sunday Morning*, seems the epitome of working-class anger in his distrust of authority, but his selfishness and political naivety are clearly dramatized, as when he condemns the idea of wealth redistribution, asserting that "if I won the football pools . . . I'd keep it all mysen, except for seeing my family right" (p. 35). He is not, in fact, genuinely driven by the idea of economic or social mobility; rather, he displays an "instinctive working-class anarchism," in Malcolm Bradbury's phrase (Bradbury 1993: 325).

Sillitoe offers a frank treatment of the short-term aspirations and satisfactions of a working-class Nottingham community; but what really resonates is the ambivalent vitality of Arthur, a lathe operator in a bicycle factory, whose bottled-up energy leads him to excessive acts of hedonism: drinking, fighting, and pursuing married women. Sillitoe conflates class rebellion with male adolescent assertion in this novel (with a strong hint that such assertiveness will continue beyond adolescence). This conflation locates the main problem in understanding Arthur Seaton: is his rebellion against authority misdirected, a delusional rechanneling of his sexuality? Or do gender and class situation conspire to keep him in thrall, with no way out for a man in this context? The continuing power of the book may reside in the fact that it is impossible to choose between these alternatives.

A parlor game that serious readers should resist is imagining what might become of a character should the action of a novel continue into the future. Such imagining is a more serious business for the novelist, however, and Sillitoe obligingly published a sequel of sorts to *Saturday Night and Sunday Morning* in 2001: the novel *Birthday*. There are some arresting moments of character interaction that trade on knowledge of the earlier book, as when Arthur recalls meeting Brenda on the street, when she is "a bit more than forty," and discovers that he is the father of her 15-year-old daughter (Sillitoe 2001: 138). However, the general impetus of the book is not to provide this kind of elaboration of the earlier narrative. Indeed, the principal character is one who played no part in the original: Arthur's older brother Brian.

It is, rather, at the level of observed social changes that *Birthday* works effectively as a sequel to *Saturday Night and Sunday Morning*. Brian is a television scriptwriter, something he turned to after failing as a novelist, and realizing that there was more money in television anyway. His occupation may not be commonplace, but it is indicative of a more general reconceptualizing of work in the information age. His father's reaction to the news that Brian is making money writing for television is revealing: "you're so lucky, our Brian," he says, "you'll never have to work again" (p. 185). That we should think of his work *as work*, and as important work, though it is ostensibly popular entertainment, is indicated in the observation of his mentor that his writing is "plugged into the hearts and minds" of ordinary people ("the kind of people which those who ran the television business hadn't a fart's chance in a whirlwind of meeting" (p. 169)). The "luck" that Jenny ascribes to his ability to – as Brian puts it – "make my living by putting words into people's mouths" (p. 223) contrasts with the material luck his father perceives: her implication is that he is fortunate to be doing work that facilitates social connection.

This perception of popular programming contrasts with Arthur Seaton's estimation of television in *Saturday Night and Sunday Morning*, which he sees as a means of pacifying the masses (p. 184), and also of creating debt, where television aerials, "installed on the never-never," swamp working-class neighborhoods (p. 28). The evaluation of Brian's profession in *Birthday* suggests a more accommodating line, a willingness to accept the cultural significance of television.

A television set is probably the most enduring symbol of the new consumer wealth that spread through British society from the 1950s onwards, and *Birthday* contains frequent references to how life has improved, materially. The characters observe that they are better off, and can take holidays abroad (p. 98); that working conditions have improved (p. 185); that people are now "well fed" and "comfortably dressed" (p. 152). The memories of such things as poor housing (p. 5), persistent hunger (pp. 142–3), and industrial accidents such as the one that befell Jenny's husband George (p. 19) all contribute to the impression of better lives for working people, and a wider share in material wealth in more recent times. That the son of his wife's cousin Paul (who is the "chief fitter at a factory" (p. 45)) can become a solicitor suggests to Arthur the existence of a meritocracy: "it must be a sign of the times that with brains you can get wherever you like" (p. 50).

Brian considers himself to be "of no class at all" (p. 227). Not all the characters see themselves this way, but it defines the essential dynamic of the book. What solidarity the characters feel for one another is based not on class but on family ties, age, or the experience of illness and disease. This latter theme suggests the flipside of the world of material comfort. Affordable food and drink are in abundance in *Birthday*, but so is cancer. The theme of toxicity is a mere undercurrent, however; predominantly, this is a work of straightforward realism that registers the spread of middle-class aspirations and tastes.

Another revealing post-Thatcher sequel to the working-class novel of the 1960s is Nell Dunn's *My Silver Shoes* (1996), in which the character Joy is resuscitated 28 years on from the opening of *Poor Cow* (a "real-time" gap, since the two novels were published 28 years apart). In this sequel, some of the former markers of class remain, a quality that distinguishes the book from Sillitoe's *Birthday*. Joy now lives in Putney in a council flat next door to her mother, and works at a job club where she has inspired many of the unemployed people seeking help. She also has a boyfriend (Jeff) who seems the ideal partner for her, since he is responsive to the sensuality that embodied her challenging transgressiveness in *Poor Cow*, and which persists in the sequel.

If the opening of *My Silver Shoes* depicts the social and material advancement of Joy, we soon realize that this is not to be a simple celebration of social improvement: almost at once Joy's well-ordered life begins to fall apart. Her mother Gladys goes into the early stages of senile dementia after a fall, while her son Jonny deserts from the army. Having found his posting in Northern Ireland unendurable, he takes up residence at home, awaiting his inevitable arrest by the military police. Joy gives up her work to care for her demanding mother, and Jeff, finding himself unable to tolerate the new domestic arrangements, eventually decides to leave her.

As in *Poor Cow*, social liberation is a gendered issue, linked to sexual liberation. Jeff and Joy are reunited after a cooling-off period in which Joy and Gladys, returning to an old haunt, take a holiday at a caravan park at Selsey Bill. Both women enjoy memories of particularly lurid sexual encounters in this episode of self-discovery, and this underscores the central theme: the continuity of these two women, linked by the need to assert themselves through their sexuality (pp. 191–4).

More clearly than in *Poor Cow*, the sexual frankness of Joy in *My Silver Shoes* is presented in economic terms. At the start of the novel Joy had appeared independent, constrained principally by a shrill mother with a narrow vision. But by the end of the book Joy and Gladys are revealed to have the same defining characteristic, the uninhibited sexuality that, in a situation of poverty, seems to be a woman's only reliable route to empowerment. In accordance with the shifting balance of power, the later Joy is significantly more assertive than she is in her earlier incarnation, while the latter-day men are inadequate.

These two sequels register the gradual disappearance of specifically working-class concerns – *Birthday* more explicitly than *My Silver Shoes* – and an increasing, though relative, sense of empowerment. What is also striking about both novels is the simple, lucid style of writing. Dunn intersperses moments of first-person address from Joy within a pared-down third-person narrative, in the manner of filmic documentary realism in which the camera observes, and the subject occasionally speaks to the camera. *Birthday*, aside from one odd moment of direct address, is written from a similarly undemonstrative third-person perspective.

Neither novel, in short, makes a development of working-class realism in the way that Raymond Williams proposed: the discontinuity of social experience is more marked than any continuity. Rather than enabling a collective view, Dunn's documentary realism tends to emphasize the isolating effects of contemporary poverty. In this respect, her recent work resembles that of Livi Michael, whose *Under a Thin Moon* (1992), for example, develops the social documentary style in a classic depiction of underclass deprivation. The novel's sharply restricted point of view emulates the sense of economic imprisonment: this is a social experience that is alienating and marginalizing, rather than collective. James Kelman's *How Late It Was, How Late* (1994) creates a similar effect in presenting oppression and economic deprivation as a given state, apparently unalterable. The focus is the plight of Sammy, a Glaswegian who has become blind after a violent confrontation with the police. The narrative comprises a depressing account of state oppression, the alienating impact of which is intensified by the interior monologue of Sammy: this creates a sense of claustrophobic, internalized oppression which "recreates" for the reader the personal plight of the oppressed individual. The narrative method attempts to embody the individual experience of poverty, and in a way that tacitly acknowledges the unavailability of collective working-class experience.

It is clear that the rapidly shifting class dynamic of British society since 1950 has largely dissolved the traditional, adversarial model of class, replacing it with a new model of inequality in which there is no longer a collective, working-class experience to which writers might appeal – at least not in the ways envisaged by Raymond Williams. Yet there is an element of class challenge in Kelman's *How Late It Was, How Late*, specifically related to literary culture. The furore over the novel's success in winning the 1994 Booker Prize, given its "bad language" (a rendering of Glaswegian dialect heavily punctuated by obscenities), did seem to strike at certain class perceptions about what kind of experience the "serious novel" should engage with.

It is not clear, however, who owns that version of literary culture from which the word "fuck" is excluded. The *Lady Chatterley* trial did not settle the matter, it seems. Yet when Barbara Pym allowed the word into the usually genteel world of her fiction, in her Booker-shortlisted novel *Quartet in Autumn* (1977), the Rubicon was probably crossed for contemporary middlebrow literary culture. Within that novel, the Rubicon is crossed for Letty Crowe when a destitute figure on an Underground platform rears up and shouts "Fuck off!," confirming for Letty that it is not the old school contemporary she thought she recognized. This moment of irruption in Pym's genteel world points to the source of the book's elegiac mood, and its lament for the manifest irrelevance of the ageing gentlewoman like Letty, and the fading social milieu to which she belongs: as for the characters, so for the readers who might identify with them.

There are reasons, then, to doubt the notion that there are stable class perceptions that may still be counted on to "police" literary language, or that are available to receive offence from instances of linguistic transgression. Yet this kind of argument, linking a novelist's linguistic innovation to a politics of class conflict, resurfaces periodically. Perhaps the most notable recent instance has been the claim surrounding another novel of working-class Scotland, *Trainspotting* (1993) by Irvine Welsh, that this novel's use of a thick Edinburgh dialect is a challenge to the linguistic norm of English literary culture. What such a claim fails to take into account is that Welsh's language is a stylized, phonetic rendering of the dialectal form, and would have been just as alienating, initially, to actual speakers of the dialect as to literary editors in London. Of course, it would be absurd to suggest that there are not clear differences of economic circumstance between the fictional worlds of Barbara Pym and Irvine Welsh; but just as Pym came to recognize (and lament) the dissolution of the class that inspired her fiction, so does Welsh (in *Trainspotting*) achieve an elegiac mood, in key moments, that offsets the book's apparent assault on middle-brow tastes. It is an intriguing paradox that, for all the drug-taking, the violence, the sexual brutality, there is a submerged community that links the characters in this seemingly atomized, multi-voiced work, a latent (but unrealized) collective that humanizes the book, and which constitutes a hidden lament for a simpler kind of community – the very sort of community that had once been enshrined in the home-and-hearth codes of the working class.

The Contemporary Novel and Middle-Class Complicity

An issue that often exercises critics is the identified "middle-class" stance of novelists presuming to fictionalize elements of contemporary political reality. A recurring complaint has been that such writers – Margaret Drabble is the usual straw doll in these discussions – treat issues pertaining to class in such a way as to reinforce the position of privilege from which they write. The nub of this critique is that the view from the Hampstead dinner table pointedly excludes the working class, and establishes a deluded liberal vantage point (corresponding in some measure to the novelist's) that masks its own vested interests. In this view, the novel, in the hands of old-guard practitioners such as Angus Wilson, Margaret Drabble, or Iris Murdoch, as well as more recent and less conventional inheritors of the liberal-realist mode of political fiction, such as Martin Amis or Jonathan Coe, inevitably becomes a hegemonic tool, a reactionary cultural force that serves, broadly, to reinforce the status quo. Given that writers of putatively "middle-class" background continue to dominate the British literary scene, targets for such a critique are never lacking.

The legitimacy of this outlook seems dubious to me. Middle-class identity, like working-class identity, has been subject to dramatic change, and this makes the identification of any particular novel or novelist as quintessentially "middle class" fraught with difficulties. It is true that many "concerned" political novels, and especially novels about the state-of-the-nation, are written from a broadly "bourgeois" position; but this may be no more than to observe that the conditions of writing and reading narrative fiction have usually been bourgeois. (And it should be remembered that these conditions have historically enabled many revealing – and sometimes self-contradictory – insights to emerge. Any novel that now projects a stable, middle-class identity will soon reveal its own contradictory circumstances – as sometimes *does* happen in Drabble, with interesting results.) We need not, perhaps, be especially anxious about the bourgeois nature of literary production. Indeed, it would seem strange to condemn a cultural form on account of its conditions of existence, since that would mean condemning it *tout court*. Most important, here, is the idea of the middlebrow trajectory of British culture as embodying a kind of long revolution: as the range of middlebrow culture and experience is extended, so do the material conditions of existence associated with the "liberal" novel become gradually less implicated in political and economic privilege, at least in a national sense.

Criticisms of the liberal or middle-class novel of social consciousness have also been based, I think, on an overestimation of what the novel can achieve, and on a misperception of what it should be expected to achieve. It is a fundamental mistake to assume that novels can effect political change, or serve particular interests, in a direct, material sense. Novels about society play a part in our understanding of ourselves, of course, and can even, in exceptional cases, contribute some indispensable piece of a generation's collective self-definition.

But political novels may have a long period of gestation. They are not written, like political manifestos, to make direct interventions in particular political moments; neither are they typically read in sufficient quantities to be taken as significant forms of influence. (Film and TV have the reach and immediacy that the novel so patently lacks.)

The complaint against the dominance of bourgeois themes and perspectives in British literary culture also implies that working-class tastes are marginalized in that culture. As Jonathan Rose has demonstrated, however, from the nineteenth century through to the middle of the twentieth, working-class literary tastes (based on the available personal testimonies) tended to follow the pre-modernist canon. Neither was this felt to be politically oppressive by the readers themselves: classic authors such as Shakespeare and Milton were often read in preference to overtly "left wing" writers; and the encounter often left these working-class readers more, rather than less, politically engaged. It is true that Rose's book identifies an autodidact tradition that may not be truly representative of working-class inclinations; but he convincingly establishes an intellectual working-class tradition that inclined toward writers like Dickens and Thackeray rather than the modernists (working-class readers had no time for avant-garde writing), and which anticipates the middlebrow literary world of Britain since 1950 (Rose 2001).

Rose laments the disappearance of this working-class autodidact tradition in the second half of the twentieth century. He objects to the reconciliation between bourgeois and bohemian values epitomized by the work of "professionals in the creative industries":

> Affluent and ambitious, profit-motivated and style-conscious, they are sincerely committed to women's equality and genuinely interested in the literature, music, art, and cuisines of non-Western peoples. But the boutique economy they have constructed involves a process of class formation, where the accoutrements of the avant-garde are used to distance and distinguish cultural workers from more traditional manual workers. (Rose 2001: 464)

This process of class formation, involving the professionalization of cultural workers, and the commodification of various forms of cultural expression, is well observed, in some respects. But Rose's argument that this has had the effect of killing the autodidact tradition, of shutting out the astute, working-class observers of bohemia, is less convincing. A simpler explanation is that the class of traditional manual workers, with a self-improving hunger for education, has disappeared from the post-industrial British landscape. New forms of menial labor and exploitation may have emerged, but these no longer identify a "class" with shared values, interests, and aspirations clearly distinct from the values and aspirations of the expanding middle classes. Neither do new forms of menial work provide the kind of community focus that manual labor once did: when phoning a call center from Britain today, one is as likely to be connected to Mumbai as to Manchester.

In the last chapter of his survey of class, Gary Day traces the transformation of class identity in the twentieth century, leading inevitably to the transformed global perspective I have been anticipating. With respect to the postwar period, he details a series of significant (and often lamentable) trends that impact especially on working-class experience, such as modern housing and the break-up of "people-centered" communities; the spread of consumerism and the alienation that follows in its wake; and (following Richard Hoggart) the development of a new mass art that obscures collective values (Day 2001: 180–83). Day properly points out the disparity between the disappearance of superficial class markers and the persistence of economic inequality in the 1950s and 1960s, seeing in this disparity the quiet emergence of an "underclass" that would not become fully visible until the 1980s. There is little here that I would want to dispute, but where I would place a significantly different emphasis is in the consideration of a ruling or dominant class. In Day's analysis, there persists a "dominant" class that "universalizes its values" through mass culture (Day 2001: 187–9). In my view, this question of dominance is dissipated, merged into the more general sense of complicity that Day gestures toward in his closing paragraph:

> We can no longer define class in terms of owners and non-owners of the means of production. We have moved from an economy where money was invested in industry to an economy where money is invested in money. The global movement of money means it is hard to give it a local class identity. . . . There is no part of cultural life that does not speak in the idiom of money. It is for that reason that we are all "middle class" now. Except, of course, for the poor, whose plight reminds us that class, and what we mean by it, is once more an issue in British society. (p. 204)

The problem for Western professional people, including successful novelists – or, for that matter, literary critics – is that their relationship to the global economic order is complicitous in ways that are not

Dominic Head

always easy to unravel. Of course, one can engage in obviously self-aggrandizing acts, like buying a second home (or, worse still, a second home abroad). But even the purchase of a first home, given the vicissitudes of the property market, can be to participate in an institution that now imposes economic inequality with a suddenness unparalleled in British history, and in a manner that undermines the nation's supposed movement toward meritocracy. Yet it is the global context that truly transforms the scale and significance of economic power, a power exercised in the simplest acts of consumerism: it may make no difference whether you buy vegetables grown in Kent or flown in from Kenya – leaving aside the environmental implications – since either purchase depends on exploitation of workers from overseas, migrant in the one case and indigenous in the other.

It is clear that recognizable and stable class identities have disappeared from British society, and from the novel in Britain. The novel of underclass experience, clearly registering a new form of inequality, has achieved some prominence, but has usually been written in a mode that is devoid of any concept of community or collective action: the rhetorical effect is to make grim predicaments seem generalized, hard facts of the contemporary political landscape. With hindsight, the disappearance of the novel of class from British literature can be said to have been signaled by deep contradictions in the novels of working-class realism that were already evident in the heyday of the 1950s and 1960s. For the past 30 years and more the engine of the novel has been fuelled by other concerns, such as gender, migrancy, ethnicity, and, more recently, by globalization, genetics, cognition. It is in response to these concerns that writers like Rushdie, Winterson, and McEwan have made their names; and it is these concerns that now throw into relief the most pressing questions of inequality.

References and Further Reading

NONFICTION

Adonis, Andrew & Pollard, Stephen (1997). *A Class Act: The myth of Britain's classless society*. London: Hamish Hamilton.
Bradbury, Malcolm (1993). *The Modern British Novel*. London: Secker & Warburg.
Cannadine, David (1998). *Class in Britain*. New Haven, CT: Yale University Press.

Davies, Nick (1997). *Dark Heart: The shocking truth about hidden Britain.* London: Chatto & Windus.

Day, Gary (2001). *Class.* London: Routledge.

Kavanagh, Dennis (1990). *Thatcherism and British Politics: The end of consensus?* London: Oxford University Press.

Rose, Jonathan (2001). *The Intellectual Life of the British Working Classes.* New Haven, CT: Yale University Press.

Williams, Raymond (1979). *Politics and Letters: Interviews with "New Left Review."* London: New Left Books.

Williams, Raymond (1983). *Towards 2000.* London: Chatto & Windus.

Williams, Raymond (1987). *The English Novel from Dickens to Lawrence.* London: Hogarth Press (first published 1970).

Williams, Raymond (1989). The social significance of 1926. In: Robin Gable (ed.), *Resources of Hope: Culture, democracy, socialism* (pp. 105–10). London: Verso.

FICTION

Amis, Kingsley (1954). *Lucky Jim.* London: Gollancz.

Barstow, Stan (1960). *A Kind of Loving.* London: Joseph.

Braine, John (1957). *Room at the Top.* London: Eyre & Spottiswoode.

Dunn, Nell (1967). *Poor Cow.* London: MacGibbon & Kee.

Dunn, Nell (1996). *My Silver Shoes.* London: Bloomsbury.

Hines, Barry (1968). *A Kestrel for a Knave.* London: Penguin.

Kelman, James (1994). *How Late it Was, How Late.* London: Secker & Warburg.

Michael, Livi (1992). *Under a Thin Moon.* London: Secker & Warburg.

Pym, Barbara (1977). *Quartet in Autumn.* London: Macmillan.

Sillitoe, Alan (1958). *Saturday Night and Sunday Morning.* London: W. H. Allen.

Sillitoe, Alan (2001). *Birthday.* London: Flamingo.

Storey, David (1960). *This Sporting Life.* London: Longman.

Waterhouse, Keith (1959). *Billy Liar.* London: Evans Bros.

Welsh, Irvine (1993). *Trainspotting.* London: Secker & Warburg.

Williams, Raymond (1960). *Border Country.* London: Chatto & Windus.

Williams, Raymond (1964). *Second Generation.* London: Chatto & Windus.

Williams, Raymond (1978). *The Volunteers.* London: Eyre Methuen.

Chapter 12

What the Porter Saw: On the Academic Novel

Bruce Robbins

Philosophy! The porter knows as much of it as I do. He doesn't know that he knows, but that's why he knows. A porter, Russell, is simple.
Ludwig Wittgenstein, in Terry Eagleton, *Saints and Scholars*

"Just a small mention"

There's a moment in Kazuo Ishiguro's *The Unconsoled* (1995) when the protagonist, a world-renowned pianist who has arrived in an unnamed European city to give a concert and a speech, is approached by a porter in the hotel where he's staying and asked to say a few words, somewhere in the course of the speech, on behalf of porters. "Just a small mention, sir. As you know, many of us, we've worked and worked over the years to try and change the attitude in this town towards our profession. We may have had a small effect, but by and large we've failed to make a general impact and, well, it's perfectly understandable that there's frustration setting in that things may never really change. But one word from you tonight, sir, that could alter the course of everything. It could be an historic turning point for our profession" (Ishiguro 1995: 296).

Academics too have been known to express a certain frustration with "the attitude in this town towards our profession." Extending the analogy, it's not hard to imagine a faculty member working up the nerve to approach a visiting novelist, laden with drinks rather

248

than luggage, and begging for a slight mention. On the other hand, given the generally unflattering treatment academics have received from the so-called academic novel, it might seem wiser for them to look for help elsewhere. Over the past half-century or so, novelists who turned their attention to the university have arguably contributed more than a little to the acute lack of respect and understanding of which academics, like Ishiguro's porter, tend to complain. From Kingsley Amis's *Lucky Jim* (1954) through the academic novels of David Lodge and Malcolm Bradbury and down to the campus fiction of the present day, there has been no need to ask whether satire would be the chosen mode. The only relevant questions have been how satiric the collective portrait would be and what institutions, schools of thought, or character types would be singled out for ridicule.

Is this a scandal? It is, of course, if one adopts a porter-like perspective. And the fact that in recent decades higher education has repeatedly been under such barbaric attack (the adjective is not too strong) from the government has made it harder for academics to adopt any posture more complicated than unconditional self-defense. But self-defense itself, if it is going to succeed, may require just that wicked unsettling of professional self-centeredness that Ishiguro performs. Like the butler of the better-known *Remains of the Day* (1989), the elderly porter of *The Unconsoled* is presented as artificially inflating his self-worth by unnecessarily magnifying the difficulty of his job. When the pianist addresses him in the elevator in the novel's first scene, it is because the porter has not put down the two heavy bags he is carrying. Patiently, without lowering the bags, the porter explains that he is committed to maintaining the standards of his profession: "there's always this idea that anyone could do this job if they took it into their heads . . . I suppose it's because everyone in this town at some point has had the experience of carrying luggage from place to place. Because they've done that, they assume being a hotel porter is just an extension of it" (p. 6). Much the same has often been said about literary criticism. Who needs a PhD in order to enjoy and evaluate the novels he or she reads? To an outside observer, the specialized forms of argument that distinguish academic critics from the laity may look no less arbitrary than the porter's refusal to put his suitcases down while riding up in the elevator. As if to entice academic high-culture bearers into entertaining a parallel with the carriers of other sorts of baggage, Ishiguro pushes his musician on just this point. He does not question the content of the expertise – the genuineness of Ryder's musical achievements is conceded – but he does question the enormous social significance Ryder and others attribute to that expertise. Ryder defends his compulsive traveling from city to city, at an obvious cost to his personal and familial life, on the grounds that he and his expert opinions are desperately needed. Is he as needed as he thinks he is? On what grounds? And who gets to decide how much need for his expertise there really is?

These questions are not rhetorical. Novelists are not inherently trust-worthy on them any more than pianists or academics are. For all their allegiance to a larger-than-academic reading public, novelists too have their local claims to press, their professional axes to grind – in particular against academics, who are competitors in the wider social field. When novelists attempt to speak in the name of "society at large," they enter into an open-ended contention of diverse and partial voices. But to see this contention as happening within the academic novel is to see the genre's higher claim to the reader's interest – a more interesting claim, certainly, than the question of how the academy comes off in any given text. Toward the end of John Wain's *Strike the Father Dead* (1962), the young hero's father, described by the jazz pianist son as "an old-fashioned professor of classics at a tenth-rate university" (p. 196), chats casually with a young colleague in metallurgy and is surprised by the following speech: "You call your son's music trivial, and not only that but ignoble. But you must know that there are a lot of people in the modern world who'd say much the same about your work . . . I don't say I agree with them, but there are thousands of people who think that with the world in its present state, facing urgent problems of food-supply and the conquest of disease, and with international politics in the state they are, it's a waste of a man's lifetime to spend it teaching people dead languages and poring over ancient texts" (Wain 1962: 224–5). Though it is instantly rejected by the classics professor – "At that, of course," he says, "I knew I was dealing with a hopeless case" (p. 225) – this speech offers an alternative framework in which the academic novel can be read, one that productively estranges us from the usual *à clef* readings and the totting up of positive and negative images. Accounting of the familiar literal-minded sort, which is sneakily encouraged by the customary authorial denial that anything herein is taken from the 20 years the author spent at University X, can thus give way to a more ambitious inquiry into why novelists should turn their attention to the university at all and what larger vision of the humanities in relation to the state of the world might be involved when they do – for example, how what they say about the doings of professors might be related to what they say about the doings of porters.

"This quiet place, where only intellectual achievement counted"

There is general agreement on a rough periodization of the academic novel: if the second half of the twentieth century is dominated by satire, the first half is dominated by pastoral (Carter 1990; Rossen 1993; Showalter 2005). The roughness of this scheme appears at once if one thinks of novels like H. G. Wells's *Love and Mr Lewisham* (1900), which refreshingly deals with urban science education rather than Oxbridge humanities and does so (no doubt for that reason) with a minimum of pastoral idealization, or Philip Larkin's *Jill* (1946), which deals with Oxford, but as the eerie site of a scholarship boy's class self-abasement, or Barbara Pym's *Crampton Hodnet* (written in 1936, though not published until 1985), whose gender-problematized Oxford is again superbly sardonic. In any case, however, the early idealizing of the university is not something academics ought to look back upon with nostalgia or gratitude. This is for at least two reasons. In this period, first of all, only a tiny percentage of the general population attended university, so that the celebration or defense of the university was almost necessarily the celebration or defense of a highly restricted class and gender privilege. It thus made a sort of case for the university which might well do more to hurt than to help the university's would-be defenders in a later, more democratic era. And second, because pastoral idealizations of the university seem to draw subversive attention to what they have excluded – a point that works against the novels' suitability for the purpose of self-defense, though in favor of their long-term literary interest.

Evelyn Waugh's *Brideshead Revisited* (1945), which Ishiguro may have had in mind in naming his protagonist, presents Charles Ryder's experience of Oxford as a life-changing discovery of beauty. Oxford makes this discovery possible, the novel insists, because it is walled off from the crass commercial civilization outside, cloistral, sequestered, and, as life goes on, "irrecoverable as Lyonnesse" (p. 29). Pastoral involves criticism, explicit or implicit, of the world outside it. And pastoral also involves a threat that the outside world will penetrate and destroy the idyllic space it has fenced off (Morace 1989: 158). Waugh's pastoral paradise is an all-male society, indeed largely if only

251

Bruce Robbins

implicitly a homosexual one. It makes the university into a site for languid masculine intimacy before the inevitable fall into compulsory heterosexuality. The protagonist owns a skull with the words "Et in Arcadia ego" inscribed in its forehead (p. 53). Lyonnesse is no sooner mentioned than, one page later, "a rabble of women" (p. 30) arrives to introduce discordance. Ignorant vulgarity, kept at bay by the university's walls, is represented in the novel's opening frame by the conscription army and later associated with new rather than old money and with a general leveling down that might also be described, from a more sympathetic viewpoint, as progress and democracy. The eccentric teddy-bear-carrying aesthete Sebastian Flyte, who is said to define the protagonist's Oxford experience, is presented later in the novel (now living with a parasitic working-class lover in North Africa) as "a remittance man" (p. 240). The phrase is a reminder that the idyllic vision of Oxford organized around "small companies of intimate friends" (p. 270) was also a rentier vision, and as such premised on very broad exclusions. Even the need to work for one's bread, as Ryder himself will, is too harsh a reality for it. Ryder, an architectural painter who is paid "to salute [the] achievement [of his patrons] at the moment of extinction," notes that his arrival in the great country houses "seemed often to be only a few paces ahead of the auctioneer's, a presage of doom" (p. 260). He can be seen as a sort of fatal servant, unwittingly helping to bring down the old aristocratic family he gives every appearance of worshiping and whose great house he nearly inherits.

C. P. Snow's *The Masters* (1951), which Elaine Showalter describes as "one of the most reverent, idyllic, and utopian academic novels ever written" (Showalter 2005), again presents the university as an all-male society. The novel's entire action is taken up with the 12 votes about to be cast by the fellows of a fictional Cambridge college in order to elect a new master. The existence of sex can barely be detected, as if from a great distance: "From one of the May week balls, we could just hear the throbbing of a band" (p. 165). *The Masters* would seem to make sex, money, and politics into non-issues. It is usually said that, as on a ship or a country house weekend, nothing remains but the play of conflicting personalities under stress. Yet the final result turns on how forces from outside the College are after all allowed to intrude. One of these is the politics of the Spanish Civil War. The major "outside" force is women. The (politically conservative) candidate whom our (politically progressive) narrator has initially favored loses the mastership, in large part, because of his embarrassing

252

and ambitious spouse, referred to as a "tormented shrew" (p. 88), who had been his student and who commits the unpardonable sin of speaking about the prize as already won before the votes have been cast.

Showalter notes the tension between Snow's "idealized view of an irrecuperable past" and the pettiness of motive and conduct we actually see, for which the accustomed term seems to be "careerism" (Showalter 2005). With one exception, an exception (the young scientist Calvert) that has no bearing whatever on the plot, Snow refuses to show the excitement of research and discovery. He does not pretend to make real to the non-academic public the challenge and difficulty, the meaning and value of the actual work these men do. Instead the screen is filled with what even we academics call, irreverently, "academic politics." Though Snow is Trollopian enough to view careerism without satire, it is as if, even in this most utopian of academic novels, we are already at the precipice, ready to plunge over the edge into satire.

This edginess is also an inconspicuous ingredient in the charm of Dorothy Sayers's *Gaudy Night* (1939). Sayers's all-female Shrewsbury College is described as a "quiet place, where only intellectual achievement counted" (p. 17). But when real intellectual achievement is presented – and it *is* presented, that being another of the novel's charms – it takes the form of inspired detective work, allusion-studded repartee between Harriet Vane and Lord Peter Wimsey, and one poem, again composed jointly by the two detectives. As for scholarship, its central exhibit is Miss Lydgate's "forthcoming work on the Prosodic elements in English verse from Beowulf to Bridges. . . . Miss Lydgate had perfected, or was in process of perfecting (since no work of scholarship ever attains a static perfection), an entirely new prosodic theory, demanding a novel and complicated system of notation which involved the use of twelve different varieties of type . . . the important Introduction which afforded the key to the whole argument still remained to be written" (pp. 39–40). By the time we are told that this "colossal work in progress . . . has been defaced and mutilated in the most *revolting* manner" (p. 75), the only appropriate response would seem to be applause.

The university's imperturbable rhythm of terms and seasons suggests that within its walls nothing really changes. But if "The University is a Paradise," as the epigraph claims, Sayers gives it one and perhaps two serpents. The sure one is the perpetrator of the revolting mutilation. The tentative addition would be Harriet herself, whose drily unromantic view of Miss Lydgate's project and its endlessly ramifying typographic complications makes the reader want to share in the mutilating. The novel's edginess, linking detective and criminal, also animates the unscholarly materialism of porters. The trail that will lead to the culprit begins with "Poor Jukes" (p. 43), the College's former porter, who has been dismissed for theft and other crimes and whose wife, it turns out, has been caring for the villain's children. (The present porter, who admires Hitler and is himself admired, must alas be left uncommented upon here.) After a lengthy exposure of all the little tensions within the college's all-female world that might have resulted in this outburst of violence, the possibility of a functioning community of unmarried women scholars is triumphantly affirmed when the mystery is solved and the criminal turns out to be not one of them but a scout, a servant. Mutatis mutandis, the butler did it. The crime expresses a resentment against "intellectual achievement" – a resentment that Harriet herself never quite expresses but embodies nonetheless. The complicity between detective and criminal comes out in the confession scene, when the villain says, "It would do you good to learn to scrub floors for a living as I've done, and use your hands for something, and say 'madam' to a lot of scum" (pp. 484–5). Harriet has said of her own work, earlier in the novel, "anyone with proper sensitive feeling would rather scrub floors for a living" (p. 31). Whether as detective or novelist, scrubbing floors is not far from what she already does.

The motive for the servant's crimes is revenge for the suicide of her husband, a former scholar hounded out of the profession years earlier when caught (by one of the College's fellows) in a piece of fraudulent scholarship. Anticipating the themes of Wain's metallurgist, her confession speech asks, in effect, what scholarly standards are worth: "couldn't you leave my man alone? He told a lie about somebody else who was dead and dust hundreds of years ago. Nobody was the worse for that. Was a dirty bit of paper more important than all our lives and happiness? You broke him and killed him – all for nothing" (p. 485). One need not agree with her in order to feel a public power in these Nietzschean questions that overflows the particular case, articulating attitudes that would not diminish, strangely enough, even when the offspring of scouts and porters had begun to find their way into the university as students and faculty. "It's a kind of blind malevolence," one of the fellows says, "directed against everybody in College" (p. 97).

In the period after World War II, the malevolent vision that informs this attack on the college moves toward the center of the academic novel. *Lucky Jim* (1954) manages what might once have seemed an impossible feat: to make a university don, even an uninspired and soon-to-be ex-don, into a post-war Everyman (Taylor 1993). It does this, however, only by making Jim Dixon into living proof that university teaching is something anyone can do. Unlike Ishiguro's porter, Jim is not especially interested in his subject, does not try to be good at it, does not believe the teacher of history has a unique mission to save the rest of society. Like the villain in *Gaudy Night*, he believes not in the stringent rules of scholarship but in life, happiness, and the right to remain employed. Amis's satire of the university thus asks to be interpreted as manifesting, however controversially, a democratizing of perspective. The academic novel has integrated something of the viewpoint of the servants.

Taking their cue from *Lucky Jim*, critics have often tended to stress the conservative impulse behind the genre's postwar satire, or what Janice Rossen calls its "pejorative poetics" (Rossen 1993: 1). There is plenty of evidence for this case. Tom Sharpe's *Porterhouse Blue* (1974), which mocks the absurdities of hallowed Oxbridge tradition, is no less mocking about all attempts to undo that tradition. *Porterhouse Blue* begins with the "Feast," a formal version of the ritualized seasonal parties with which Barbara Pym and Malcolm Bradbury also begin their best-known academic novels. The Feast establishes the College's dietarily deadly thralldom to the past, otherwise described as its "amiable inertia" (p. 11), which is suddenly threatened by the modernizing master, a Benthamite accused of being "an advocate of change for change's sake" (p. 20). The rest of the novel is about how the threat of change is deflected. The fellows are outraged, but the most effective agent of resistance to change is Skullion, the porter, who acts not on their beliefs but on his own. "Skullion could think of nothing good in change" (p. 11).

The novel takes some distance from Skullion, a man in whom "centuries of endured servitude had bred a fierce bigotry nothing would easily remove" (p. 41). Yet it also indulges the porter of Porterhouse when he insists for example that the gentlemen he has served for decades are not "rich bastards . . . who just exploited you" (p. 14). And it positively gloats at the porter's discomfiture of the liberal master. The key both to the novel's plot and to its politics is the moment when master gives the porter the sack. As the right-wing chorus remarks, "Bad publicity for a socialist . . . Can't turn them out into the street. Old retainers. Wouldn't look good" (p. 125). "That's one of the nice things about these damned socialists. The first people to be hurt by their rage for social justice are the working classes" (p. 155). Placed by the master's enemies before a television camera, the indignant Skullion "expressed his admiration for scholarship and deplored research. He extolled wisdom and refused to confuse it with knowledge. Above all he claimed the right to serve and with it the right to be treated fairly" (p. 181). Appearances to the contrary, this is not simply the conservative voice of Merrie Olde England. The porter also speaks in the much more up-to-date voice of a state that has pledged itself to something resembling full and fair employment.

Satire and the Welfare State

James English, following Malcolm Bradbury, A. S. Byatt, and others, describes academic novels of the post-war period as "texts of the welfare state" (English 1994: 132; Taylor 1993: 68–9). This seems right in a profound if also a complex sense. The Education Act of 1944 (universal free schooling based on the 11+ examination) and the dramatic democratizing of higher education that followed, made possible by the intense experience of national solidarity in World War II, were part of "a rapidly enlarging system of government benefits and entitlements to provide a social safety net of unprecedented breadth." As a result, English concludes, "[at] no time in British history has education occupied such a privileged place in political discourse, or carried such a burden of societal hopes and expectations" (English 1994: 129–30). These hopes and expectations are most visible in the familiar novelistic forms of rebelliousness and disillusionment. Rebellion and disillusion are perhaps inevitable from the moment when the welfare state, symbolized first and foremost by the university, becomes the privileged mediator of postwar upward mobility. The welfare state can thus be blamed for the protagonist's betrayal of his or her community of origin, a betrayal that, from *Great Expectations* on, is always a more or less salient component of the upward mobility story. Much postwar satire of the university asks therefore to be interpreted as an expression of ambivalence about upward mobility itself.

On the other hand, the welfare state can also be taken as legitimizing the upward mobility story by extending its benefits to others. This is one reason why, alongside the rebellion, the "societal hopes and expectations" that define the project of the welfare state also remain vigorously alive within the academic novel, however unconsciously. The collision between (old) scholarly standards and the (new) right to employment is one instance – as it happens, an important one for *Lucky Jim*. Consider the key dialogue between Jim and Gore-Urquhart, who is about to become his benefactor, just before Jim's drunken anti-lecture: "'You're ambitious?'" 'No. I've done badly here since I got the job. This lecture might help to save me from getting the sack'" (p. 219). Keeping his job, the one thing Skullion stands up for, is also what Dixon stands up for, at least before falling down in a stupor. Amis may prefer the old semi-feudal patronage of the Good Rich Man, but in besting the posh Welch family, Jim acts out the more democratic principles of the welfare state, which has now become a sort of impersonal, institutional patron. What's wrong with Mrs Welch can be seen "most clearly, really, in her attitude towards the welfare state . . . She argues, you see, that if people have everything done for them . . ." (p. 81). It seems significant that in the novel's climax, a comic chase scene, Christine is driven off to the railway station in Welch's car and Jim is obliged to give chase by means of a local bus, which of course stops to pick up and deposit other passengers. No matter what your hurry, no one must be left behind: this is the morality of public transport. And Amis quietly vindicates it, for in the end Jim gets the girl when – if only thanks to Welch's abominable driving – the bus wins the race. The same muted celebration of the welfare state can be observed when Wain's *Strike the Father Dead* stages its ultimate reconciliation of father and son in a hospital, a state institution saturated with memories of World War II's collective sacrifices and fast-fading national solidarity.

The genre's political and historical vision makes sense, that is, only if we also consider (1) the academic novel as a displaced or disguised version of the upward mobility story and (2) the university as a figure for the welfare state in general, which has become the frame in which the ambiguities of upward mobility are played out. Peter Widdowson notices in David Lodge and Malcolm Bradbury a "firm commitment to notions of cultural decline in the twentieth century, of history as a destructive process" (Widdowson 1984: 9). But in *The History Man* Bradbury has little genuine interest in the Marxist doctrine of "historical inevitability" (p. 26) he is supposedly satirizing. The progressive version of history that matters most to the novel is the upward mobility of its protagonists, Barbara and especially Howard Kirk, who begin in "the grimmer, tighter north, in respectable upper-working class cum lower-middle class backgrounds" (p. 18) and rise in the world along with increased funding for higher education. How does Bradbury feel about these conjoined rises? Though grim northern respectability certainly informs his satire, he seems unable or unwilling to impose a corrective "decline" upon either the private ascent or the democratization of public resources that makes it possible. The critique of the university may seem simple, but the attitude toward upward mobility is ambivalent – and thus ambivalence is also the deeper narrative truth of Bradbury's take on the university.

Like other satirists, Bradbury sees the university as a haven for pretentious political extremists. But the "gleeful skewering of radical chic" trumpeted by the Penguin cover is not an accident of authorial political orientation or a mere market strategy. For the protagonist's left-wing convictions are organic to the trajectory of the "scholarship boy" (p. 18). However sincerely Howard may hold his convictions, they also follow a logic that works behind his back, legitimizing his upward mobility by suggesting that his rise, enabled by public expenditure as well as personal effort, returns its value to the public – that it belongs not to Kirk alone, but to all of those who have been, like him, disadvantaged by birth. Barbara Kirk calls her husband "a radical poseur" who has "substituted trends for morals and commitments . . . there's nothing in you that really feels or trusts, no character" (p. 32). In doing so, however, she is merely repeating charges of insincerity and inauthenticity that have been made about the upwardly-mobile scholarship boy since Richard Hoggart's founding analysis and that inevitably cluster around successful self-transformation (Hoggart 1959). The real questions at issue are, first, whether the university will be allowed to serve as a site for self-transformation, and second, whether the progressive (though hardly revolutionary) ideology of the welfare state will be allowed to legitimize the university's role by pointing toward an ultimate democratic redistribution of educational benefits.

With a little interpretive latitude, Barbara Kirk's list of charges against her sexually predatory husband might be rewritten as a mission statement of the modern university. Enjoying the mind's freedom to shake loose from the firm bedrock of given "character," taking a critical distance from what one habitually "feels and trusts," and exploring new modes of being and feeling are all declared pedagogical goals. These are much the same values J. M. Coetzee's David Lurie articulates in *Disgrace* (1999) shortly before he is accused of sexual harassment – "He is all for double lives, triple lives, lives lived in compartments" (p. 6). They are also the values Bradbury himself puts in the mouth of his sexually needy surrogate in *Rates of Exchange* (1983): "He travels, he thinks, for strangeness, disorientation, multiplication and variation of the self" (p. 25). If the academic novel makes this legitimizing case to the public, it would seem to do so, ambivalently at best, in the lexicon of extra-marital and/or unconventional sexuality. From this perspective, one might say that sex, which figured in Wells and Larkin primarily as a distraction from scholarship, comes later in the century to stand for the true if necessarily unofficial meaning of higher education. The wild beginning-of-term parties in *The History Man*, designed so as to facilitate adventurous social and sexual mingling among non-partners, would thus be a figure for the new university itself, conceived as a site of deliberate social experimentation. The reader is told nothing of the motives behind Howard Kirk's cold, systematic, somewhat impersonal promiscuity, but others understand his and the novel's other seductions as a response to "need" rather than desire (p. 185), and even (however ironically) as a form of therapy. "Another Miss Phee, getting the help," Miss Callendar says as she surrenders (p. 212). Couplings like these among students and colleagues, open to the scrutiny of others and continuous with the analytic discourse of the classroom and the rescue discourse of the welfare state, might almost be considered official exercises.

Of course, sex can also uphold, more or less, a morality that is also more or less official. In the course of exchanging jobs at their respective universities, the two protagonists of David Lodge's good-natured *Changing Places: A tale of two campuses* (1975) divert their desire from the inter-generational to the intra-generational: from students, who allow the protagonists a fantasy of limitless and cost-free self-transformation, to their colleagues's wives, who gradually return them, rejuvenated, to their usual obligations and proper social slots. Like education itself, the sex here is "only a stage." This is even more true of the scholarly conference, which is more transitory still. The conference, which has become as much a set-piece of the academic novel as the department meeting, exemplifies ephemeral sex that does not interfere with established social arrangements. Hence the comic premise of Lodge's *Small World* (1984) that the conference, especially the international conference, is a sort of modern pilgrimage and ritual of fertility.

As an institution representing the new, statutorily egalitarian opportunities of the welfare state, the university has also been exemplary for its self-conscious gender politics, a workplace in which men and women are expected to mix with uncharacteristic freedom and equality. This is no doubt one large structural reason why, beginning with *Lucky Jim* and continuing through imitations like Howard Jacobson's *Coming from Behind* (1983), masculinist backlash against feminism, homosexuality, and "political correctness" is so much in evidence. In

Jacobson's case, the attempt to synthesize the regular-guy perspective of *Lucky Jim* with the alienated Jewish figure of Philip Roth's *Portnoy's Complaint* leads to a somewhat over-strenuous insistence on the hero's heterosexuality, or his heroic refusal to be political correct about homosexuality. The climax of the novel, a sort of conversational jousting for the prize of a job at Cambridge and a version of Jim Dixon's anti-lecture, allows the hero to substitute a sexual for a scholarly triumph. In such novels, ambivalence about the welfare state takes the form of ambivalence about the new sexual equalities and freedoms, expressing itself in a familiar blend of satire and disavowed vicarious enjoyment. From the point of view of the genre as a whole, however, it is arguable that the strangest secret behind campus sexual license, whether farcical or not, is the existence of masculine desire for intelligent, well-educated, articulate women – a desire that Amis's great progenitor notoriously could not even imagine. In Lodge's *Nice Work* (1988), for example, the older male industrialist's desire for a younger female faculty member is actually a desire not for comfortable superiority but for uncomfortable and unaccustomed equality – more specifically for a woman who, like him, loves her work. An adulterous sexual escapade is again rejuvenating, but what saves the marriage is the wife, under the influence of the female academic's example, getting a job and becoming more of her husband's equal.

"Sado-Monetarism" on the International Stage

> *You and I, Robyn, grew up in a period when the state was smart: state schools, state universities, state-subsidised arts, state welfare, state medicine – these were things progressive, energetic people believed in. It isn't like that any more.*
>
> David Lodge, *Nice Work*

The de-legitimation of the welfare state is hard to periodize. To judge from the academic novel at least, many of the "progressive, energetic people" who seemed to believe in and benefit from the state in the period when it was smart were also quite prepared to bite the hand that fed them. In fiction, there is thus no clear break between the satire of Amis and Sharpe, written while the welfare state was thriving, and the novel's response to post-1978 efforts to dismantle the welfare state and squeeze higher education in the vice of corporate profitability – what Bradbury calls in *Rates of Exchange* "the age of Sado-Monetarism" (p. 21).

The signs are easy to miss, but they are there. Consider, for example, the sexual harassment subplot of Coetzee's *Disgrace* (1999). The father of the student whom David Lurie has seduced tells him, "We put our children in the hands of you people because we think we can trust you" (p. 38). One of Lurie's colleagues asks, "Don't you think . . . that by its nature the academic life must call for certain sacrifices? That for the good of the whole we have to deny ourselves certain gratifications?" (p. 52). The university does not behave badly to Lurie. If the reader still cannot wholeheartedly take its side, it is in part because the state, which speaks through the university, has its own problem of "trust." How can we believe it acts for "the good of the whole" when, in the name of democracy, it compels the university to submit to a "rationalization" that – like the university itself in its pastoral mode – profits the few at the expense of the many? The stage had already been set for Lurie's departure from the university when the conditions of his employment were drastically altered: "Once a professor of modern languages, he has been, since Classics and Modern Languages were closed down as part of the great rationalization, adjunct professor of communications. Like all rationalized personnel, he is allowed to teach one special-field course a year, irrespective of enrolment, because that is good for morale. For the rest he teaches Communications 101, 'Communications Skills,' and Communications 201, 'Advanced Communications Skills'" (p. 3).

The "rationalization" that began in the UK with the Thatcher administration's cuts in funding and imposition of corporate-style bottom-line discipline, and was then continued by successor governments, was of course part of the larger international movement that has come to be called "globalization." Its symptoms are thus to be found on the same global scale. In the Canadian Jeffrey Moore's *Prisoner in a Red-Rose Chain* (1999), a similar story underlies the farce surrounding "the Department of Comparative Art, a mongrel born of the former Comparative Literature and Comparative Philology Departments and later infused with some tired blood from Film Studies and Art History" (p. 148). The cross-disciplinary misunderstandings and other absurdities of the "the annual Comp Art party" (p. 148) reflect, among other things, the absurd budgetary constraints that have been imposed on the academy from outside. What seems to be conventional academic satire, then, may also strike a very different target: the fiscal discipline under which the university is bending and breaking.

The British university's legitimation crisis is invisible in Lodge's *Changing Places* (1975), but this crisis has come to the self-conscious center of *Nice Work* (1988), which offers its public a skeptical industrialist's view of cutting-edge work in the humanities. To Vic Wilcox, the industrialist hero, what people do in the humanities is not work at all. He tells Robyn Penrose, the feminist critic with whom he is thrown together, that "reading is the opposite of work" (p. 240). And the pressure of his alien perspective makes itself felt on the heroine, who passes it on to her boyfriend: "doesn't it worry you at all? That most people don't give a . . . damn about the things that matter most to us?" Wilcox, Robyn says, "has been getting at me about arts degrees being a waste of money" (p. 152). His question has become her own: *"'Who pays? There is no such thing as a free lunch.'* . . . Why should society pay to be told people don't mean what they say or say what they mean?" (p. 153).

As I've tried to suggest, questions like this have never been entirely foreign to the genre of the academic novel, and that is one of the genre's virtues. But it takes a certain magnanimity to recognize this virtue at a moment when the hostile perspective of scouts and porters has been channeled into the politically threatening form of authoritarian populism. And it is not obvious, therefore, what sort of response might be appropriate. The old defenses don't work for the new universities, as Robyn tells her professor father: "was it a good idea to build so many new universities in parks on the outskirts of cathedral cities and country towns? . . . [This] perpetuates the Oxbridge idea of higher education as a version of pastoral, a privileged idyll cut off from ordinary living" (p. 220). Henceforth, it seems, the university can only be defended in the name of what it contributes to "ordinary living." Robyn offers one defense when her competence in German, combined with old-fashioned sexism of a sort that would have trouble surviving in the academy, allows her to help Vic outwit his tricky German suppliers. Though Lodge borrows the convention of the inheritance from his source, Gaskell's *North and South*, the real equivalent of inherited capital in *Nice Work* is educational capital. The new knowledge economy, one might say, is a business–academy partnership demanding public respect even for forms of knowledge whose practical usefulness may not be immediately evident. Robyn's boyfriend, who has already (in the epigraph to this section) drawn his own conclusions about the moribund state sector, offers a more oblique case when he escapes to an arbitrage job in the City. There, he says, deconstruction is already being realized in the domain of finance: "I regard myself as simply exchanging one semiotic system for another, the literary for the numerical" (p. 225).

It is because of the rising dominance of finance capital, Lodge suggests, that British industrialists like Vic are in such trouble. The case for higher education is increasingly made, therefore, in national terms. Pressed to account for her work and its value, Robyn finds herself falling back "on arguments that I don't really believe any more, like the importance of maintaining cultural tradition" (p. 152). This anticipates A. S. Byatt's answer to the same question in *Possession: A romance* (1990). As Byatt makes clear, conceptual innovation and interpretive flair are the versions of the critic's labor least likely to be absorbed by the public. The popular view of the literary critic, when it is respectful, will instead stress connoisseurship, the ability to recognize and evaluate, to verify date and authorship, along with Sayers-like detective work – here, the discovery of a cache of nineteenth-century love letters. But these skills must be supplemented by the maintaining of cultural tradition, or what Byatt calls "traffic with the dead" (p. 116). And even this oldest of cases for the humanities must itself be supplemented by a nationalist impulse. When Byatt refashions the "who will inherit the estate?" plot so as to center on a writer's papers rather than a rich person's house, she puts those papers at risk of being dispossessed, bought up and carried off by the limitless funds of the insatiable Americans. The national patrimony, she tells her readers, is in danger. The bearers of cultural baggage should rally round.

In *Nice Work*, it is Robyn herself who (via a job offer in California) is threatened with expropriation by the Americans. If what is affirmed in the ending on Vic's side is family solidarity based around work, what is affirmed on Robyn's side is the solidarity of the work unit. For all its foibles, the British university closes ranks and stands firm. And it is to Lodge's credit that, in the very moment of triumph, he notes what is left out. Robyn's reading of *North and South* as an affirmation of "instinctive class allegiance" (p. 49) proves true of *Nice Work* as well: again, the working class serves only as a catalyst to produce solidarity between wings of the middle class whose quarrel, in light of their larger divergence from the workers, comes to seem trivial. On the last page, Robyn's decision to "stay on" in England is provoked by a visible lack of communication between the students on the lawn and the black gardener who is mowing it.

Its indulgence for easy jokes at the expense of non-native speakers, like *Small World*'s throwaway about a Turkish critic who quotes from "Bill Hazlitt" (p. 214), should not distract from the genre's distinctive recent commitment to the international dimensions of its subject. It is as if British higher education, undervalued by its own government, had turned to that hopefully more complimentary reflection of its value to be found elsewhere in the world, where demand for its wisdom and credentials continues to run strong. At any rate, that is one narrative impulse to be discovered among the sometimes obnoxiously xenophobic humor of Bradbury's *Rates of Exchange* (1983). Bradbury's book-length tour de force of bad English, as spoken in a fictional Soviet bloc country, is both irrepressibly comic and, from time to time, poetically estranging. And the poetic estrangement proves itself to have a serious point. In a novel that begins and ends with an academic carrying his baggage through an airport, Petworth's value to his hosts is shown after all to have had nothing to do with the content of his lectures on linguistics; it has had everything to do with his right to travel freely across borders that are closed to the Eastern Europeans. Will he leave the country bearing a forbidden novel in manuscript in his bag? To ask this question is to be obliged to ask whether the gift of love he received on his trip – from the novel's beautiful author – was merely another mispronunciation of his name, a tribute not to who he thinks he is, but to who he is to the comic foreigners. Seen from a global perspective, is the professor only a porter?

Notable academic novels of recent years have chosen to see Oxford through the eyes of international visitors, whether teachers, as in Javier Marías's *All Souls* (1992), or students, as in Amit Chaudhuri's *Afternoon Raag* (1993). There is no government de-funding or quantifying of research in these novels. It is as if, seen from far enough away, the university could once again become a pastoral oasis into which history does not intrude. The 90-year-old porter at the beginning of *All Souls* "literally did not know what day it was and spent each morning in a different year, traveling backwards and forwards in time . . . certain days he believed it was 1947, for him it really was 1947 or 1914 or 1935 or 1960 or 1926 or any other year of his extremely long life" (pp. 4–5). Against this backdrop, it is no surprise that the hero's lover describes a lover's "role in life" as "not to last too long, not to persist or linger" (p. 186). Chaudhuri's Oxford sets a similar standard of permanence that makes everything within it seem transient and thus insubstantial. The first sentence of *Afternoon Raag* is: "Each year, in Oxford, new students come and old ones disappear" (p. 1). "I had a feeling of being surrounded, as on a ship or a train, by personal routines and habits that would not be known again" (p. 7).

Here one does not choose between love objects but vacillates, not unpleasantly, between them, thereby entering into harmony with the transience that Oxford encourages. "The students do not really matter, because within the college walls there is a world . . . that clings to its own time and definition and is changed by no one" (p. 75).

And yet even this supremely lyrical rescue of the university-as-pastoral is structured, narratively speaking, by the old tension between town and gown. Chaudhuri's student narrator speaks of an "inexplicable pride" (p. 34) that keeps him from riding buses – adding as if in an afterthought a mention of the Indian bus driver with whom, it seems, he might not want to be associated. And the novel ends in a moment of communion, mediated by D. H. Lawrence, between the narrator and a much poorer fellow Indian. Without the university, we are to understand, this might not have happened.

Acknowledgments

My thanks to Dehn Gilmore of Columbia University for a brilliant improvisation on the Waugh/Ishiguro relation.

References and Further Reading

NONFICTION

Carter, Ian (1990). *Ancient Cultures of Conceit: British university fiction in the post-war years*. London: Routledge.

English, James F. (1994). *Comic Transactions: Literature, humor, and the politics of community in twentieth-century Britain*. Ithaca, NY: Cornell University Press.

Hoggart, Richard (1959). *The Uses of Literacy*. Harmondsworth: Penguin.

Leonardi, Susan J. (1989). *Dangerous by Degrees: Women at Oxford and the Somerville College novelists*. New Brunswick, NJ: Rutgers University Press.

Morace, Robert A. (1989). *The Dialogic Novels of Malcolm Bradbury and David Lodge*. Carbondale, IL: Southern Illinois University Press.

Rossen, Janice (1993). *The University in Modern Fiction: When power is academic*. New York: St Martin's Press.

Showalter, Elaine (2005). *Faculty Towers: The academic novel and its discontents*. Philadelphia, PA: University of Pennsylvania Press.

Taylor, David J. (1993). *After the War: The novel and English society since 1945*. London: Chatto & Windus.

Widdowson, Peter (1984). The anti-history men: Malcolm Bradbury and David Lodge. *Critical Quarterly*, 26(4), 5–32.

Bruce Robbins

FICTION

Bradbury, Malcolm (1975). *The History Man*. London: Secker & Warburg.
Bradbury, Malcolm (1983). *Rates of Exchange*. London: Knopf.
Byatt, A. S. (1989). *Possession: A romance*. London: Chatto & Windus.
Chaudhuri, Amit (1993). *Afternoon Raag*. London: Heinemann.
Coetzee, J. M. (1999). *Disgrace*. London: Secker & Warburg.
Ishiguro, Kazuo (1989). *The Remains of the Day*. London: Faber.
Ishiguro, Kazuo (1995). *The Unconsoled*. London: Knopf.
Jacobson, Howard (1983). *Coming from Behind*. London: Chatto & Windus.
Larkin, Philip (1976). *Jill*. Woodstock, NY: Overlook (first published 1946).
Lodge, David (1975). *Changing Places: A tale of two campuses*. London: Secker & Warburg.
Lodge, David (1984). *Small World*. London: Secker & Warburg.
Lodge, David (1988). *Nice Work*. London: Secker & Warburg.
Marías, Javier (1992). *All Souls*. London: Harvill Press.
Moore, Jeffrey (1999). *Prisoner in a Red-Rose Chain*. Saskatoon, SK: Thistledown.
Pym, Barbara (1985). *Crampton Hodnet*. New York: E.P. Dutton.
Sayers, Dorothy L. (1995). *Gaudy Night*. New York: HarperCollins (first published 1936).
Sharpe, Tom (1974). *Porterhouse Blue*. London: Secker & Warburg.
Snow, C. P. (1951). *The Masters*. London: Macmillan.
Wain, John (1962). *Strike the Father Dead*. London: Macmillan.
Waugh, Evelyn (1945). *Brideshead Revisited*. Boston, MA: Little, Brown.
Wells, H. G. (1993). *Love and Mr Lewisham: The story of a very young couple*. London: Everyman (first published 1900).

Index

Index

Lightning Source UK Ltd.
Milton Keynes UK
UKOW051218280512

193431UK00004B/17/P